INTRODUCTO[...]

IN[...]

CONTEMPORARY THEOLOGY

ROBERT L. REYMOND

**PRESBYTERIAN AND REFORMED
PUBLISHING COMPANY**

To
Those Students of Mine Who Love
To "Talk" Theology

THE AUTHOR

Dr. Robert L. Reymond holds degrees from Bob Jones University and has done post-graduate work at Fuller Theological Seminary and New York University. In addition, he was a Visiting Scholar at Union Theological Seminary, New York City, during the summer of 1964. From 1961 to 1968 he served on the Bob Jones University faculty in the Graduate Department of Old Testament, teaching Semitic languages and theology. In 1968 he joined the faculty of Covenant Theological Seminary, St. Louis. In addition to his teaching duties he edits the Biblical and Theological Studies Series, a component part of the International Library of Philosophy and Theology published by the Presbyterian and Reformed Publishing Company. He is also associate editor of the Craig Press, Nutley, New Jersey.

Dr. Reymond has travelled throughout the Middle East, and is a member of the American Schools of Oriental Research, the Society of Biblical Literature and Exegesis, and the Evangelical Theological Society.

Besides several monographs, Dr. Reymond's published articles have appeared in *Christianity Today, Biblical Viewpoint,* and the *Quarterly* of the Creation Research Society.

PREFACE

The idea for this little book grew out of a careful reading of John B. Cobb, Jr.'s *Living Options in Protestant Theology*.[1] In this very interesting volume, one I recommend for its careful scholarship and clarity of expression, Cobb analyzes in depth the theological systems of nine leading contemporary theologians.[2] His method of approaching each system, in his own words, is as follows: "The criticisms made of each position are intended as *internal* criticisms only. By this I mean that they are intended to expose the actual situation in the theology in question and not to judge it by any standard of orthodoxy or personal preference."[3] Now, admittedly, there is a great deal to be said for a methodological approach which concentrates on the detection of inconsistencies within systems of thought. But a thoughtful examination of Cobb's work only strengthened my previously-held conviction that unless a theological system is judged in the light of the absolute norm of the Old and New Testaments, it will never be viewed in its true light. After all, that for which each theologian is professedly searching is *Truth*; and simply constructing a system of thought which will survive internally the superficial application of the law of contradiction does not insure *ipso facto* that it possesses *ultimate* truth. Cobb's work tends to cloud this fact. Though he makes several penetrating criticisms of these men, the unwary reader is left with the impression that if only the 'theologian in question would remove certain specified inconsistencies from his system it would deserve a rational man's assent. In reality, the systems, when viewed from the standpoint of Orthodoxy, are so clearly sub-Christian in their disavowal of the cherished doctrines of Protestant Orthodoxy that only by the broadest and loosest interpretation of the word "Protestant" can they be included in a proposed treatment of living options in Protestant theology.

3

Actually, when evaluated in the light of a true Reformation theology, none of them can be offered as a viable option.

The purpose of the present book is to present six of these same systems, this time evaluating each from a Biblically-oriented frame of reference. I intend thereby to mark out the only path which, in my opinion, the Christian student of contemporary theology should follow. Like any author, I can only hope that I have clarified certain ultimate issues in theology today.

I want to acknowledge the labors of Mr. Robert D. Bell, one of my students, who carefully edited the original manuscript, the patience and love of my wife, Shirley, who many times had to "fix it herself" during the writing of this book, and the concern for the publication of Christian books of Mr. Charles H. Craig of the Presbyterian and Reformed Publishing Company. To all three I extend my sincere gratitude.

Finally, appreciation is hereby expressed to the Westminster Press for their kind permission to use Cobb's format in the way which I have done. I have acknowledged by notation the several places which reflect my dependence upon his work.

NOTES

1. Published by The Westminster Press, Philadelphia, 1962.
2. E. L. Mascall, L. Harold DeWolf, Henry Nelson Wieman, Emil Brunner, Karl Barth, Rudolf Bultmann, Paul Tillich, H. Richard Niebuhr, and Reinhold Niebuhr.
3. Cobb, *ibid.*, p. 14.

CONTENTS

INTRODUCTION

"There is today a recognized need for conservative, evangelical textbooks designed for use in Bible institutes, Christian colleges and theological seminaries. While there is no dearth of so-called 'scholarly' material in many of the fields of study pursued in Christian institutions, much of this material from the student point of view is either too technical and detailed for general use or too negative and destructive from a Biblical point of view." [1] Having found the condition which Unger here describes quite prevalent in the field of contemporary theology, I have endeavored to write a small volume which, on the one hand, will avoid much of the labyrinthine intricacies of modern theological thought, but which, on the other, will still present to the collegian and layman without falsification or over-simplification the salient ideas of six leading theologians of the present day. This is done with the conviction that if these modern thinkers are properly understood, much contemporary theological writing which is now imponderably dense to the student will become transparent to his understanding.

No apology is made for the conservative presuppositions of this book. Indeed, it is increasingly becoming the conviction of modern philosophers and theologians that no reasoning is without its presuppositions. According to Van Til, ". . . circular reasoning is the only reasoning that is possible to finite man." [2] And with this decision Rushdoony concurs when he writes: "All reasoning is either from God to God-given and God-interpreted facts, or from man to man-made interpretations of brute factuality. All reasoning is circular. . . ." [3] This book, then, rests quite frankly upon three presuppositions:

(1) The Bible is the Word of God written, inerrant and infallible in the autographs and remarkably preserved in the apographs. As

such, the Scriptures are possessed of certain attributes. First, they are *necessary* for a true knowledge of all the ways and works of God, this attribute opposing humanistic rationalism.[4] Second, they are *authoritative,* or self-attesting and self-authenticating, this attribute protesting against human autonomy.[5] Third, they are *sufficient* to meet man's spiritual need to know the whole counsel of God, this attribute challenging all manner of sectarianism.[6] And fourth, they are *perspicuous,* this attribute opposing chiefly a clericalism which would insist that no ordinary church member may interpret Scripture for himself directly.[7]

(2) The system of doctrine expressed in the *Westminster Confession of Faith* adheres, in my opinion, more closely to the doctrinal teaching of the Scriptures than any other systematic statement of faith and serves as my "hermeneutic" for a correct understanding of the Scriptures.

(3) The only saving Gospel is outlined by Paul in I Corinthians 15:1-4, and any other "gospel," however plausible or sophisticated it may appear to the "modern mind," is not *the* Gospel (Galatians 1:6-9), and its advocate stands under apostolic anathema.

We are certain that for many such an approach is stultifying and prejudicial, but we are equally certain that only by such a procedure will progress be made toward a valid criticism of the systems discussed herein; consequently, all theological value-judgments will be made in the light of these three assumptions.

Perhaps the Introduction to a work on contemporary theology is the place to ask and to answer the question, why should the Christian study contemporary theology? In general, simply to be intellectually alert and aware of current trends, the Christian student of theology should know what is happening in the field of modern theology. For example, he should be aware that Continental theology has undergone three significant shifts in emphasis in this twentieth century: from the optimistic liberalism of the first decade the emphasis shifted in the 1920's under the influence of Barth and Brunner to a dialectical religious experience, and then in the early 1940's under Bultmann's persuasive voice an existential theology became dominant, and finally, since mid-century the emphasis has been shifting away from Bultmannism toward what has been called, for lack of a better name, post-Bultmannianism, or the effort to relate the Christian faith more successfully and fruitfully to history.

These facts must be recognized, for it is these same influences that American theology feels, albeit in most cases belatedly. But far too often the Christian is concerned only with a basic understanding of his own position with the unhappy outcome that he neither knows nor appreciates his position. Certainly he cannot evaluate the true worth of his religious heritage. What if the surgeon were interested in medicine only to the extent that it was practiced in his hospital? Would he not justifiably be regarded as non-professional and uninformed? Surely, the Christian collegian and layman, and particularly the candidate for the Christian ministry, should cultivate an interest in current theological trends and seek to understand the systems which are possessing the minds of young and old, layman and minister, in order thereby to be able to refute their error.

Furthermore, although one might think he already knows what *ought* to be said and done relative to the several alleged options in contemporary theology even before he studies them, history has shown the danger of attempting to determine what *ought* to be in isolation from what *is*. This is simply to say that as the student of Orthodoxy seeks for himself the teaching of Scripture, rather than conducting his research in a theological and historical vacuum, he should carry out his task consciously and consistently in the full light of past creedal statements and present theological development. Even those systems judged heretical should be studied. Only then will the orthodox student's theological position become truly satisfying to him epistemologically and pistically, and relevant to his day.

Finally, the Christian should bear in mind that, since God "governs all his creatures and all their actions," the liberal and neo-orthodox theologies of the present day are part of God's overall plan and purpose for his world and this age. Today many Bible students believe that the prophetic Scriptures indicate that in the last days of this present age apostate Christendom will build an ecumenical church. If this be so, an ecumenical theology will, of necessity, have to have been constructed. Is it not likely, then, that current efforts to find a theological system which will satisfy the large communities of faith within Christendom have their place in a divinely foreordained apostasy from the Word of God? [8] In my opinion, this is more than mere likelihood. And if so, a knowledge of contemporary theology will greatly aid one to evaluate the progress of the modern ecumenical enterprise.

In this book the main emphasis will be on the methodologies (the controlling principles that guide to an affirmation) inherent within the systems of the respective theologians treated. This is done because I believe that a theological position must be understood in terms of its methodology. Indeed, the proponents themselves of recent expositions of the content of faith have indicated an awareness that theological divergences among them arise largely from differences in methodologies employed, and thus they themselves see the necessity of explaining more fully the principles that guide them to their conclusions. The student may refer to the *Prolegomena* which head Tennant's *Philosophical Theology,* Barth's *Church Dogmatics,* and Tillich's *Systematic Theology* as examples of such explanations. Furthermore, a student does not demonstrate an understanding of a theological system merely by being able to recite the isolated views of a particular theologian in a given number of areas. Until he understands the grounds upon which the systematician affirms what he does, he cannot intelligently judge the worth of the system. Finally, a determination of the theologian's methodology is important because that with which he is primarily concerned, namely, essential Christian truth, raises the question of *authority,* and in every case, the authority is the pre-scientific "given" (though this is not always forthrightly recognized) which determines the methodology to be employed. More and more it is being recognized that the starting point, the methodology, and the conclusion in any rational system are all inextricably woven together. Consequently, pinpointing the methodology through analysis will enable one more readily to determine the authority which has been accepted pre-scientifically, that is, presuppositionally. This, in turn, will reveal whether the theologian can hope to arrive at essential Christian truth.

It only remains to classify the theological positions found in the following chapters. First to be discussed will be two theological systems based upon a favorable attitude toward the use respectively of traditional philosophy and scientific empiricism as constituent elements of the theological undertaking, that is, systems stressing a natural theology as the point at which the theological edifice begins. Second, the discussion will turn to two theological systems based upon (overt) hostility toward philosophical reasoning and stressing the dialectical relationship between God and man, which in turn focuses on the religious experience as the foundation for and essence

10

of the theological edifice. Finally, two theological systems will be treated which relate themselves to philosophical existentialism, a philosophy which is itself hostile to traditional philosophy because of what it regards in the latter as naive uncritical beginning assumptions. Since this volume is intended to aid the uninitiated but interested student to draw meaningful and relevant conclusions concerning the men discussed, a criticism will attend the treatment of each man and be limited mainly to points of a Biblical nature.

In any volume where selectivity prevails, many other significant theological systems and trends could have been discussed. In the present case these include the Neo-Augustinianism of the Sphere-Sovereignty school of Herman Dooyeweerd, the Neo-Thomism of Étienne Gilson and Jacques Maritain, the post-Bultmannian school, the *Heilsgeschichte* school, the newly-emerging Pannenberg school on the European continent, the theological *aggiornamento* of Vatican II, and the radical ("death of God") theologies here in America. Allusions will be made in the appropriate places to many of these omissions, but inasmuch as the present volume is an introductory guide to the field, the systems explored, in my opinion, are representative of mainstream theological thinking and will serve as an adequate introduction to the "vocabulary" of contemporary theological thought.

NOTES

1. Merrill F. Unger, *Introductory Guide to the Old Testament* (Grand Rapids: Zondervan Publishing House, 1951), preface page.

2. Cornelius Van Til, *Metaphysics of Apologetics* (unpublished classroom syllabus), p. 16.

3. Rousas J. Rushdoony, *By What Standard?* (Philadelphia: The Presbyterian and Reformed Publishing Company, 1959), p. 29.

4. Cf. *Westminster Confession of Faith*, I, 1-3.

5. *Ibid.*, I, 4. Of course, the Holy Spirit must illumine the unbeliever's darkened mind in order that he might acknowledge Biblical authority (this work known theologically as the *testimonium Spiritus Sancti*).

6. *Ibid.*, I, 6.

7. *Ibid.*, I, 7. For a thorough discussion of these attributes, consult Cornelius Van Til, *An Introduction to Systematic Theology* (unpublished classroom syllabus), pp. 134-136.

8. As an example of what is meant here, Van Til, in the Preface to his *Christianity and Barthianism* (Philadelphia: The Presbyterian and Reformed Publishing Company, 1962), writes: "Barth's theology is rapidly becoming the rallying point for modern ecumenism. Roman Catholic and New Protestant theologians alike rejoice as Barth replaces the Christ of Luther and of Calvin with a Christ patterned after modern activist thought."

PART I: THEOLOGICAL SYSTEMS STRESSING NATURAL THEOLOGY

CHAPTER I

A BRIEF HISTORY OF NATURAL THEOLOGY

Before we look at two theological systems which place an emphasis upon a natural theology, it will prove beneficial to define a few terms and to trace historically the rise and development of natural theology.

"Natural theology" we shall understand in this survey to be the use of rational conclusions as a philosophical prolegomenon in "constructive relationship with other beliefs derived from revelation." [1] Cobb writes: "The idea of natural theology presupposes a Christian revelation that essentially confirms and supplements reason, rather than either displacing it or functioning as its ground." [2] A word of caution is in order here. One should be careful not to confuse natural theology thus defined with (1) *natural revelation,* which is the term employed in orthodox theology to indicate the location of general (that is, non-saving) revelation, namely, in the created universe; or with (2) a completely unbiblical *natural religion,* which seeks no other authority or source of religious knowledge than nature and natural reason.

All natural theologies share certain family characteristics. Ramm lists the following: (1) a genuine belief in the trustworthiness of human rational processes to find the truth about religion; (2) an effort to ground faith in empirical foundations; (3) a belief that the image of God in man (*imago Dei*), weakened in the fall, is still essentially intact; and (4) the subjection of religious propositions to the same kind of verification—namely, demonstration—that scientific assertions undergo. [3] In these systems faith in God is considered just as rational and worthy of acceptance as faith in confirmed scientific law.

15

From the earliest days of the Church a form of natural theology existed in formal theological expression. For example, in his first Apology Justin Martyr affirms many analogues of Christian doctrines in Greek philosophy. More to the point, however, this view is implicit in much early Christian teaching that the convert to Christianity could assume that the God about whom he had learned in Greek philosophy was the same God who had revealed himself in Jesus Christ. The writings of Athenagoras, Irenaeus, Clement of Alexandria, Origen, and even Tertullian are replete with explicit statements to this effect (although it is true that Tertullian has been traditionally credited with having fathered the view that there is absolutely no communion between Jerusalem and Athens, between the Church and the Academy, and with having declared: *"Credo quia absurdum est"*—"I believe because it is absurd!").[4]

Thomistic Natural Theology

It was not until the thirteenth century that the first and still normative definition of natural theology was framed.[5] In the preceding century in the teachings of Averroes (1126-1198), the famous Arabian philosopher and interpreter of Aristotle, and more fully later through his followers and Siger of Brabant, a contemporary of Thomas Aquinas, the view was crystallized that the conclusions of philosophy and faith definitely contradict and oppose each other and that one must simply accept and live with this opposition. This teaching has been labeled by philosophers as the doctrine of "twofold truth"—what is true in philosophy may be false in theology, and vice versa. This view, of course, rules out a natural theology as defined above, but it is mentioned here because it was in coming to terms with this conclusion that Aquinas developed his now-famous natural theology.

Thomas Aquinas (1225-1274), "the Angelic Doctor," could not accept the view that truth derived by reason was in opposition to truth derived by revelation. For him truth is one. Through his philosophical work Aquinas concluded rather that truths derived from the two sources supplement each other. Thus he distinguished three types of truth. First, there are truths, which, though consistent with reason, are discernible only from revelation—such as those of the Trinity and the vicarious atonement. Second, there are truths

16

derivable by philosophical speculation which are also revealed for the sake of those who have neither the time nor the capability for such mental exercise—such as the existence of God and some of his attributes. And third, there are truths about which revelation is silent—and which are therefore the proper domain of philosophical labors, such as the laws of logic. For Aquinas the last and highest truth arrived at by reason and the first and lowest truth conveyed by revelation was the existence of God. Consequently, Aquinas expended a great amount of thought and exposition in developing his celebrated five rational proofs for the existence of God, to be dealt with later in connection with the theology of E. L. Mascall.

Thomas Aquinas is likewise famous for his definitive treatments of the attributes of God by way of negation and of human knowledge of God by way of analogy. With regard to the first, Aquinas is certain that although the divine essence by its immensity far surpasses every form to which human intellection reaches, by taking the way of negation (*via negationis*) and determining what God is not, human intellection may tell something at least of what God is. A very simple example would be the conclusion that since God is not in time as we are in time, God, therefore, is eternal. One cannot help but wonder how Aquinas knew before he reached his conclusion that God is not in time as we are in time. Could it be that he assumed the validity of his conclusion in order to construct his premise?

Concerning the second concept—man's knowledge of God by way of analogy, Aquinas treated three terms: univocism, equivocism, and analogy. A term predicated *univocally* of God is a term applied to God in an *identical* sense to that which is applied to man. When predicated *equivocally*, the term is applied to God in a completely different sense to that which is applied to man. Aquinas denied both of these methods of predicating about God. He reasoned that if it be predicated of God that he is the cause of nature in the univocal sense that a father causes his son, then God becomes virtually identified with nature. The result would be pantheism. Nor can we say that just as man is good so God in a univocal sense is good. In both cases God is different from the father and the good man. On the other hand, we cannot say that everything known about God is known equivocally (or ambiguously), that is, in some sense completely different from the meanings we grant to terms. Then

17

complete discontinuity would exist between God and man's knowledge about him, and sheer agnosticism would be the result for man epistemologically. How then is God known and in which sense is anything predicated of him? Aquinas is quite sure that the answer is by proportionality or analogy. In other words, <u>God is not known directly but rather proportionally</u>. Thus the assertion, "Just as man is good, so God is good," means by way of analogy (*via analogiae*) "Just as man is good with reference to manhood, so God is good with reference to Godhood." This proportionality between God himself and his effects and perfections in creation Aquinas called "the analogy of being" (*analogia entis*). Hence, through his concepts of negation and analogy, Aquinas restricted man's knowledge of God to a negative theology and the analogy of being.[6]

The natural theology of Thomas Aquinas as set forth in his *Summa Theologica* and *Summa Contra Gentiles,* comprised in the main of his theistic proofs, negative theology, and analogy of being, is still normative for the Roman Catholic Church. And although the medieval Church's Thomistic and scholastic theology was severely criticized by the Reformers during the time of the Reformation, still some Protestants, including Luther and Melanchthon,[7] accepted with varying degrees a natural theology hardly distinguishable from the Thomistic kind.

Deistically-constructed Natural Theology

For the second major form of natural theology we must move forward historically to the seventeenth and eighteenth centuries. In the former century with the rise of modern science under the influence of the *Principia* of Sir Isaac Newton (1642-1727), the world and the universe (at least what part of it was known) came to be viewed as matter whose motion is governed by mathematical laws. And since these mathematical laws presupposed a Supreme Intelligence, it seemed only right to attribute the very creation of matter, including man, to this Intelligence. Moreover, the very fact that man was capable of such rational conclusions convinced the rationalist that man by virtue of his reasoning powers was of a high moral order and different from all other matter. This Intelligence was understood to have given man a moral law, capable of being grounded in the reasonableness of rewards and punishments after

18

death. Hence the existence of a Supreme Intelligence, a moral law, immortality, and blessedness after death all were supposed capable of demonstration by reason alone. This theological position came to be known as Deism. Lord Herbert of Cherbury (1582-1648), the "father of Deism," enumerated five points of Deism, all capable of being intuitively perceived: (1) the being of God, (2) the duty to worship him, (3) the practical-moral character of divine worship, (4) the duty to repent of sins and to forsake them, and (5) divine retribution, partly here and partly hereafter.

Then arose the question of the relation of the Christian faith to this deistic construction. Three views were soon advanced. First, one might regard Christianity as in opposition to Deism, as did Voltaire (1694-1778), for example, in his *The Bible Finally Explained* and Thomas Paine (1737-1809) in his *Age of Reason*. The rejection of Christianity by these men obviously classify their views a natural religion, however, and not a natural theology as earlier defined. Second, one might regard Christianity as simply identical with the deistic position, in which case Christianity's additional elements should be dismissed or minimized. Here the reader might note Matthew Tindal's *Christianity as Old as the Creation, or the Gospel a Republication of the Religion of Nature* (1730) and John Toland's *Christianity Not Mysterious* (1696). Although this position in a general sense may be regarded as a natural theology, it fails to qualify under our definition as a natural theology. Third, one might believe that Christianity includes not only the deistic beliefs but also additional elements as rational extensions of those beliefs. As an example here, John Locke (1632-1704) justified the acceptance of the Christian religion on the ground of its fundamental reasonableness and value in practical living. Only this third position can be understood as embodying a natural theology as previously defined. During the rationalistic eighteenth century—the Enlightenment Era, this expression of Christianity, agreeing with, yet further extending, the beliefs of Deism, was very popular and widespread.

Deism gradually collapsed under the weight of two influences. Historically, its (necessary) Newtonian view of the world gradually eroded. But much earlier, its collapse was accomplished systematically by Hume's *Dialogues Concerning Natural Religion*, in which he argues against the dogmatic assertion of the creation of the universe by a divine Intelligence by denying the traditional concept

19

of cause and effect. There was at least the possibility, according to Hume, that the universe is the result of chance. And with the downfall of Deism the natural theology extending from it was gradually superseded in the nineteenth century by the next two forms of natural theology.

Hegelian Natural Theology

To set forth the third and fourth major expressions of natural theology in church history, we must first take a short detour into the field of philosophy. This brief study is also very necessary for a proper understanding of the nineteenth-century theologians discussed in Chapter IV.

Modern philosophy is generally said to have originated in Descartes' *Cogito, ergo sum*—"I think, therefore I am." This seventeenth-century philosopher, by taking such an approach to the acquisition of truth and certification, placed a premium upon the ability of human reason alone to gain knowledge. Descartes' view, known as rationalism and formally defined as the epistemological position which asserts that knowledge can be obtained by respecting the internal demands or compulsions of reason, was more persistently developed in the writings of the great Continental Rationalists—Spinoza and Leibniz. Baruch Spinoza (1632-1677) writes in his unfinished *Treatise on the Improvement of the Understanding* in answer to the question of the method to be employed in the acquisition of knowledge: ". . . the intellect, by its native strength, makes for itself intellectual instruments, whereby it acquires strength for performing other intellectual operations, and from these operations gets again fresh instruments or the power of pushing its investigation further, and thus gradually proceeds till it reaches the summit of wisdom." Believing that reason or intelligence is the distinguishing characteristic of man, he further taught that the highest form of religion is the rational contemplation of God and that the *summum bonum* or highest good of life—the goal of ethics— is to live according to reason. Gottfried Leibniz (1646-1716) in his metaphysical treatise *Monadology* (Propositions 31-32) declares that our reasonings are founded on two great principles: (1) the (Aristotelian) law of contradiction which states that contradictories cannot both be true and (2) sufficient reason, "in virtue of which

20

we hold that no fact can be real or existent, no statement true, unless there be a sufficient reason why it is so and not otherwise." Viewing the world as the expression of perfect Reason, he constructed an idealistic metaphysics based upon his novel doctrine of a divinely (rationally) pre-established harmony in man and the world of nature.

Reacting against Continental Rationalism were the noted British Empiricists—Locke, Berkeley, and Hume. Simply stated, empiricism is the epistemological theory which attributes the origin of all knowledge to experience. We could do no better here in our representation of John Locke (1632-1704), who conceived of the human mind at birth as a blank paper (*tabula rasa*), than quoting from *An Essay Concerning Human Understanding* (II, I, 2) his famous words: "Whence comes [the mind] by that vast store, which the busy and boundless fancy of man has painted on it with an almost endless variety? Whence has it all the materials of reason and knowledge? To this I answer, in one word, from experience. In that all our knowledge is founded, and from that it ultimately derives itself. Our observations, employed either about external sensible objects, or about the internal operations of our minds, perceived and reflected on by ourselves, is that which supplies our understandings with all the materials of thinking. These two are the fountains of knowledge, from whence all the ideas we have, or can naturally have, do spring." George Berkeley (1685-1753), denying at the outset Locke's material substance as a source of our ideas though still affirming that knowledge was won through sensation, suggested God as the cause of the individual's perceiving external objects. God creatively posits finite spirits into existence, but he thinks external objects into existence through the minds of these spirits. David Hume (1711-1766) agreed with Berkeley against Locke that matter as something beyond sensation is an unverifiable inference, but carrying sense empiricism to an extreme, he drew the same conclusion about spirit. For him there is no mind, there is no cause-and-effect relationship in the traditional sense. Only psychologically-conditioned habit remains. All experience is simply impressions of sensation that are innate.[8]

It was this apparent deadlock between rationalism and empiricism that confronted Immanuel Kant (1724-1804). As Avey states, "He came to the conclusion that the Leibnizian tradition placed too much confidence in human reason and led to dogmatism, whereas the

Humean tradition represented too little confidence and led to skepticism." [9] Allegorically represented, it might be said that rationalism, on the one hand, had the "string" of reason (logic and understanding), and empiricism, on the other, had the "beads" of sensation and experience; but to Kant, as long as the two were kept apart, the "necklace" of true knowledge seemed illusory. How could the two be brought into fruitful conjunction? Or, framed philosophically, how are *a priori* synthetic judgments possible? Kant proceeded to give his answer in his distinguished criticism of human reason.

In his *Critique of Pure Reason* Kant agrees with Hume that this world consists of the movement of experienced qualities that cannot in themselves explain or justify our ideas of substance and causality. But he charges Hume with trying to reduce to sensory appearance what can never be so reduced, namely, the presuppositional frameworks which determine for sensory appearances the form they have. "There can be no specific items in space and time for one who has no capacity to perceive space and time." [10] Therefore, making a distinction between *reality* and *appearance,* Kant, in deference to the empiricists, granted that knowledge arises from sensations in the mind and posited an objective world of reality (*noumenal*) as the wellspring of sensations. On the other hand, in deference to the rationalists, Kant affirmed that space and time are *a priori* forms of experience and that the mind, in contradiction to Locke's *tabula rasa,* is structured to think along the lines of twelve categories—unity, plurality, totality, and causality, to name a few. This latter concession means that the mind itself structures or *creates* according to its own categories of thought the particular "form" (*phenomenon*) of sensation which comes to it from the world of reality. In other words, the human mind can never attain any knowledge of the thing-in-itself (*das Ding an sich*) of the noumenal world; the mind can only gain an apparitional knowledge of the thing-in-itself because of the mind's predisposition to impinge upon the thing-in-itself its own structuring categories. In other words, the noumenal realm is always separated from knowledge by the reasoning process itself. In this manner Kant sought to synthesize the rationalistic and empiricistic methods of arriving at knowledge by affirming that each needs the other. On the one hand, because knowledge includes judgment and only thought combines sensations into judgments,

22

without the categories of thought, sensations alone produce no knowledge. On the other hand, were no sensations to enter into the categories of thought, the categories would be empty abstractions and in themselves would not constitute knowledge. In short, "thoughts without content are empty; percepts without concepts are blind."

With this short philosophical excursion behind us, we may return to our discussion of the rise of Hegelian natural theology.

Kant's most revolutionary contribution to his philosophical successors was his attribution of a creative role to the mind; it had an immediate impact on philosophical and theological thinking. Cobb writes: "Kant severely restricted this role by positing an objective noumenal source of the content of experience. But just as Berkeley had rejected the material substances of Locke, so Kant's successors rejected the objective noumena of Kant. Berkeley had assumed that the objectivity of sensory stimulation must still be explained and hence had argued for God as its cause. But the idealist successors of Kant could regard creative mind as the source of the whole of its experience." [11] Illustrative of this development are Johann Fichte (1762-1814), who taught that the noumenal is the Ego, and Friedrich Schelling (1775-1854), who came to regard Kant's creative mind as the source of the whole of the experience of man, the noumenal as well as the phenomenal. Finally, G. W. F. Hegel (1770-1831) embodied the truest example of German idealism; instead of separating the realms of the noumenal and the phenomenal as Kant had done, he "regarded the phenomenal as an embodiment of the pure rationality of the noumenal." [12] In other words, Hegel concluded that there was a universal mind in which all persons and objects participate. The real is the rational and the rational is the real. Thought and being are one!

With this metaphysical view as his frame of reference, Hegel, employing a three-term dialectic of thesis, antithesis, and synthesis, worked out an elaborate system of categories in order to show precisely the unified differences of the Absolute Mind. Within such a system, never could there arise a hindrance to the smooth working of the Absolute Mind, because for every thesis there arose an antithesis, both of which would give way to their synthesis, which would immediately become the thesis for the next progressive round. "By such a dialectical procedure Hegel deduced a long list of categories.

23

The final category contained explicitly all that the first contained implicitly." [13] Even Christianity is viewed as the result of such a dialectic process.

It was a philosophy of religion influenced by Hegelianism that became the philosophical prolegomenon of the natural theologies of the liberal A. E. Biedermann (1819-1885) and the more conservative I. A. Dorner (1809-1884). Hans Martensen (1808-1884), Kierkegaard's object of resentment in the Danish Church, was also an Hegelian theologian. It is not our purpose in this chapter to elucidate the systems of these theologians,[14] but suffice it to say that few thinkers today would deny the incompatibility of Hegelian philosophy and Christianity. Indeed, few would deny that these men failed to remove the antagonism between Christianity and a philosophy which by nature sought to supersede it.

Creative Evolution

The fourth and last major form of natural theology to be discussed in the present survey is a natural theology based upon some form of creative evolution. In the eighteenth- and nineteenth-century Anglo-American world, neither Hume's criticism of rationalism was taken too seriously nor Kant's influence felt too strongly. The orderliness of the cosmos as pointing to God as its originator and sustainer remained a part of common-sense religion. The great shock to Anglo-American natural theology, according to Cobb, was the rise of Darwinian science following the publication of Charles Darwin's *On the Origin of Species by Means of Natural Selection* (1859).

Apart from sheer rejection of Darwinian evolution (which the Bible believer felt compelled to do in order to remain true to his faith commitment to the *creatio ex nihilo* doctrine of Biblical creationism) and sheer acceptance of it (which when carried consistently to its logical conclusion led to atheism and agnosticism), three major alternatives arose. First, in order to save religion, anxious theologians resorted to Kantian philosophy, thereby reducing the whole Newtonian world to the phenomenal realm and vindicating religion in the superior realm of the noumenal. Also, under Ritschlian influence the realms of fact and value were distinguished and the Newtonian world was relegated to the former. Second, Hegelian idealism was employed to show the ultimate unreality of the Darwinian world.

24

Francis H. Bradley (1846-1924) took this approach, affirming that the Absolute contains all history and progress, while Josiah Royce (1855-1916) taught that every finite aspect of the universe must be interpreted as a unique expression of the Absolute. Third, some philosophers of religion felt that the essential naturalism of the Darwinian thesis could be retained, but substituted a theistic for the mechanistic force that dominated it. Thus was developed a form of "theistic" or creative evolution—the fourth type of natural theology. This fourth type is represented by the "Process-Philosophers," who emphasize "nature as *process*" rather than "nature as *system.*" Henri Bergson (1859-1941) in his *Creative Evolution* identifies the "*élan vital,*" or vital impulse or process in the world, with God, who is a continuity of energy, a ceaseless agency of change. Samuel Alexander (1859-1938) in his *Space, Time and Deity* conceives of God as both the push or *Nisus* toward higher levels of existents and the *next unrealized level.* Here God himself is evolving. Alfred North Whitehead (1861-1947) views God in his *Process and Reality* as (1) the primordial created fact, or unlimited conceptual realization of the absolute wealth of potentiality, (2) the principle of concretion, or that actual entity from which each temporal concrescence receives that initial aim from which its self-causation starts, and (3) a consequent nature, or the presupposed actuality of conceptual operation in unison of becoming with every other creative act. Henry Nelson Wieman (1884-   ) in his *The Source of Human Good* sees God as the process operating in the world toward the production of value or worth, the process of creativity of good. In *American Philosophies of Religion* he identifies God with one aspect of the universe, namely, that activity in our midst which shapes life toward that progressive attainment of mutual support and meaning.

All such views repeat the ancient Heraclitian error of overemphasizing *process* to the neglect of *structure.* Their God is immanent, impersonal, and nothing more than an aspect of the process of nature and as such not even deserving of the name "theism." F. R. Tennant (1866-1957), an English scientist-philosopher, although holding with these Process-Philosophers that there is a force at work in nature that transcends all Newtonian natural categories which may be designated God, still affirms the existence of a personal (though finite) God on cosmic teleological grounds.

25

Our historical survey is now finished. Today, of these four major forms of natural theology—the Thomistic, the deistically-constructed, the Hegelian, and the creative evolutionary, only the Thomistic natural theology of the Roman Catholic system and certain forms of creative evolution are regarded by many as viable possibilities for natural theology. In other words, the theologian today who desires to construct a natural theology as the basis for his theological edifice thinks of the God who supplements his natural theology as being either Thomistically transcendent or a process within nature. In the next two chapters E. L. Mascall will represent the former; Henry Nelson Wieman will represent the latter.

NOTES

1. John B. Cobb, Jr., *Living Options in Protestant Theology* (Philadelphia: The Westminster Press, 1962), p. 18.

2. *Ibid.*

3. Bernard Ramm, *Varieties of Christian Apologetics* (Grand Rapids: Baker Book House, 1961), p. 16.

4. It is true that in Tertullian's *On the Flesh of Christ*, he employs the thought, "It is certain because it is impossible."

5. I am indebted to Cobb's *Living Options in Protestant Theology*, Chapter 1, for the main outline of this present chapter.

6. For a penetrating analysis of Thomas's natural theology showing the unbiblical methodology resident within it, consult Cornelius Van Til, *A Christian Theory of Knowledge* (unpublished classroom syllabus), pp. 119-124.

7. Herman Dooyeweerd, *A New Critique of Theoretical Thought* (Philadelphia: The Presbyterian and Reformed Publishing Company, 1953), I, 511-515.

8. For a brief treatment of the rationalist and empiricist failures to make their respective cases, consult Gordon H. Clark, *Religion, Reason and Revelation* (Philadelphia: The Presbyterian and Reformed Publishing Company, 1961), pp. 50-58.

9. Albert E. Avey, *Handbook in the History of Philosophy* (New York: Barnes & Noble, Inc., 1961), p. 165.

10. *Ibid.*, p. 166.

11. Cobb, *op. cit.*, pp. 27-28.

12. *Ibid.*, p. 28.

13. Clark, *op. cit.*, p. 66.

14. For discussions of these systems, consult Hugh Ross Mackintosh, *Types of Modern Theology* (London: James Nisbet & Co., Ltd., 1937), pp. 130-134; and J. L. Neve, *A History of Christian Thought* (Philadelphia: The Muhlenberg Press, 1946), II, 122-127.

CHAPTER II

MASCALL'S THOMISTIC METHOD

ABOUT ERIC MASCALL

Eric Lionel Mascall was born in Sydenham, Kent, England, in 1905. He was educated at Pembroke College, Cambridge (B.A. in mathematics), Ely Theological College, University of London (B. Sc.), Oxford University (D.D.), and Cambridge University (D.D.). He is an Anglican priest and theologian, a Tutor at Christ Church, Oxford, and a Lecturer in the Philosophy of Religion in the University of Oxford. He had twice served as Bampton Lecturer (Oxford, 1956; Columbia University, 1958).

His published works may be divided into the philosophico-theological ones: *He Who Is: A Study in Traditional Theism*; *Existence and Analogy: A Sequel to "He Who Is"*; *Words and Images: A Study in Theological Discourse*; and *Via Media*; and the ecclesiastico-theological ones: *Christ, the Christian, and the Church*; *Corpus Christi*; and *The Recovery of Unity*.

In recent times he had written against the "new morality" and "secular Christianity" in his *The Secularization of Christianity*.

Treatments of Neo-Thomism and Mascall which will be beneficial to the American reader are David H. Freeman's chapter on Neo-Thomism in his *Recent Studies in Philosophy and Theology* and Cobb's chapter on Mascall in his *Living Options in Protestant Theology*.

The theological writings of Eric Mascall brilliantly reflect a philosophical or rational theology which is part of a larger movement known today as Neo-Thomism. Neo-Thomism, as the name indicates, denotes a re-examining of, as well as a return to, the natural theology of Thomas Aquinas. It represents the philosophico-theological phase of the overall effort of the Roman Catholic communion to re-assert herself in the twentieth century, particularly in the English-speaking world.

As would naturally be expected, Neo-Thomism has been given new and sophisticated exposition chiefly through the writings of Roman Catholic scholars, such as Étienne Gilson, Jacques Maritain, and R. Garrigou-Lagrange.[1] However, some Anglo-Catholics, such as F. J. E. Woodbridge and John D. Wild here in America, and Mascall in England, have given expression, outside the perimeter of Roman Catholicism, to what may be classified as Neo-Thomism. In the case of the Anglo-Catholic group, they do not write out of any "communal compulsion" to defend an empirical church body but, as Mascall himself declares, from the "conviction that the rational case for theism is as strong to-day as it was in the first or in the thirteenth century."[2]

Mascall is fully aware that the approach to theology which he advocates is philosophically and logically reprehensible to both philosophers and theologians.[3] Nevertheless, he countercharges that there are only two real alternatives to natural theology as a basis for Christian theology.[4] First is the mystic's contention that knowledge of God is attained through the religious experience itself, which offers its own sufficient proof (the "I was there when it happened, so I really ought to know"—type of apologetic). In rebuttal, Mascall, while allowing that an experience with God gives knowledge of him, yet insists that such an experience is not the normal way to learn of God and that a religious experience is no substitute for natural theology. Second is the contention of the essentialist (one who holds that the concept of the *essence* of a being includes its actual *existence*), following the Anselmic ontological argument for God's existence, that God's existence is self-evident in the very concept "God." Anselm (1033-1109) in his *Proslogium* (Chaps. II and III) affirmed that the very concept of

28

God implies his existence because such a concept conceives of the most perfect being that can be imagined, and the lack of his existence would contradict the concept since one can have a concept of a God with existence which is greater than the "impossible concept" of a God without existence. Mascall replies that this argument only proves that man is not capable of forming a concept of God that does not include his existence. But man's concept of God's existence is not the same as God's existence.[5]

Actually, there is another possibility open to Mascall were he of a mind to consider it, namely, a theology based uncompromisingly on the authoritative, written revelation of Holy Scripture, and specifically on what it teaches, for example, in Romans 1-3 concerning man's natural inclination in his fallen state to suppress all revelational truths concerning God's nature, his own depravity, and his need of a Savior to redeem him from the guilt and power of sin— in short, a theology pursuing the methodology of the great Reformed creeds. But, as we shall see, this course he fails to take.

The "Five Ways"

In formulating his natural theology, Mascall begins with Thomas's five proofs for the existence of God (his famous "Five Ways" are found in his *Summa Theologica, I, 2*).[6]

The first way is the argument from motion or change. Understanding change in the Aristotelian sense of the actualization of potentiality, Thomas argues that every change requires an explanatory cause that is inherent in neither the potentiality nor that which is actualized. A proximate cause can also be the effect of a more remote cause; but since it is impossible to conceive of infinite causal regress, for in that case there would be no first mover and consequently no motion at all, Thomas concludes that "it is necessary to arrive at a first mover which itself is not moved by anything; and everyone understands this to be God."

The second way is the argument from efficient causation. The very being of an effect requires an efficient cause outside itself, but again, since it is impossible to conceive of infinite causal regress, there must be a first efficient cause, itself uncaused, and to this, Aquinas observes, "everyone gives the name of God."

29

3.   The third way is the argument for the necessity of a first cause from contingency. Thomas argues that everything about us is capable of not existing. And if there were ever a time when nothing existed, nothing ever could have existed. But because something does exist, a prior cause is necessary. To avoid infinite regress, Aquinas argues for the necessity of a first necessary being; and this first necessary being, Aquinas writes, "all men speak of as God."

4.   The fourth way is the argument from degrees of perfection in things. Thomas reasons that the degrees of perfection observable in things can be understood only against the backdrop of an absolute norm. Thus the fact that beings exist with limited perfection implies their immediate dependence upon a being that is perfect in itself. Moreover, if a thing possesses only limited perfection, it must receive it from a thing which possesses it unconditionally and without limitation, and this being, Thomas affirms, "we call God." The fact that Thomas does not expressly make use of the denial of infinite regress in this argument does not alter the fact that this denial is implicit even here.

5.   The fifth way is the argument from purpose. The final end or purpose of entities, Aquinas alleges, demands a supreme intelligence which directs all things to their natural and purposive end. The final cause, the goal at which all purposes tend, "we call God."

Mascall's Reconstruction

The five proofs for God's existence as framed by Thomas all depend upon two ideas: first, the cause-and-effect relationship, and second, the idea that an infinite regress is repugnant to the intellect. Mascall is convinced, however, that Thomas's theistic proofs did not intend to emphasize the cause-and-effect relationship as such or the intellect's aversion to infinite regress as much as something else, namely, the *finitude* inherent in the entities of this world.

This novel interpretation, important to an understanding of Neo-Thomistic natural theology, means that each of Thomas's arguments "points to some aspect of finitude and insufficiency on the part of the entities in our world, on the basis of which we are driven to recognize a self-sufficient cause of a wholly different order." [7] "Their primary function, as I believe, is not to provide us with five different proofs of God's existence . . .," writes Mascall. "Their function is to exhibit to us five different characteristics of finite being, all of which show that it does not account for its own existence. In the last resort St. Thomas has only one datum for an argument for the existence of God, namely the existence of beings whose existence is not necessitated by their essence; that is, beings in which essence and existence are really distinct." [8]

Mascall then asserts that the one necessary requirement for the acceptance of Thomas's sometimes unclear argumentation is the "simple recognition that there are finite entities and subsequent reflection on what this means." [9] Mascall writes: "The highly Aristotelian form which St. Thomas gives to his argument for the existence of God is not essential to it and moreover . . ., for us at the present day, it clouds to some extent the real issue. What *is* necessary is the recognition of finite being as being in which there is a real distinction of essence and existence, as something which is *there* and yet need not be there, as perfect in its degree and yet not self-subsistent perfection; as being whose very limitation declares that whatever it is and has it receives from without, as an effect implying a cause that possesses in its own right all that it communicates. . . . It is this recognition that things . . . cannot account for their own occurrence—that is the necessary basis of the cosmological or existential approach to theism." [10]

But Mascall is also aware that such a step as the acceptance of the existence of objective, finite entities is not possible to many intellectuals because of their epistemological views. Thus he sets about to refute their views. Against the empiricists of the Humean order—the greatest threat to his system—who reduce all experience to impressions of innate sense data which cannot prove the existence of any entity and who then assert that our awareness of objects is the creative and distorting act of the mind, Mascall urges that along with the *senses,* man has an *intellect,* whose "proper object . . . is not being in general but the being of sensible things." [11] Thus he writes: "Man . . . does not consist of two beings, one sensitive and the other intelligent; he is one being who both senses and understands. Thus, says Gilson, 'we can form a certain knowledge of singulars. By the senses we attain directly to the things known, thanks to our perception of their sensible qualities, and by the intellect we attain to these same things, thanks to the abstract concepts which we form of them.' " [12] In other words, Mascall

31

declares that the human mind has not only sensations of objective finite entities but also an intellect which judges the validity of the sensations and ascribes finite existence, in harmony with the senses, to the objects whose existence is given by the senses. The intellect, it is true, can at times err, but it will not normally do so. In this way, Mascall accredits finite existents.

Mascall recognizes that this construction is not really "proof" of the existence of finite beings, but it is, he is assured, the philosophical description of a fact of common experience. And "the fact and not the theory is the basis for the natural knowledge of God." [13]

According to Mascall, the primary implication of the entire argument for the existence of finite beings is the existence of God as their cause, to whom must be ascribed self-existence, infinity, self-sufficiency, and necessity. For to ascribe anything less to him is simply to postpone the question of the true cause and so to postpone the question of God. It should be quite clear from this that, in spite of all of his efforts to modernize Thomas's Five Ways, Mascall still leans the entire weight of his argument upon the cause-and-effect relationship and the aversion of the human mind to infinite regress.

Mascall knows that he has developed his argument sufficiently to satisfy many people that God exists, but he knows also that actually he is not yet "out of the woods" logically. For in predicating of God existence and causality, not to mention infinity, self-sufficiency, and necessity, he has, in his statements about an infinite God, employed terms that derive their meaning from their relation to the finite sphere. Mascall anticipates a very serious objection to his argument in the following words: "You have already asserted, we shall be told, that the only existence which you can apprehend is that of finite beings; you denied, in so many words, that you were an ontologist. But now you are saying that you have apprehended the existence of a being which is more than finite. Again, you have told us that the causality which God exerts on finite beings is altogether different from any causality which finite beings themselves can exercise; your whole argument for God's existence depends upon your assertion that there is something about finite beings, namely their existence, which no finite cause can confer. But since the only causality of which you, as a finite being, can be aware is the causality which finite beings exercise, in attributing causality to

God you are using the word 'causality' in a sense to which, on your own hypothesis, it is impossible to attach any meaning. You are in fact in an insoluble dilemma. If you assert existence and causality of God in the same sense in which you assert them of finite beings, you are rendering God incapable of fulfilling the very function for whose performance you alleged him to be necessary. But if you assert existence and causality of God in an altogether different sense from that in which you assert them of finite beings, you are making statements about God to which you can, *ex hypothesi,* assign no intelligible content. God therefore is either useless or unthinkable; this would seem to be the conclusion of the matter. We seem to be on the brink of an ontological argument for the non-existence of God." [14]

To rebut this objection, Mascall falls back upon Aristotle's concept of *analogy,* just as Thomas did before him, and devotes to its exposition an entire chapter in *Existence and Analogy.* His first step is to agree with Thomas that when one is discussing God, all predications about him are analogical, and not univocal or equivocal.[15] Then, again with Thomas, he distinguishes within the concept of analogy (1) an analogy that holds between two beings in consequence of the relation each bears to a third, and (2) an analogy that indicates a relation which one being bears to another. Mascall sees only the latter type as applying to predications about God. This type itself he divides into two.

The first sub-type is the analogy of attribution which *attributes* to God *virtually* the perfections found in creatures *formally*; that is to say, he is able to produce those perfections found in the creature, but it does not necessitate God's possessing them formally himself. The second sub-type—the analogy of proportionality—implies that the analogy under discussion is found formally in each of the two beings but in a sense commensurate with or proportional to the nature of each being. Thus a man possesses life in a sense proper to man, and God possesses life in that supreme sense proper to self-existent being itself. Thus by "combining in a tightly interlocked union both analogy of attribution and analogy of proportionality," the analogical relation between God and the world is made "really satisfactory." [16] But even so, Mascall affirms that the doctrine of analogy renders only "some intelligibility in what by its very nature must be a mystery." [17]

33

From this discussion of Mascall's theology, it is clear that Mascall differs very little from Thomas in point of view. Both affirm the existence of God from arguments dependent upon the cause-and-effect relationship and the denial of infinite regress; both declare that all predication about God is analogical. There appears to be only one minor difference: Mascall seems to be more willing than Aquinas to rest his argument at points on "common sense" or common experience.[17a]

Criticism

At this point the discussion will turn to a criticism of Mascall's Thomistically-constructed natural theology. This criticism will attempt to refute not only Mascall's methodology, but also that of Thomas himself as well as some Protestant theologians who approve of the theistic proofs. The refutation may be divided into two main parts—from logic and from Biblical statement. We shall look at both in turn.

Refutation from logic. From the standpoint of formal logic, Mascall's argument is replete with difficulties.

(1) His own admissions weaken his argument. He admits, as Cobb shows, that "a certain habit of mind is required in order that the data of natural theology be allowed to present themselves to the viewer." [18] In short, his argument lacks the self-authentication of a compelling argument. Again, by Mascall's own admission, few if any thinkers prior to the great Scholastics perceived of the existence of things in terms of finiteness, and even they did so under the influence of Scriptural teaching. Cobb asks pointedly: "Can we say that what we learned to see under the influence of revelation is in fact the one natural way of seeing things." [19] Finally, his "proof" for the existence of finite entities—so vital to his argument as a whole—namely, that man possesses not only senses but also an intellect which ascribes existence to objects, is really not a proof at all, but rather constitutes his "given," based upon what he perceives to be "common experience."

(2) His argument violates the rules of formal logic. Mascall's entire argument may be reduced to the category of cause and effect. Although he employs none of Thomas's "Five Ways" uncritically, especially so, the cosmological argument, still a simple paraphrase

34

of his argument might run, "This world, as a finite existent, implies God, as its infinite cause." Now once he has chosen the "rational" method to demonstrate the validity of the Christian claim to the existence of the Christian God, he should be able to prove his affirmation by formally valid logic. But we do not think he can for the following reasons.

(a) An argument from the standpoint of formally valid logic must be able to define its terms. Throughout his argument Mascall employs the term "cause." For its definition, however, he relies on the concept of analogy and affirms that God is a cause in the sense that is proper to him, but precisely what that sense is, Mascall is unable to say. He even admits that his analysis of the *analogia entis* between God and his effects and perfections in creation has left much mystery, the Scriptures being necessary for the elucidation thereof.

(b) An argument from the standpoint of formally valid logic must use each major term in only one sense throughout the argument. But Mascall does not hesitate to affirm that all predication about God is analogical, that is, nothing is predicated of God and the world in a univocal sense. Hence, when Mascall argues that since a finite world exists an infinite God must exist but self-consciously employs the term "exists" in two different senses—one applicable to finite entities and one applicable to infinitude, he becomes guilty of the fallacy of equivocation.

(c) An argument from the standpoint of formally valid logic must seek out and rid itself of its unproven assumptions. Mascall's argument contains both obvious and hidden ones. As examples of the obvious assumption, the following may be noted: (1) assuming for the moment that the argument as formulated by Mascall is valid, Mascall's identification of the arrived-at "self-sufficient cause" with the *Christian* God is an inference, a "leap," not a proposition demonstrated by the argument itself. (2) Inasmuch as Mascall does not *prove* anything concerning the world, not even that it is composed of finite entities (this latter assertion based solely on the *assumption* that our intellects would not deceive us in our experiencing in common finite existents), he really winds up assuming that this world is an effect, which, as we shall see presently, involves him in another logical difficulty.

An example of a hidden assumption is his unstated distinction between description and explanation. For him not to make this distinction would prove fatal to his argument. Simply defined, description tells how a thing is; explanation tells why a thing is. Now the presupposition of every theistic proof is the existence of a phenomenon which is capable of being described but which demands for its explanation a reason lying outside of it. In scientific inquiry today, the opinion has increasingly prevailed that explanation is only more inclusive description, that the distinction between the two concepts is only one of degree. Thus a complete description of a phenomenon would include its complete explanation. Because of a lack of knowledge at present, explanation may be desirable, but the possibility at least exists that experimentation could produce a complete description which would describe in terms of natural law what was before considered an explanation.

Cobb is right that there is a certain "common-sense" distinction between description and explanation, but the point we are making is that the burden is Mascall's to demonstrate this distinction. And until he does so, his theistic proof is logically suspect.

(d) An argument from the standpoint of formally valid logic must avoid the logical fallacy of *petitio principii* (begging the question), or circular reasoning. Yet Mascall's argument commits this error at least three ways. (1) Earlier we noted that Mascall really *assumes* that this world is an *effect*. But if this is done, the proposition to be proved is already assumed, because an effect as an effect logically demands its cause. This is circular reasoning, for an effect can only be an effect if there is first a cause to produce it, but this is the very point that the argument is intended to prove. Now it is true that Mascall never argues for the finite existence of the entire world. The finite existence of any part of it, he concludes, would prove the same thing. But this conclusion only involves him in still another dilemma. His final conclusion, it should be recalled, is that God is the cause of the entire world and not just a part of it. To conclude this, however, he must argue that, if any part of the world is finite and thus dependent upon an infinite cause, the whole world is finite and thus dependent upon an infinite cause. This is to argue for the same essential nature of a whole from the nature of its parts. But *a whole can be essentially different from its parts*, as Gordon H. Clark has shown with an amusing illustration: "Salt is good to eat—on eggs at least; it is a preservative of pork and olives; it is also, essentially, a chemical compound. But its constituent parts are sodium and chlorine. They are essentially elements. They are also essentially poisonous to the human system. The salt on pretzels tastes good, but who would put a piece of sodium on his tongue? It simply is not true that parts singly have the same characteristics as the wholes of which they are components." [20] (2) Throughout his argument Mascall tacitly denies that a regressing series of causes can regress to infinity, the reason for such a denial being that otherwise there would be no first cause. Of course, an infinite regress is incompatible with a first "self-sufficient cause," but since the argument must be logical to be valid, the existence of the first cause—the proposition to be proven—cannot be appealed to ahead of time to support the premise that an infinite regress is out of the question. (3) It was noted above that Mascall assumes the distinction between description and explanation and, moreover, that the presupposition of every theistic proof is the existence of a phenomenon which is capable of being described but which demands for its explanation a reason lying outside of it. Obviously, Mascall must assume this distinction. On the other hand, to make the distinction involves circular reasoning. As Cobb writes, "If we believe that the distinctive category of explanation can be applied to cosmic activity, we must suppose that the cosmos is personal, for there is no such thing as a nonpersonal explanation that is other than generalized description. But we are then assuming what we are supposedly inquiring about. Either the cosmos is personal and we do right to seek an explanation of the world, or the cosmos is not personal and we can only describe phenomena." [21] Thus in assuming such a distinction, Mascall assumes the truth of the very thing for which he is arguing, and thereby commits the logical fallacy of circular reasoning.

(e) An argument from the standpoint of formally valid logic, as David Hume pointed out long ago, should not ascribe to a cause any properties beyond those necessary to account for the effect. Agreeing with Hume, Clark rightly affirms: "The cosmological argument, if otherwise sound, might give us a God sufficiently powerful to be the cause of what we observe; but no more. In spite of the remark of some orthodox theologians that that is already a good deal, one must reply that it is not the omnipotent creator described in the Bible." [22] In the light of this logic, Mascall's theistic proof totally fails to demonstrate the existence of the

Christian God. But even more repugnant to Christian theism is the fact that Mascall's argument, if valid, would prove the existence of either a good God who is not omnipotent or an omnipotent God who is not good, because *the observed effects of this world include sin and calamity.*[23] If the God of the cosmological argument is a *good* cause of the world, according to logic he is not omnipotent because he would want to rid the world of sin and evil. Since, however, sin and evil are actually present, apparently he cannot overcome them. If the God of the cosmological argument is an *omnipotent* cause of the world, again according to logic he is not good, because he would then have the power to rid the world of sin and evil but obviously does not wish to. Now the problem of the presence of sin in a world sovereignly governed by a holy God is a very real one for the Christian apologist and should not be dismissed lightly or handled in a cavalier fashion, but suffice it to say here that the theistic proofs have no answer to the problem. Only in revelational verities will any valid solution ever be found.

From the standpoint of formal logic, we may conclude that Mascall's argument for the existence of God is invalid. Clark is correct when he writes: "It is not possible to begin with sensory experience and proceed by the formal laws of logic to God's existence as a conclusion." [24]

If the theistic proofs are not valid, are they at least *useful?* Opinion varies among Christian scholars at this point. Some have discarded them as utterly worthless. Others contend that though they are not formally valid, they are nonetheless helpful as *testimonia.* No doubt, any answer requires qualification. If they are used with the express intent to logically persuade the unbeliever to accept Christian theism, they are not only not logically valid, but also they are even anti-Christian in that (1) they imply that men are rationally able to pass judgment on the question of God's existence when in reality the unbeliever is spiritually blind (Rom. 1:22); (2) they imply that man is "neutral" with reference to God, needing to have God's existence proved to him, when in reality he is a covenant breaker who possesses already all the evidence required to condemn him in the sight of God (Rom. 1:20) and who actually has every reason to conclude that God does *not* exist; and (3) their use as supposedly rationally logical deductions is the employment of illegitimate means to win men to Christ, for if the Christian apologist *knows* them to be logically problematical and chooses to use them just the same, even if he is successful in his witness, he is taking advantage of the unlearned who do not see their faults. And ultimately, he will do untold harm to the convert's spiritual growth, for now the convert must learn from another source that he in fact was not in a position at the time of his conversion to judge the Word of God, a fact that he might now never learn. If, on the other hand, the Christian apologist uses them in such a way that they obviously presuppose Biblical revelation (specifically, what that revelation has to say about man's blindness and enmity toward his Maker) and directs their appeal to the knowledge of God which every man already possesses as a bearer of God's image, that is to say, if he grounds them in the Creator-creature relationship and self-consciously employs them, not as logically valid arguments, but only as means to make the covenant breaker epistemologically self-conscious and hence God- and covenant-conscious, then they could be valuable; but then the Christian apologist will discover that he will only have been pro-claiming the Gospel, as it should be proclaimed, in an authoritative manner, the effectual working of this proclamation being left to the sovereign operation of the Holy Spirit of God.

Mascall is neither ignorant nor lacking in a knowledge of logic. Such refutation will not take him by surprise; he is no doubt aware of the factors which logically invalidate his argument. In fact, he even agrees that there is a real difference between the God of philosophical theology and the God of the Scriptures and that the former is poor and barren beside the latter.[25] Nevertheless, he is still assured, on the basis of a kind of assumed intuition in man, that the God of his natural theology and the God of Christian theism are the same God. Moreover, Mascall is not alone in this opinion. The vindication of Christian theism by means of the rational proofs for God's existence is a common apologetic approach. But the questions must be squarely faced: Is this approach in harmony with all that the Scriptures teach concerning God and his self-revelation to man, and man's ability and willingness to understand and to heed these verities *prior* to his conversion? More particularly, is such an apologetic Pauline? Did Paul urge the natural man, by means of the theistic proofs, to accept the truth of the Christian claim that a God with a certain specific nature exists? Or did he believe that such a means was unnecessary, indeed, even harmful, in that it granted, by the very nature of the appeal itself, that the natural man prior to his spiritual conversion was capable of perceiving spiritual truths? To these pertinent questions we address ourselves now.

Refutation from Biblical statement. The Pauline apologetic is located in Romans 1:18-32, 2:14-15, I Corinthians 2:14, Acts 14:15ff., and Acts 17:11ff. In these passages Paul under divine inspiration teaches certain crucial things pertaining to the present problem. First, Paul teaches that God has revealed his eternal power and Godhood in his creation (Rom. 1:20) and his law through the activity of man's conscience (Rom. 2:14-15). The rain and the fruitful seasons reveal God's goodness to man (Acts 14:17). Second, Paul teaches that man, even in his present fallen condition, is aware of the Creator's existence (Rom. 1:19-20): "That which is known of God is manifest in them, for God manifested [it] to them. For his invisible attributes, even his eternal power and Godhood, since the time of the creative activity (which brought) the world (into existence), is completely visible, being continually perceived by means of the things having been made" (private translation). Furthermore, he teaches in Romans 1:32 that the wicked and unbelievers "thoroughly know by experience" the ordinance of God that they who are accustomed to practice evil are worthy of death. And, as if this were not enough knowledge to grant to the unbeliever, Paul declares in Romans 2:14-15 that "when the Gentiles who do not have law do by nature the things of the law the same, even though they do not have law, are a law unto themselves, who show that what the law demands is written in their hearts, by the fact of their conscience bearing witness and their thoughts, meanwhile, alternately accusing or defending themselves" (private translation). Thus Paul concludes that the accusing conscience evidences a knowledge of a moral law resident within man.

Because of this religious knowledge which he possesses, man knows of God and is essentially a *homo religiosus*. The explicit teaching of Paul in Romans 1:21-23 and Acts 17:23 is that *man must worship.* But Paul also teaches that *what* man worships depends upon his nature. In Romans 1:18-23 and I Corinthians 2:14, Paul declares that it is not man's nature to live in accord with true religious knowledge. Rather, his very nature, now depraved, instructs him to suppress all such truth in unrighteousness and to exchange as his object of worship the glory of the incorruptible God for the likeness of the image of corruptible man, birds, four-footed creatures, and creeping things. In short, *man by nature must worship, but he will not worship God*. Moreover, the Scripture teaches that such spiritual truth as man possesses is being continually reinforced by the additional revelation pressing in upon him from the existing universe and from even himself. But does he heed this revelation? No, he continually suppresses it because it is *now* his nature to do so. Were he, for one moment, to admit the truth of such revelation, he would also have to admit his own creaturehood, his rebellion and disobedience, and the justice of his condemnation before God. He would even have to worship the Creator rather than the creature. Consequently, he refuses to admit the fact of revelation. Would not these Scriptural facts alone rule out the theistic proofs as means of convincing the unbeliever of the truth of God's existence? He already knows that God exists but suppresses this knowledge. Would he not suppress the same knowledge even if it could come to him by means of the rational proofs?

The theistic proofs as traditionally formulated and employed actually involve an improper use of natural revelation. What is the purpose of this form of revelation? Prior to his fall, man would have possessed an immediate awareness of the revelation which obtained between his Creator and the universe. He would have known that God is the Creator as soon as he knew anything at all about the universe.[26] But since the fall, natural revelation has included the wrath of God (Rom. 1:18) and has had for its purpose the rendering of man inexcusable before God. Paul expressly declares in Rom. 1:19 that God revealed himself in nature to men "so that they may be (*eis to einai*) without a defense." Is it not clear then that God never intended natural revelation to be a sort of "neutral area" upon which natural theology could build a case for Christian theism? We can only conclude that Mascall's intent, as well as his argument, is unscriptural.

So far we have examined and criticized only Mascall's argument for the existence of God on the basis of the existence of objective finite entities. But Mascall incurs further difficulty when he attempts to bring this philosophically-constructed God into conjunction with the God of revelation. One example may suffice to illustrate this point. The God of Scripture is a personal God. As such, he is gracious, merciful, longsuffering, abounding in loving-kindness, and forgiving. On the other side of the ledger, he is wrathful and righteous in his judgments. He will by no means acquit the evildoer. Now it will be recalled that Mascall argues from the existence of finite entities which do not contain the ground of their own being to a source of all being that necessarily contains the ground of its own existence. Such a being, Mascall insists, must be self-sufficient and necessary, genuinely transcendent to and independent of the world. To support this conception, Mascall feels compelled to affirm the impassibility of God, that is, that God is absolutely changeless and unaffected emotionally by what happens to men, even though this view introduces a serious tension between the God of Scripture and the God of his rational theology. For Mascall, God is altogether free from the vicissitudes and evils of this world; not to affirm this makes God essentially part of this world order. Although God loves man, he loves not in any sympathizing way, but in such a way that he offers "concrete practical help." All such ideas as God grieving because of our sin, rejoicing at our repentance, and feeling for us in our suffering must be understood in a purely metaphorical sense.[28]

Now no real Christian would deny that to contemplate the influence of the suffering and sin of this world upon its Creator raises deep mysteries which stagger the most powerful minds. Yet acknowledging such influence is not nearly so problematical to the Christian mind as its denial because the Scriptures plainly indicate that God grieves, rejoices, and responds to devotion and rebellion.[29] Mascall's construction of God's impassibility serves as a good illustration of how the God of Scripture is invariably made to conform to the philosophically-constructed God of natural theology.

This exposition and criticism of Mascall's Thomistic methodology has shown that God's existence cannot be demonstrated logically on the basis of the observation of objective existents. And the Christian can be pleased that it cannot. If it could, it would be a strong argument in favor of the *non-existence* of the God of Christian theism, not to mention the lie which it would make of all that the Scriptures teach concerning the nature of man and his attitude toward God and spiritual things. Even if it could, its conclusions have to be supplemented by the additional revelation of Scripture which requires a "leap" on the part of both proponent and opponent, for the question—why this body of revelation and not another—is not an idle one. And finally, as we have seen, the supplementing revelation is invariably distorted at some point or other. Mascall has fallen into the error of all natural theologians: he has allowed his philosophical presuppositions so to control Scriptural revelation that the latter ceases to call men to turn fully away from themselves to *full* faith in Jesus Christ as Savior from sin and as Lord of the life.

NOTES

1. Cf. Gilson's *Le Thomisme* and *God and Philosophy,* Maritain's *The Three Reformers* and *The Dream of Descartes,* and Garrigou-Lagrange's *Dieu, son existence et sa nature.*

2. E. L. Mascall, *Existence and Analogy* (London: Longmans, Green and Co., Ltd., 1949), p. x.

3. Cf. John B. Cobb, Jr., *Living Options in Protestant Theology* (Philadelphia: The Westminster Press, 1962), pp. 34-36, for a brief discussion of the objections raised by the philosopher and theologian to natural theology and Mascall's answers to them.

4. E. L. Mascall, *He Who Is: A Study in Traditional Theism* (London: Longmans, Green and Co., Ltd., 1943), pp. 16-34. Cf. *Existence and Analogy,* pp. 21-28.

5. Mascall, *Existence and Analogy,* pp. 22-23.

6. Mascall, *He Who Is,* pp. 40-56.

7. Cobb, *op. cit.,* p. 39.

8. Mascall, *Existence and Analogy,* pp. 77-78; cf. also pp. 68-69.

9. Cobb, *op. cit.,* p. 40.

10. Mascall, *op. cit.,* pp. 84-85.

11. *Ibid.,* p. 55.

12. *Ibid.,* p. 54.

13. Cobb, *op. cit.,* p. 41.

14. Mascall, *op. cit.,* pp. 86-87.

15. The reader may recall from an earlier discussion of Thomas in Chapter I that a term used *univocally* of God intends a sense precisely *identical* to the sense that is intended when it is used of man; a term used *equivocally* intends a sense completely *unrelated* to the sense intended when used of man; but a term used *analogically* is the *via media* between them—indicating attribution or proportion.

16. Mascall, *op. cit.,* p. 113.

17. *Ibid.,* p. 121.

17a. J. Oliver Buswell, Jr., in *A Systematic Theology of the Christian Religion* (Grand Rapids: Zondervan Publishing House, 1962), I, 75-77, is convinced that Thomas thought of his arguments for God's existence not as "complete demonstrations in the sense of syllogistic logic" but rather as "inductive probability reasonings, helpful to men who already have some knowledge of God." With this opinion neither Clark, Carnell, nor Van Til (as I understand them) would concur, all of them contending that Thomas is completely *empiricistic* throughout the development of his argumentation, even maintaining that "nothing is in the intellect which is not first in the senses." As I indicate in the following section, I am personally persuaded that these last three men more accurately represent Thomas's intent.

18. Cobb., *op. cit.*, p. 48.

19. *Ibid.*

20. Gordon H. Clark, *Religion, Reason and Revelation* (Philadelphia: The Presbyterian and Reformed Publishing Company, 1961), p. 42.

21. Cobb, *op. cit.*, p. 60.

22. Clark, *op. cit.*, p. 40.

23. The effects of this world also include much that is, from *empirical* observation, meaningless and purposeless, a fact fatal to the teleological argument. What, on *empirical* grounds, is the purpose behind the untimely death of a young father of four children? What, in fact, on *empirical* grounds, is the purpose behind the sin and calamity of this world? Only revelational verities can give the solution (cf. Rom. 8:28).

24. Clark, *op. cit.*, p. 35.

25. Mascall, *He Who Is,* p. 81.

26. Cornelius Van Til, *An Introduction to Systematic Theology* (unpublished classroom syllabus), p. 73.

27. Mascall, *Existence and Analogy,* p. 142.

28. *Ibid.,* p. 136.

29. For support of the position herein taken that God does "feel" love, joy, grief, etc., cf. Charles Hodge, *Systematic Theology* (Grand Rapids: Wm. B. Eerdmans Publishing Company [n. d.]), I, 428; J. Oliver Buswell, Jr., *A Systematic Theology of the Christian Religion,* I, 55-57.

CHAPTER III

WIEMAN'S EMPIRICAL NEO-NATURALISM

ABOUT HENRY NELSON WIEMAN

Henry Nelson Wieman (1884-   ) was born in Rich Hill, Missouri, the son of a Presbyterian minister. He did his undergraduate work at Park College (B.A., 1907); then upon graduation from San Francisco Seminary (Presbyterian), he spent a year in Germany studying under Eucken at Jena and under Windelband and Troeltsch at Heidelberg. After a short pastorate in Davis, California, he went to Harvard University and earned the Ph.D. degree (1917), studying there under Ernest Hocking and Ralph Barton Perry.

He taught in the philosophy department at Occidental College (Los Angeles) from 1917 to 1927, and then accepted the position of Professor of Philosophy of Religion at the Divinity School of the University of Chicago, formally retiring from that position in 1947. Since his retirement he has taught at the Universities of Oregon, Houston, and Southern Illinois.

His writings, reflecting the influences of his Harvard professors, Bergson, Dewey, Whitehead, and Tillich, include *Religious Experience and Scientific Method, The Wrestle of Religion with Truth, The Issues of Life, The Source of Human Good* (his most famous work), *The Directive in History, Man's Ultimate Commitment,* and *Intellectual Foundation of Faith.*

A very interesting volume of essays about Wieman is *The Empirical Theology of Henry Nelson Wieman,* edited by Robert W. Bretall.

*   *   *   *   *

Neo-naturalism is primarily a brainchild of the first half of this century. In Chapter I, we saw that Darwinian science, with its appearance and pronouncements, evoked many kinds of religious response. One such response was that the concept of a transcendent God remains intact in spite of Darwinian evolution if the evolutionary process simply be regarded as the means by which this God creates (Mascall). Neo-naturalism, however, views the inference from evolutionary creativity in nature to a transcendent God as weak and unnecessary and chooses to identify the on-going process in some way with God. This view differs, then, from pure evolutionary naturalism in this respect, namely, that the mechanistic necessity that dominates in a Darwinian world is rejected and replaced by a force that drives unceasingly toward spiritual being and value. The methodology of neo-naturalism is a radical empiricism, and "its clearest systematic exponent is Henry Nelson Wieman." [1]

Wieman is not concerned to establish his religious faith upon an empirical foundation just to see if it can be done. Rather, as a moralist, his central concern is to discover that value operative in human life which can transform humanity, which, as he sees it, is in dire need of transformation and salvation from evil. And, he insists, this value must be found in human existence, otherwise we are only deluding ourselves. A "God out there"—whether understood in the Thomistic, traditionally Protestant, or Barthian sense—is of no value in meeting man's real needs. What man needs is a knowledge of the "ultimate good" within humanity and an openness toward it, for only an openness toward this value will bring about his much-needed rescue from evil.

In the next few pages we want to see why and how Wieman arrives at these conclusions and how he relates these conclusions to Christian thought.

The Empirical Method in Religious Inquiry

In his "Intellectual Autobiography" [2] Wieman declares that his study of John Dewey forced him to conclude that "inquiry concerning what makes for the good and evil of human life must be directed to what actually and *observably* operates in human life.

Otherwise, the inquiry will produce misleading illusions." [3] He declares: "The transcendent, the supernatural, the ineffable, the infinite, the absolute being itself, and other such ideas inevitably lead inquiry astray unless they can be identified with something which *observably* operates in human life." [4] Being convinced that nothing can transform man unless it actually operates in human life, Wieman contends that "in human life, in the actual processes of human existence, must be found the saving and transforming power which religious inquiry seeks." [5]

Anticipating the objection that inquiry directed only to that which is observable can yield knowledge of only that which is observed, Wieman insists that "what is observed is not necessarily identical with what enters immediately into sense experience. Rather, what we observe is what we infer from sense experience by predicting specific consequences and observing or failing to observe under required conditions what was predicted. Perception, including sense experience, can engage the total personality with all its resources of inquiry—intuition, inference, wonder, meditation, speculation, faith, love, aspiration. Perception always involves sense experience. But profound perception brings into action every means and every power by which knowledge is attained." [6] It is clear from this statement that Wieman understands the empirical method, in a most profound sense, to include intuition and inference, meditation and speculation; but it must also be clearly kept in mind that he directs his inquiry into what saves man from evil *toward the observable processes operative in the universe in general and in human life in particular* and not toward the "other-worldly." Herein Wieman's empiricism comes to the fore and controls him in his affirmations about God (just as his understanding of God, as we shall see, controls him in his methodology).

In the natural theologies of Thomism and Boston Personalism, for example, the existence of God and certain facts about him are inferred from more immediately given data. In the solipsistic "leap of faith" constructions of the dialectical and existential theologians, the religious experience as wholly the act of God forever remains non-descriptive and non-verifiable. Wieman is convinced that only in an empirical theology such as his own [7] where "God is given directly in experience and hence subject to direct description and verification" is there an escape from the speculative inferences of

47

the natural theologies on the one hand and the arbitrariness of the "leap of faith" theologies on the other.[8] We have already seen that for Wieman all talk about God as a transcendent, absolute being is illusory and misleading unless it can be identified with something that observably operates in human life. Here he stands against both the classical natural theologies and traditional Protestantism. Against Tillich, Niebuhr, Barth, and Brunner, Wieman writes: "Perhaps no one of them would accept any wording save his own. But the central point . . . common to them all [is that] human inquiry cannot get knowledge of any specific character which will identify with assurance the essential nature of the ultimate referent of our faith and our ultimate concern." [9] Against all these constructions, Wieman pits his empirical description of God as a "non-subjective reality that is directly accessible to normal experience." [10]

Reality as Process

Admittedly, Wieman does not first construct an ontology and then introduce his theory of value. Rather, he develops the former in conjunction with and in the interest of the latter. But for purposes of enhancing the reader's understanding of Wieman we will first examine his view of reality.

A study of the history of modern philosophy, specifically the radical empiricism of David Hume, will reveal that great energy has been expended to show that the concept of substances underlying qualitative entities is vulnerable to critical analysis. The empirical argument usually runs that if all concepts arise in sense experience, one can have no concept of substance. All that can be thought or spoken of is an endless flow of qualities. Wieman agrees with this, at least to the degree that the real can no longer be understood in terms of substance, since no empirically accessible substance can be identified with God. But he will not agree with the Personalists who infer from human personality the personality of God. Wieman's tack is completely different.

Wieman interprets all the things which are looked upon as the substantial entities that make up this world no longer as substances but rather as "strands" that, in conjunction with one another and with the perceiving and feeling mind as itself a strand, make up qualities. He writes: ". . . qualities do not inhere in the mind or in the organism—although mind and organism are necessary strands of existence in that conjunction of strands which is quality as experienced by us. Neither do qualities reside in objects. The brown stick is not brown, the painful fire or the delightfully warm fire is not painful or delightfully warm when these objects (here called strands of existence) are taken by themselves out of conjunction with all the other things necessary to yield the experience of brown or painful or warm. This conjunction with other things is not merely conjunction with a sensitive organism or with a conscious mind, although these are included in every conjunction where quality and value occur in our experience. But no less essential to a conjunction that is brown or painful or warm are the air, the sustaining earth and everything else that analysis and experiment reveal to make a difference to the qualities experienced at that time and place. The sensitive organism and the mind have no privileged position, and they are no more bearers of the quality felt—or creators of it or projectors of it—than are the other strands equally necessary to the occurrence of that quality at that time and place. . . . If these assertions are true [and Wieman thinks they are], the evidence indicates that quality is not in any of these strands or created by any or borne by any of them; quality is the conjunction of them. Quality is not a relation between the organism and the object, such as stick or fire. Quality is the conjunction of all the strands necessary to the occurrence of the quality." [11]

Qualities for Wieman become then the events which are consciously experienced by the organism and in which the organism stands as one strand. He continues: "We are identifying qualities with events. Every event consciously experienced is a quality or complex of qualities; every quality experienced is an event. Every quality, every experienced event (the two are identical), is also a conjunction. *Quality, event* and *conjunction* are words that denote the same actuality. Every experienced event can be analyzed into strands; it can also be analyzed into qualities." [12] Furthermore, "no event is ever repeated and no quality is ever repeated because a quality is the conscious experience of an event. . . . In actual experience the quality is never the same from one time to another and it never continues the same during the time we are experiencing it. . . . Thus quality and event have the same character; they are never repeated, they are always changing." [13]

49

If the reader wonders what all this means, perhaps Cobb's summary of Wieman's Heraclitian thought at this point will be helpful: "The sticks and stones, tables and books, vegetables and human bodies, which were once regarded as the individuals out of which the world is composed, are now seen as strands that in various conjunctions with one another and with strands of perceiving and feeling constitute events. Events are the conjunctions of such strands, or rather the events are the actualities through analysis of which we isolate these strands. . . . These events, which constitute the ultimate reality, are qualitative in nature. That is, they are complex qualities that may be analyzed into simpler qualities in particular relations. Among these qualities no priority can be given either to sensory or emotional elements. They occur in conjunction, and this conjunction is the given reality itself." [14] So important does Cobb consider Wieman's vision here for the rest of his construction that he gives further exposition and illustration: "What still seems to us more 'common sense' is an understanding of reality as composed of separate entities in interaction. In this view my mind constitutes one such entity, and my body, my typewriter, and the paper on which I am writing constitute other such entities, along with the chair on which I sit and the table that supports the machine. These entities seem to be primary realities and my act of typing seems to be secondary. [In Wieman's thought, however,] the typewriter *is* a togetherness of qualities and potentialities. But these qualities do not exist simply in themselves. They occur only in conjunction with the sensitive organism and mind of man. By the same token this organism does not exist in itself. It always occurs as an interaction with its environment. What is primary, what is the source for all other knowledge, what is prior to all speculative inference, is the event of my typing, which includes all the qualities of color and sound and touch as well as of emotion, memory, and expectation that constitute it." [15]

What does all this mean? How has Wieman interpreted reality? *In nuce,* the focus of reality has been shifted, in Cobb's words, "from substances to events," "from static to dynamic categories": ". . . within an event, however broadly or narrowly conceived, there is a qualitative flow rather than unchanging being. The qualities are the concrete, objective realities that constitute events and hence processes. Therefore, process is the all-inclusive term for reality. We may speak of the one total cosmic process, or we may speak of the myriad of processes that make it up. The point is that the most concrete division of the whole, whether into few or many parts, always yields qualities, events, or processes." [16] For Wieman, then, reality is process in which humanity is involved.

For the study of religion, this means for Wieman, since religion is very much a part of reality for him, that religious verities, including God, are to be viewed as related to and included within the all-encompassing reality of process and open to the same scientific investigation and analysis as any other discipline. He writes: ". . . identity and difference, change and permanence, existence and possibility, structure and quality, mind and matter, substance and form, better and worse, right and wrong, good and bad, God and man—all the categories sought by metaphysics or other philosophical inquiry can be uncovered by proper analysis of the perceptual event." [17] Only by empirical induction, according to Wieman, will speculation and arrogant dogmatism be removed from religious inquiry: "Any claim to truth beyond the evidence is not a mark of sanctity or virtue or humility. Rather, it displays either the arrogance of faith or an irresponsible childishness. Often these two go together. No appeal to divine revelation, the sanctity of authority, direct communion with God or any other source allegedly superior to the tests required to guard the fallible human mind from error [namely, observation, agreement between observers, and coherence] can escape the condemnation just asserted. The false garb of humility and holiness only makes the arrogance more pernicious and the irresponsibility more dangerous. The simple fact is that the human mind is addicted to error as the sparks fly upward. Hence it must submit humbly to tests of truth; and nowhere is this more imperative than in matters high and holy." [18] Wieman insists then that the empirical approach be rigidly followed in the study of ontology.

Qualitative Meaning and Creative Interchange

Wieman identifies God with the creative process in nature responsible for all good. But to grasp Wieman's equation of the two, we must look at his understanding of what constitutes good and how it is produced.

51

"Good" as qualitative meaning. Wieman maintains that one may analyze and describe the events which constitute reality in two ways: he may concern himself with the strands, the conjunction of which comprise the event, or with the "connection between a quality [event] now occurring and the qualities of past events such that memories are awakened and anticipation is aroused." [19] If he follows the former path, though the meaning that pertains to the strands is likewise a connection between present and past qualities, not so much memory and anticipation of qualities as anticipation of order and sequence of events (that can be followed with minimum regard for quality) is awakened. Thus the event takes on instrumental value, but not qualitative value, because interest focuses on the quality only as a means of identifying the strands of the event. But if he follows the latter path, meaning focuses on qualities as such; and as memory of past qualities is awakened and anticipation of future qualities is aroused (both accomplished in connection with the present quality), the present quality is enriched and transformed into *qualitative meaning.* For Wieman only qualitative meaning carries intrinsic value, hence it is only qualitative meaning that is good. But this good is *created good.*[20] *Creative good,* we shall see shortly, Wieman identifies with God.

Thus far we have seen that Wieman identifies "good" with qualitative meaning, "that connection between events whereby present happenings enable me to feel not only the quality intrinsic to the events now occurring but also the qualities of many other events [past and future] that are related to them." [21] But why identify "good" with qualitative meaning, for is it not perfectly conceivable that one man could derive qualitative meaning from torturing another man? Wieman counters that such an example contains implicitly a false equation of intrinsic good and moral good, the latter not being what he intends by good. Qualitative meaning (or genuine created good) is not necessarily moral; it may indeed be immoral if judged by a particular standard. But it is good in the sense that it enriches experience and increases total human growth. Even suffering and pain, if endowed with communicable meaning, become qualitatively meaningful and hence good, and may serve the creative good as it adds to and enriches total human experience.

If such an understanding of created good seems childishly naive in a world filled with evil men who need no encouragement in their aim to inflict pain and death on their neighbors, Wieman is confident that such a conclusion is due to a failure to comprehend how and why this good is produced. And this brings us to what he terms "creative interchange."

Creative interchange as the event of human good. For Wieman, man, as everything else, is evolving. Under the impulse of the creative good (God), brute matter gave place to the appearance of life, then certain limitations within the biological organism were overcome to produce man, and now with man's ability to open himself up to the interests of others through creative interchange the single organism is no longer limited to its own perspective. Beginning about two hundred thousand years ago when the sub-human rose to the human level,[22] creative interchange, in Wieman's opinion, inaugurated a genuine victory or advance in the evolutionary process over earlier periods in this planet's history.

In two different places Wieman gives us his understanding of the aspects of the total event that produces human good. This process or event he calls at times "creative event," at other times "creative interchange," and refers thereby to the situation "in which individuals encounter other persons or possibilities with openness and sensitivity,"[23] or, said another way, to the person-to-person process of refreshment and renewal by living contact with another in thought, word, and deed. In *The Source of Human Good* he speaks of these aspects as "subevents" and lists four: "emerging awareness of qualitative meaning derived from other persons through communication; integrating these new meanings with others previously acquired; expanding the richness of quality in the appreciable world by enlarging its meaning; deepening the community among those who participate in this total creative event of intercommunication." [24] In his later *Intellectual Foundation of Faith* he describes these aspects as "spiritual activities" and examines five: the expansion of the range of what the individual can know, control, appreciate as good, and distinguish as evil; the deepening and correcting of the appreciative understanding of oneself and of other persons; the progressive unifying or integration of all the personality's acquisitions; the increasing of the capacity to undergo failure, defeat, suffering, loss, and guilt in such a way that their consequences will be creative rather than destructive; and the increase of freedom.[25] Men should remain open to "creative interchange"; to do anything else is evil.

The process of creativity of good (which between persons creates creative interchange), Wieman, as an empirical moralist, identifies with God: "This divine creativity . . . can be called God if the word 'God' refers not to a person but to what creates personality progressively when required conditions are present; creates the world relative to this progressively created mind of man; sustains man as he cannot sustain himself; saves man from evil as he cannot save himself; transforms man so that he can forgive and love and appreciate what he could not by any intentional striving on his own part; endows man with all the spiritual activities previously listed under five heads." [26] We see then that Wieman rises from an understanding of reality as process to an understanding of that process creative of human good as "God." Thus God for Wieman remains well within the area accessible to human analysis and empirical description; but as the process creative of good, he is in turn worthy, Wieman is equally convinced, of man's service, which demands among other things the worship and devotion characteristic of historic religion.

This last affirmation, however, raises two questions: first, if we may return one more time to the man who experiences increase in good (qualitative meaning) by torturing another man, how is it possible to serve a process creative of good understood in such a way that it includes what heretofore has been adjudged as wicked; and second, if God is only the source of human good, again how is it possible to serve him, since to be God he must, for some at least, stand over them, not only as savior from evil, but also as lord and judge?

The first question raises the entire problem of evil in the world, and Wieman does not shy away from it but faces the issue squarely. He admits that commitment to the process creative of good (as he has defined good) might very well involve one in actions heretofore regarded as evil as judged by a given moral code, indeed, it might lead to one's own deprivation and death. He writes: "Anything is good if it sustains and promotes the release of that kind of intercommunication among men termed the 'creative event.' It is evil

54

if it does the opposite. One act or course of conduct is better than another if it provides more amply the conditions enabling the creative event to produce qualitative meaning; it is worse if some alternative would be favorable. Kinds of legislation, types of economic order, methods and goals of education, habits and moral practices, forms of religion—these and any other proposals for changing or maintaining the established state of affairs are evil if some practicable alternative should enable men to communicate more fully and freely in a manner fostering creative transformation. They are good if they facilitate this event more fully than anything else under the circumstances." [27] And continues Wieman in another place: "With commitment to creativity death can be accepted as a necessary condition for the most complete attainment of the ruling purpose of one's life. Unless individuals in one generation die, the innumerable individuals in subsequent generations will not have space and opportunity to develop and make their contribution to the growth of cultural resources required for the progressive creation of man. . . . My own death and limitation of my own power I cannot accept as good merely because other individuals are benefited thereby. But if I give myself to the divine creativity sufficiently to attain the great good which it can do for me, I shall in that very act of commitment find all things good which promote the work of this creativity because I have identified myself with it so that what is good for it is good for me. When this occurs, I can accept my own death and my limitation of power when these are seen to be the necessary conditions for the effective operation of this creativity throughout human history. . . . In so far as one's death and other limitations of power are the necessary conditions for the most effective work of this divine creativity, the individual committed to the living God who works throughout history in this way will accept as good his own death and other limitations which contribute to the progressive creation of man." [28]

Now if it should be objected that one might not want such a God and refuse to commit himself to such a process, Wieman admits that such is the case. But he is also positive that there is no other *real* alternative. Commitment to the "transcendent God" of traditional Orthodoxy provides no real help of another kind. It only denies the ultimate reality of evil. Nor will Wieman affirm out of an *a priori* optimism that good will ultimately triumph over evil.

He sees such a claim "very doubtfully supported by evidence." [29] Instead, such a claim, for Wieman, not only denies the reality of evil but also sickens the human spirit inasmuch as "men drugged with this belief cannot live with power in the face of things as they are." [30] Is there then any ground for hope? Wieman suggests that the first ground for hope is the evidence that the world has certainly been growing better if better is understood in the sense in which he has defined good, that is, in the sense that there has been an increase of qualitative meaning. The second ground of hope is simply that we possess no knowledge of any evil that can destroy creativity, although it may be and has been obstructed at times.[31] Beyond this Wieman refuses to prognosticate, though he seems strongly to teach an ultimate dualism by his claim that evil as the opposite of good may likely always exist, at least as a possibility. [32] Nonetheless, he strongly urges men to commit themselves to the creative process in true faith and trust as the only real choice in life, contending that to do anything else is to side with absolute evil. This commitment, if made, will demand of men service, worship, and devotion.

In the light of the foregoing discussion, Wieman's answer to the second question could almost be predicted: the creative process as the source of human good is not only man's savior from evil but also *is* his lord and judge. If anything is clear to Wieman it is that man is not the author of his own good. Rather, the creative process acts sovereignly within mankind as its lord; all that man can do is to commit himself to it in utter dependence. He cannot even foresee a specific goal or end. The process ever remains man's lord and judge while saving him from his own evil.[33] In traditional language this means that man is saved by faith, completely apart from a "righteousness" of his own.

The Creative Process and Christianity

If Wieman said nothing else, his thought could justifiably be termed a philosophy of religion. However, though it is true that "he does not deeply care whether the gospel he proclaims be called Christian or not," [34] he is deeply concerned that men commit themselves to God and also recognizes that he himself "found God within the Christian tradition and that this is the situation for Western

56

man." [35] Furthermore, although it is also true that in his most recent writings Wieman is not as convinced as he formerly was that Christianity provides a faith possessed of sufficient power to guide Western culture,[36] it will be helpful to see how he has related his understanding of God to Christian thought in *The Source of Human Good*. It should be noted, however, that even in this volume Wieman is not concerned with Christian theology as such; rather, he is interested in what he perceives was the influence of Jesus' life, death, and resurrection on the disciples, and the influence of the Christian Church on the world.

Jesus' influence on the disciples. As might be expected, Wieman sees Jesus' influence on his disciples as illustrative of creative interchange. In fact, he views the "event" of Christ, which includes the continuing fellowship of the Church, as the third of the three greatest victories of creative activity in this planet's history. The first two were the appearance via evolution of the living cell and the arrival of man upon the scene by the same process. The Christ event, as the third, is overcoming the obstacles to the transformation of the world into richness and fulness of meaning.[37]

Wieman speaks first of Jesus' life. In conjunction with the social, psychological, and historical situation of the time and the heritage of Hebrew prophecy, Jesus by his life (not by his teachings necessarily or by his actions) accomplished, albeit unintentionally,[38] *four* things in the intercommunication within his little band of disciples. First, he broke their personalities down and remade them in such a way that the thought and feeling of each got across to the other. They became deeply and freely receptive and responsive each to the other. Second, the meanings that each derived from the others were integrated with what he already possessed, thus transforming him and lifting him to a higher level of fulfillment and giving him more capacity to understand, to appreciate, and to act with power and insight. Third, this openness to one another expanded the world about them and made it richer with meaning and quality, for now they could see through the eyes of others, feel through the sensitivities of others, and discern the secrets of others' hearts. And finally, there came more depth and breadth of community between them as individuals with one another and between them and all other men, this following from their enlarged capacity to get the perspectives of all whom they encountered.[39]

But Jesus' death was equally important, for as long as he lived, the creative interchange they knew was bound by cultural and religious limits. To the disciples Jesus was the Messiah, but as the Messiah he must do what the prophets had said the Messiah would do, namely, give to the world the blessings of Hebrew heritage. Thus his death removed the distinctly Jewish obstacles which would have prevented such salvation from being brought to all men. Wieman writes: "When Jesus was crucified, his followers saw that he could never carry to fulfillment the mission of the Jewish people as they conceived it; hence there was no good in him of the sort that had led them to follow him. They had thought that he would save the world by making supreme over human existence the good as seen in the perspective of Jewish culture. Now they saw that he never could do anything of the sort. . . . They reached that depth of despair which comes when all that seems to give hope to human existence is seen to be an illusion. This was the immediate consequence of the Crucifixion." [40]

But Wieman maintains that the "power of the Resurrection" altered all this. The resurrection gave to the creative interchange experienced by the disciples universal applicability. Of course, Wieman would not wish to be understood as himself believing in or teaching the bodily resurrection of the man Jesus. What was resurrected was the "life-transforming creativity" which they had known in fellowship with Jesus. Writes Wieman: "After about the third day, however, when the numbness of the shock had worn away, something happened. The life-transforming creativity previously known only in fellowship with Jesus began again to work in the fellowship of the disciples. It was risen from the dead. Since they had never experienced it except in association with Jesus, it seemed to them that the man Jesus himself was actually present, walking and talking with them. Some thought they saw him and touched him in physical presence. But what rose from the dead was not the man Jesus; it was creative power. It was the living God that works in time. It was the Second Person of the Trinity. It was Christ the God, not Jesus the man." [41]

The Church and creative power. Christ's creative power is transmitted to us today by the continuing community, which we know as the Church, and its ritual, myth, and Bible. Wieman declares: "Christ . . . is not merely the man Jesus. Christ is the domination by the creative event over the life of man in a fellowship made continuous in history." [42] He continues: "This lifting to domination [of the creative event in the lives of the disciples] could not . . . by itself alone, accomplish the salvation of man. It had to be perpetuated in history. Otherwise, it could not reach you and me. . . . This domination is not perpetuated in the sense that any group of people lives continuously under the supreme control of this creative interchange, but it is rather perpetuated by ritual, myth, and Bible, so used and interpreted that people can always recover a sense of the supreme importance of the source of all good to be found in creative interaction. Hence the ritual and myth, the symbols and the Bible, become the 'means of grace.' The church is the historic continuity of these means by which men may recover a renewed access to that way of life in which creative interchange dominates the life of man as it did in the fellowship of Jesus." [43]

Concerning the interpretation of the Church's symbols and Bible, Wieman claims that ritual and symbolism in the Church are non-cognitive, but he is equally insistent, against Tillich, that these non-cognitive symbols awaken in the communicants' experiences qualities which have structures which can be known only by cognitive symbols. Sin becomes thereby the domination of created good over creative power in the concern of man, the devil is pride and rebellion against creative interchange, salvation becomes the victory of creative good over created good, and the cataclysmic winding-up of all things portends perhaps another creative crisis in the future.[44]

With this understanding of the Church, Wieman sees it as the only agency that is free and commissioned to demand that the conditions of creative power be met. If the Church will do this through its leaders, it will lead the way in the march of humanity toward an ever-growing richness in total human existence.[45]

In the foregoing pages we have seen how Wieman constructs his natural theology. After arriving at an understanding of reality as process and interpreting the process creative of human good as God, he supplemented this construction by singling out the Christ-event, or the continuing fellowship of the Christian Church, as the community where creative interchange has been permanently established and where men are called to devotion to the creative process rather than to created goods. Thus Wieman's neo-naturalism serves as the foundation for his Christian understanding.

Many things might be said by way of criticism of Wieman's total *Weltanshaung,* but we will limit our remarks to a criticism of his ontology, axiology, and Christian perspective.

Wieman's ontology. As we have seen, Wieman develops a theory of reality in which neither substance nor person but "event" is that which is ultimately real. But these three by no means exhaust available ontologies, as he is well aware. For example, the idealist claims that reality is of the essence of spirit, the materialist argues for matter, the voluntarist for will, the existentialist for self, and the pluralist for perhaps all of these. Now Cobb is correct when he affirms that Wieman's entire theological position is dependent upon his ontology: "Wieman's creative event cannot seriously be regarded as God unless we agree that what he understands by events constitutes that which is ultimately real. *If* Wieman's ontology is correct, *then* it may well follow that Wieman's theology is also correct. But on what basis are we to decide as to the correctness of his ontology? By what neutral criteria shall we judge alternative ontologies." [46] Cobb answers his own questions: ". . . however we decide ultimately to answer such questions, we shall be forced to enter extensively into philosophical discussion of highly debated questions. If our acceptance of Wieman's theology depends upon our agreement with him on . . . speculative ontological questions, then Wieman's position does not have the freedom we have sought from speculation." [47] Could it be that Wieman has been governed in what he regards as empirical investigation by a pre-scientific assumption of what God can and can not be? If Cobb is correct, and I think he is, Wieman can hope to make his case only if his ontology is accepted, but this the consistent Christian will never do.

It is for certain that underlying Wieman's ontology is the *a priori* acceptance of biological evolution. If one has kept abreast of developments in evolutionary thinking, he will know that the supporting evidence for biological evolution is even slimmer than what it was when Darwin published his *Origin of Species* in 1859. Morris lists ten lines of evidence that supposedly prove evolution to be factual, and demonstrates that each of them can be understood better in terms of special creationism.[48] The evidences from classification, comparative anatomy, embryology, biochemistry, and physiology are merely evidences of similarity of one kind or another which can be as easily understood in terms of creation by a common Creator. The evidences from geographical distribution, vestigial organs, breeding experiments, and mutations simply call attention to the fact that some biological changes can and do take place, but these changes can be explained well within the limits of the Biblical "kinds," with provision in genetic structures for such variations as adaptation to different environments might require. And the evidence from paleontology, by far the most important of the supposed lines of evidence, is greatly weakened, if not rendered completely sterile, by the fact that the much-publicized "geologic column" which is used to date the earth is actually non-existent except for its appearance in the textbooks on geology and by the fact that its very construction by the geologist involves both the *a priori* acceptance of the theory of evolution and the fallacy of reasoning in a circle. Reasoning in a circle occurs when, on the evolutionary principle that simpler organisms must be dated earlier than more complex organisms, the age of strata is determined by the fossil evidence and then the fossils are dated by the strata in which they are found!

If the evolutionist is ever to make his case scientifically, he must alter two firmly established scientific findings: he must first *prove* that spontaneous generation can occur and has occurred and he must *disprove* the Second Law of Thermodynamics which simply states that all systems or processes tend toward less and less organization and order. Pinnock certainly appears to be right when he concludes that the evolutionist teaches evolution more out of *religious* than out of scientific necessity.[49]

The Christian man accepts, on the question of origins, the Biblical cosmogony, a unique account in ancient literature. It is one of *creatio ex nihilo,* the sort of creationism averse to all evolutionary speculation.

Scripture ascribes the creation of the universe and of man to the triune God. God the Father was the Originator of the creation (I Cor. 8:6, Eph. 3:9, Heb. 1:2), and God the Son (John 1:3, Eph. 3:9, Heb. 1:2) and God the Holy Spirit (Gen. 1:2, Psa. 104:30, Job 26:13) were Agents through whom the creation was accomplished. The triune God, Biblical revelation teaches, did not create out of a sense of a need to complement himself (Acts 17:25)

61

for he was exactly the same ontologically after his creative activity as before (Psa. 90:2). Rather, he created all things simply because he willed to do so (Rev. 4:11) and for the purpose of glorifying himself (Isa. 43:6-7). In short, the God of the Old and New Testaments reveals himself as self-contained and self-sufficient, in no way ontologically correlative to his creation.

The Biblical cosmology carries for the Christian man of science three clear implications. First, he looks upon the universe as created by God and hence *real*. He looks upon himself as created in God's image as a *real* image-bearer. He refuses to speak of man as an accident of nature as did Sir James Jeans in *The Mysterious Universe* or as a gruesome result of nature's failure to take antiseptic precautions as did Sir Arthur Eddington in *New Pathways in Science* or as "unreal" except as he participates in Wieman's qualities. He also recognizes the *reality* of his personal Creator, who is both his Lord and his Savior. But he also recognizes ontological discontinuity between his Creator and himself. He refuses to talk of being in general or to speak of God as a process within nature as does Wieman. Rather, he speaks of God's being as distinct in essence from and as the origin of all created being (Isa. 40:18, 25).

Second, in his search for meaning in the universe, he knows that he may claim to know a fact only as his knowledge of that fact conforms to God's interpretation of that fact by virtue of the creative act and by subsequent special interpretative revelation. It is true that he will gather information about many things in nature that will exceed in quantity the information recorded in Scripture, but he knows that his gathered information must nonetheless conform to the information which God has chosen to reveal in the Bible if it is to be valued as true.

And finally, he knows that the Scriptures determine for him, at least in broad outline, what is and is not scientifically possible. He consults the Scriptures before he makes a final pronouncement in any matter, and assumes no position or principle which would ultimately deny the supernatural or the miraculous.

Because these implications really register with him, the Christian rejects all such views of God, the universe, and reality as are suggested by Wieman. And by so doing, he undercuts Wieman's efforts to construct a theory of being which avoids the speculative questions raised by opposing ontologies. In fact, his rejection of Wieman's system and his replacement of it by his own only serves to point up the fact that the very existence of variant ontologies demands of Wieman in the construction of his thought not only empirical but also *a priori* decisions. Even while he is being the most empirical in his descriptions, Wieman never ceases to reflect the pre-scientific judgments which determine the directions which his descriptions take. For example, his *a priori* rejection of the Christian God determines his description of God as process.

In the light of Wieman's declared intention to believe only that which can be empirically verified, one can not help but be amused at Wieman's own account of his "call" to the lifetime task of investigating the problems of religious inquiry. "Throughout high school and up to the month of April in my senior year at college," he writes, "I was sure that I should be a journalist. . . . But shortly before my graduation, I came to my room after the evening meal and sat alone looking at the sunset over the Missouri River. Suddenly it came over me that I should devote my life to the problems of religious inquiry. I never had a more ecstatic experience. I could not sleep all night and walked in that ecstasy for several days. Since that evening in April I have never doubted my vocation." [50] Where is empirical investigation here? This certainly resembles the subjective experience of the mystic! And how can Wieman validate this experience empirically apart from speculation? Admittedly, Wieman's understanding of empiricism, as we have seen, allows for speculation, but how then can he avoid the speculation of all natural theologies and the solipsistic arbitrariness of the "leap of faith" theologians? In my opinion, he cannot!

Wieman's axiology. In his theory of value, Wieman defines the good as qualitative meaning, which refers to the enrichment which the organic strand in an event experiences as memory of past events is awakened and anticipation of future qualities is stimulated. The total event in which this grows he calls creative interchange, and the creative process, or source of human good, he calls God. Opposition to the creative process is absolute evil.

By now it should be obvious that Wieman's theory of value is contingent upon his ontology just as surely as his ontology is determined by his view of God. And since we have rejected his ontology as highly speculative besides being unscriptural, we could for similar reasons reject his theory of value and end our criticism here. However, there are certain unresolved elements in his axiology which ought to be noted.

Admittedly, Wieman can understand and define the good any way he pleases, but when his understanding of this good is detached from moral good as the latter is determined by a fixed standard, then good becomes extremely relative and the way is paved for religious, social, and political antinomianism. Wieman can object all he wants that in his construction he serves God while the orthodox Christian serves a law which he thinks is God's, but there is no verifiable way that Wieman can prove that he is serving God or good unless he measures his service by a recognizable fixed standard. The Christian is confident that he has such a standard in the written Word of God. For him God determines what is right and what is wrong. Good is good because God says it is good and wrong is wrong for the same reason. For his standard Wieman must point to a process which he imagines that he sees in nature but which has no scientific legitimation. Furthermore, this process creative of good, which Wieman regards as God, includes acts of sadism and criminality which can still retain in themselves intrinsic value and thus be in themselves good. Is this not illustrative of Orwellian "doublespeak"? It certainly seems so. Such a God will motivate to service of himself only those modern minds which are able to enter into Wieman's extremely abstruse thought, after autonomously accepting his unscriptural religious *a priori*'s.

Cobb rightly questions whether Wieman's creative event can really motivate to service of itself when men realize that by such service they may be giving themselves up to deprivation and to death. To this question Wieman replies that men innately desire good, and, if shown that it is this process that creates good, they will serve it. To this Cobb rejoins: "To the extent that one is really persuaded that his *preference* for the good is the *only* reason for seeking it, his willingness to sacrifice in its service is likely to diminish." [51]

The Christian God motivates to service by appealing to the total human personality with its faculties of reason, love, and will. In response to divine love, the Christian serves his God, who, while decreeing evil, still regards evil as evil and promises ultimate victory over it. Wieman believes that this view denies the reality of evil,[52] but this it most emphatically does not do.

Lest it be said that the problem of evil—admittedly a difficult problem—was completely ignored, we make the following remarks, though by no means dogmatically, but merely to suggest the manner in which we feel the problem should be approached and the solution sought.

Theologically, the problem of evil relates to the doctrine of God's providence and is usually framed by Christian thought in the form of a question: How can the all-powerful God, who is also all-holy, tolerate the existence of evil in the universe which he governs? The question becomes all the more acute when evil is related to God's decrees.

Historically, the problem is an old one. Persian Zoroastrianism sought solution in an ultimate and co-eternal dualism between the principles of good and evil, a view which was to appear later in the semi-Christian garb of Manichaeism. Though the Greek philosophers were not interested in the question in the same way that Christian philosophers were to be, nonetheless they clearly saw the problem. Plato seems to have concluded that God simply is not in control of some things, evil being among them. Aristotle's God, being thought-thinking-thought, is for all practical purposes unconcerned with the world. The Christian philosopher, Augustine, in some places, suggests that evil does not exist, for to *be* is to be in some sense *good*. This means that everything that is is good; there are just some better and some lesser goods. Leibniz, centuries later, suggests that what is regarded as evil, if considered from a larger world perspective, will be seen to be merely the "shadows" which appear in any great work. This world will then be seen as the best of all possible worlds. And in more recent times, many modern philosophers, for example, F. R. Tennant and the Boston Personalists, simply maintain that God is good but finite, for being good, if he were also omnipotent, he would certainly rid the world of such a blight upon it.

None of these solutions is a viable option for the Christian who desires to be true to Scripture. He cannot admit that God controls some things in his universe but not all things. Neither can he believe that God is unconcerned with evil. He cannot accept an ultimate and co-eternal dualism. Neither can he deny the reality of evil or believe that this is the best possible world. He certainly will refuse to admit that his God is finite. Furthermore, he is sure that the existence of evil relates to an ultimate glorifying of his God. So whatever he says about evil he says within the following scripturally-prescribed limits: first, God is in sovereign control of all things, including evil; second, though it is not ultimate and co-eternal, evil is nonetheless real; third, though it constitutes a disruptive intrusion into a once-perfect world, evil is at the same time a divinely-decreed intrusion which will ultimately be overcome by God for his own glory; and finally, in its historical connection, calamity (criminal acts, wars, death, etc.) is one means employed by God to punish his race for its rebellion against him.

The most popular solution among Christians to the question of where the responsibility for evil lies is the claim that God created man with a free will and decreed to permit him, if he so chooses, to exercise his will in an evil direction. Thus it is man who is responsible for evil and not God, for God did not force him to sin. The important elements to be noted here are God's permission and man's free will. This solution is supposed to exonerate God of all responsibility for the existence of evil in his universe. But a moment's reflection reveals that permission, when applied to God who actively controls all things, makes no real sense. And as for man's free will, though it is true that man sins because he *wants* to sin (could this be due to the presence of an evil nature within him?), there is good reason to doubt whether man is as *arbitrarily* free as he imagines himself to be. Is he not under parental influence (Prov. 22:6)? Can not the weather influence how he feels? Can he be sure that at the moment he made a particular decision he was not suffering from an unknown physical malady that influenced him in his decision-making? Moreover, he has an evil nature which continuously influences him.

Ascription of free will to man is not the only means whereby man may be justly held to be responsible for his sinful acts. Knowledge of the good and a relationship to Adam are quite adequate to accomplish this. Consequently, progress toward solution might better be made by substituting for God's permission and man's free will the sovereignty of God and man's responsibility, for no Christian denies either of these terms.

If the problem of evil is viewed in this light, namely, as an apparent contradiction between God's sovereign control of his universe and man's responsibility to him for evil committed, it can be maintained that God, as absolute Sovereign, can decree evil and yet not be guilty of any crime for there is no power above him to which he must answer for his acts, and that man, the creature under divine law, can yet be held responsible for violations of that law. Furthermore, reflection will reveal that the *ultimate* problem resides, in man's thinking, between two clearly taught divine activities—God as King and God as Judge—and not between God and man (as two ultimate and competing powers) at all. God *as King* fulfills his will in all things, including the acts of men, and yet God *as Judge* holds men responsible for their evil acts. This places the "human" problem within the nature and plan of an all-wise, all-good God; and the Christian man is content to leave it with him, confident that what seems to be irreconcilable for him is completely reconcilable in the plan of the infinitely incomprehensible God.

Admittedly, these conclusions are reprehensible to Wieman, but his are no less so to the Christian. The Christian rests in the belief that he has faced the issue as squarely, if not more so, than Wieman, and that he has, in contrast to Wieman's mere personal opinion, an objective revelation from God concerning the matter. In any event, he know that he has a divine standard for measuring his and Wieman's actions, something that Wieman lacks.

Wieman's Christian perspective. My final criticism concerns Wieman's understanding of the relationship between his concept of creative interchange and Christianity. The reader will recall that Wieman claims that Jesus' life produced creative interchange in his little band of followers, later to become universalized after his resurrection in the form of the Church. If we have interpreted Wieman correctly, creative interchange is that situation in which people become open and sensitive to each other and serve the creative good rather than created goods. Now this openness refers either to an attitude reflected in what has been understood traditionally as *poor* human relations or to a sensitivity to others which results in sympathetic and genuine good will between individuals and in society, or to both. If it refers to either the first or the last of these alternatives, for obvious reasons no right thinking person will want to follow Wieman. Only the middle alternative will commend itself to good men. But this is precisely the kind of creative interchange that seems not to have been dominant over the disciples as one examines the Gospels. They debated with each other as to who was the greatest among them (Mk. 9:34, Lk. 22:24). James and John secretly sought special position over the others from Jesus (Mk. 10:37) which angered the other ten (Mt. 20:24). They rebuked both those who brought their infants to Jesus for his prayers (Mt. 19:13) and those who came themselves for healing (Mt. 15:23). Because a person was not of their "group," they forbade him to cast out demons in Jesus' name (Mk. 9:38). And James and John upon one occasion wanted to destroy an entire village because it had spurned their master (Lk. 9:54). In the end Peter denied knowledge of Jesus (Mt. 26:74), Judas betrayed him to his enemies (Mt. 26:14-16), and all forsook him at his arrest (Mt. 26:56). Where is the openness and the sensitivity that Wieman claims to see in this little fellowship? Did he discover this empirically? Admittedly, Jesus did make a profound impression on his disciples, even evoking from them faith in his messiahship. But an empirical examination of the Gospels reveals that the disciples before the crucifixion possessed little sensitivity toward each other and little, if any, real understanding of Jesus and his mission. It was actually not until after Jesus' resurrection and the Pentecost experience that they exhibited their first real understanding of the ministry of Jesus. Even then, for several years they still clung to certain decidedly Jewish expectations (Acts 1:6, 10:1-48, Gal. 2:11-12). There is much empirical evidence, therefore, that Jesus evoked little of Wieman's creative interchange from the disciples before his crucifixion and immediately after his resurrection. A study of the extant facts just will not permit Wieman to make his case.

As for Wieman's understanding of Jesus' resurrection, it is charitable to simply say that it is a complete travesty of Scripture interpretation, if it is interpretation at all! It is simply Wieman's subjective understanding of the event. In the attempt to be empirical, he rejects the most important piece of evidence that he possesses—the Scriptures. Furthermore, it is an insult to the intelligence of the disciples to make them out to be such dupes that they were so taken in by an experience which they had had with the living Jesus that after a short passage of time it induced them to actually think that they saw and touched him in physical presence, though he remained as dead as a doornail! Such handling of Scripture will commend itself to no one who knows the Scriptural accounts.

Wieman completely misses both the true mission of Jesus and the real task of the Church. No doubt the Church should call men to live at peace with one another and to work for the betterment of mankind, but this is not its primary task. Its primary task is to witness to the atoning work of her Lord before a lost world and to call men to repentance and faith in Jesus Christ.

In conclusion, Wieman's lack of genuine knowledge of Scripture vitiates his entire scheme and casts a reflection on the integrity of his avowed purpose to examine with candor all the available evidence.

We have completed our examination of "one supreme effort" (Cobb) to develop an empirical neo-naturalism. In our opinion, Wieman has not avoided speculation, nor has he projected a theism that will motivate one to continuous surrender to right moral action. Wieman calls men consciously to worship and to serve an evolutionary process in order thereby to achieve life's greatest good, but with Cobb I do not think this is really possible. Augustine expressed the need of every human heart when to the Christian God he wrote: "Thou madest us for Thyself, and our heart is restless, until it repose in Thee."

NOTES

1. John B. Cobb, Jr., *Living Options in Protestant Theology* (Philadelphia: Westminster Press, 1962), p. 31.

2. Henry Nelson Wieman, "Intellectual Autobiography," *The Empirical Theology of Henry Nelson Wieman* (Edited by Robert W. Bretall; New York: The Macmillan Company, 1963), pp. 3-18.

3. *Ibid.,* pp. 8-9 (italics mine).

4. *Ibid.,* p. 9 (italics mine).

5. *Ibid.,* p. 4.

6. *Ibid.,* p. 9.

7. Wieman does not regard Christianity as so final that the creative good of which he speaks cannot be produced by other religions as well. He knows, however, of no such religion. Cf. *The Source of Human Good* (Chicago: The University of Chicago Press, 1946), p. 287.

8. Cobb, *op. cit.,* pp. 91-92.

9. *The Source of Human Good,* p. 33.

10. Cobb, *op. cit.,* p. 92.

11. Wieman, *The Directive in History* (Boston: The Beacon Press, 1949), pp. 7-8.

12. *Ibid.,* p. 14.

13. *Ibid.*, pp. 14-15.
14. Cobb, *op. cit.*, p. 93.
15. *Ibid.*, pp. 93-94.
16. *Ibid.*, p. 94; cf. *The Directive in History*, p. 19.
17. *The Source of Human Good*, p. 183.
18. *Ibid.*, p. 211.
19. *The Directive in History*, p. 16.
20. *The Source of Human Good*, p. 17.
21. *Ibid.*, p. 18.
22. Wieman, *Intellectual Foundation of Faith* (New York: Philosophical Library, 1961), p. 61.
23. Cobb, *op. cit.*, p. 99.
24. *The Source of Human Good*, p. 58; cf. pp. 58-69.
25. *Intellectual Foundation of Faith*, pp. 61-62.
26. *Ibid.*, pp. 66-67.
27. *The Source of Human Good*, p. 82.
28. *Intellectual Foundation of Faith*, pp. 88-89.
29. *The Source of Human Good*, p. 87.
30. *Ibid.*, p. 88.
31. *Ibid.*, pp. 89-90.
32. *Ibid.*, p. 92.
33. Cobb, *op. cit.*, p. 100.
34. *Ibid*, p. 105.
35. *Ibid.*
36. *Ibid.*, p. 101, fn.
37. *The Source of Human Good*, p. 274.
38. *Ibid.*, p. 275.
39. *Ibid.*, pp. 39-41.
40. *Ibid.*, p. 44.
41. *Ibid.*
42. *Ibid.*, p. 269.
43. *Ibid.*, p. 42.
44. *Ibid.*, pp. 272-274.
45. *Ibid.*, p. 292.
46. Cobb, *op. cit.*, p. 116.
47. *Ibid.*, pp. 116-117.
48. Henry M. Morris, *Evolution and the Modern Christian* (Philadelphia: Presbyterian and Reformed Publishing Company, 1967), pp. 16-17. Cf. Chapters 2 and 3.
49. Clark H. Pinnock, *Set Forth Your Case* (Nutley, N.J.: The Craig Press, 1967), p. 39.
50. "Intellectual Autobiography," *The Empirical Theology of Henry Nelson Wieman*, p. 6.
51. Cobb, *op. cit.*, p. 112.
52. *The Source of Human Good*, pp. 87-88.

PART II: THEOLOGICAL SYSTEMS STRESSING THE RELIGIOUS DIALECTIC AND THE RELIGIOUS EXPERIENCE

CHAPTER IV

THE THEOLOGICAL SITUATION IN THE NINETEENTH CENTURY

The nineteenth century was an infamous period in the history of the Church insofar as Biblical Orthodoxy is concerned. A terribly destructive Biblical criticism was exhibited in the work of Graf, Keunen, Wellhausen, Cornill, and others. Philosophers and theologians alike were prone to discredit any ability to know God. Kant, in denying to man any knowledge of *das Ding an sich* of the noumenal world, limited man to a knowledge of the phenomenal world (which man himself allegedly had created by his own reasoning process) and to "pious guesses" about the noumenal. Fichte even did away with the noumenal, saying it was the Ego. In biology and geology respectively, Darwin introduced his theory of organic evolution by means of natural selection, and Lyell, working from a theory of uniformity in nature, postulated long periods of time for the development of geological deposits, a view apparently compatible with the theories of organic evolution. Furthermore, a general antipathy toward the supernatural pervaded the great academic centers of learning. There was an overlooking of the Biblical doctrine of the awfulness of sin. Ritschl, it is said, declared that he would walk into heaven erect! In general, no need was felt for the atoning work of Christ. "God will forgive; it is his profession," was the flippant response to the evangelical appeal of the earnest parish minister. And this was the legacy willed to the Church of the twentieth century.

Because of the attacks of this liberal brand of Christianity upon the theological orthodoxy of the Church, many scholars no longer regarded the theology of the Reformation to be tenable. The Reformers' doctrine of the depravity of man, for example, was manifestly untrue, was it not, in the light of all that man had been able to accomplish toward the betterment of himself and society? Indeed, the twentieth century, it was said, was to inaugurate a new and glorious era in the history of man. The preaching of the Social Gospel of Henry Churchill King, Gerald Birney Smith, and Walter Rauschenbusch here in America was to usher in the Kingdom of God. The twentieth century would be "the Christian century." But then the world was plunged into the chaos and destruction of the First World War, and a few short years later came the American stock market crash. No doubt for many in the Western hemisphere it was almost as if some giant demon had turned off all the lights around the world, plunging the universe into darkness.

What influence did such a turn of events have upon the liberal theological enterprise? Certainly for many young theologians trained in the great liberal theological centers of Europe it meant a re-examination of their liberal foundations. Liberal theology had not been equal to the task of bringing in the Kingdom of God! Thus there appeared on the scene the new voices of Karl Barth, Emil Brunner, Eduard Thurneysen, Friedrich Gogarten, and others, all crying out that the world was in the throes of *Krisis* and standing under the judgment of God. Out of this movement—now known as Neo-orthodoxy—developed several theological systems which have made profound impressions upon the theological world, all having in common (at least overt) hostility to philosophical reasoning and a stress upon the uniqueness of the religious experience as the foundation of the theological structure. Cobb describes these systems by the term "theological positivism," [1] while Ramm labels them "autopistic" ("credible in itself") systems.[2] The purpose of this chapter is to present in greater detail the family characteristics and historical background of these systems, emphasizing mainly the theological situation in the century immediately preceding this one.

The family characteristics of these systems, according to Ramm, are as follows: (1) a great stress upon the inward and subjective experience of the gospel, truth being defined in terms of inwardness and subjectivity; (2) much emphasis upon the suprarationalistic or paradoxical character of Christian teaching; that is to say, Christian doctrine is not capable of rational (logical) analysis; (3) a rejection of natural theology (including the theistic proofs) because (a) it presumes that there is no breach between man and God, thereby committing the sin of immanentism, (b) it assumes that the human mind can by itself discover God, and (c) the knowledge of God gained through it leaves the thinker cold, complacent, without passion, unchallenged, and untransformed; (4) a strong doctrine of the blinding effects of sin; the *imago Dei*, in general, is viewed as defaced; and (5) an emphasis upon both the transcendence and hiddenness of God.[3] In addition, a pseudo-Calvinistic answer is given to the question: "What prompts the religious experience?" "God gives the condition of the Moment," or, "Revelation creates its own response," or, "Faith is a gift of God," are the replies.

The exponents of this view trace their position back as far as the New Testament. They point out that the New Testament writer felt no compulsion to justify his affirmations by appealing to analogies in Greek philosophy or to elucidate his faith systematically along the line of philosophical categories. Certainly this is true, but it should be pointed out that the New Testament writer was setting down, under divine guidance, God's message to man and needed not to justify his statements (this should in no way be taken to imply that the New Testament writer was irrational), whereas (it hardly needs saying) the same cannot be said of these contemporary theologians. Furthermore, the New Testament writer *did* have an apologetic presupposition or basis upon which to write: the theism and revelational truth of the Old Testament scriptures.[4]

Much of the Church's theological utterances after the Apostolic Age until the sixteenth-century Reformation was consciously framed in philosophical categories of thought. But there were exceptions who resisted (sometimes with little success) the impulse to rely upon Greek philosophy to make Christian theology intelligible, such as Tertullian (c. 160-230) and the later Augustine (354-430). Then too, the mystics, such as Pseudo-Dionysius (fifth century), Bernard of Clairvaux (1090-1153), Meister Eckhart (1260-1327), and Nicholas of Cusa (1401-1464), may be regarded as standing historically in the line leading toward the contemporary autopistic systems, in that they emphasized faith almost to the exclusion of reason as the ground of religious certainty. But even with these exceptions, by and large the Reformation was a legitimate protest against the corruption of the pure faith of the early Church and the first five ecumenical councils by Greek and Scholastic philosophy.

The vital force of the Reformation lay in its return to the Scriptures of the Old and New Testaments as the final authority in matters of faith and practice. Cobb distinguishes four influences upon the great Reformer, Martin Luther (1483-1546), which led him to regard Scripture and the theological pretensions of philosophy as incompatible opposites.[5] First, he was inclined toward the primacy of Scripture through the influence of the Brethren of the Common Life, who preferred the simplicity of personal faith to the intellectual subtleties of philosophical theology. Second, under the influence of the humanism of his day, he preferred in any debate to return to the original sources of authority. Third, as an Occamist, Luther felt a natural tension between reason and revelation, the former being understood nominalistically.[6] And fourth, inasmuch as the Church had justified its practice of indulgences through an interpretation of the Bible based upon Scholastic hermeneutics, Luther, in his attack upon the practice, was necessarily forced to reject Scholastic theology. This led Luther again to the principle of *sola Scriptura*. To these should be added a fifth (and in my opinion, the most important) reason: Luther believed the Bible to be the authoritative Word of God, and hence, he came to regard it as the final arbiter in theological debate. Luther was also averse to philosophical doctrines of God for two reasons.[7] First, since God has revealed himself to man, any attempt on man's part to come to him in some other way, according to Luther, is absurd, unnecessary, and sinful. Second, for Luther any doctrine of God obtained by the speculation of philosophers is but a product of the human mind, having no reference to the true and living God, and is therefore idolatrous.

In later life Luther modified his earlier views somewhat, moving back toward a natural theology. But it was Melanchthon, the *praeceptor Germaniae,* in editions of his *Loci Communes* subsequent to the 1521 edition, who increasingly reintroduced a use of Aristotelian philosophical tools into systematic theology.

The other great systematizer of the Reformation was John Calvin (1509-1564), whose *Institutes of the Christian Religion* reflects the Reformation principle of *sola Scriptura* and refuses to allow a systematization to draw Biblical theology into the "audacious curiosity" of the natural theology of the Scholastics. Dooyeweerd writes: "Calvin expressed the true critical religious attitude concerning knowledge of God, an attitude grounded in the humble insight into the essential boundary between the Creator and the creation, in timidity with respect to the deep mystery of God's majesty. The scholastic motive of nature and grace is not found in Calvin's thought. . . ." [8] As a result, Calvin rejected as idolatrous any effort to know God apart from Scripture.

Unfortunately, a thoroughgoing scholasticism pervaded both Lutheranism and Calvinism in the seventeenth and eighteenth centuries. Among Calvinist scholars, scholastic beginnings may be found, for example, in Petrus Ramus (1515-1572) and Theodore Beza (1519-1605), reaching a high-water mark in the writings of Gisbertus Voetius (1589-1676). However, the writings of David Hume, through their cogent argumentation against Christian doctrines grounded in philosophical conclusions, "reopened for theologians the possibility that faith must work out its form and content in independence of all speculative reason."[9]

Nineteenth-century European theology may be viewed as an effort to accomplish just such an end. But by this time, the reader may recall, the thinkers of the Enlightenment, through their labors in Biblical criticism, philosophy, theology, and science, had raised a big question over the possibility of knowing anything absolutely about God. Consequently, those theologians who had never committed themselves to the Reformers' doctrine of Scripture as the inscripturated self-revelation of God were reluctant to affirm God's ontological reality on the basis of revelation, as the sixteenth-century Reformers had unhesitatingly done. As a result, the theological enterprise took a novel turn. Theologians began to frame theological affirmations in confessional terms as an account of the faith of the religious community (because this was an empirical fact which no philosopher could deny) rather than in revelational or dogmatic terms. Inasmuch as such a "faith" was really a description of experiential faith, both individually and collectively, and not the description of a faith that was necessarily the exclusive work of God, nineteenth-century theological expression became, for the most part, anthropocentric. It is within this theological context that we now discuss in the remainder of this chapter the nineteenth-century theologians Schleiermacher, Ritschl, Kierkegaard, and Nietzsche.

Prior to Schleiermacher's influence upon Christian theology, theology was traditionally acknowledged to be "thought about God," and the theologian was one who interpreted God's revelation to man. But with the publication of his systematic theology, *The Christian Faith,* in 1821/22, Schleiermacher introduced a new meaning for theology. Theology now became an explanation of the feeling of dependence which a man achieved after passing through a religious experience. This man-centered emphasis in theology has earned for Schleiermacher the title of "father of modern theology."

At the very outset of *The Christian Faith,* Schleiermacher divides human life or consciousness into three broad areas: Knowing, Doing, and Feeling. The relation between these areas he explains as follows: "Life . . . is to be conceived as an alternation between an abiding-in-self *(Insichbleiben)* and a passing-beyond-self *(Aussich-heraustreten)* on the part of the subject. The two forms of consciousness (Knowing and Feeling) constitute the abiding-in-self, while Doing proper is the passing-beyond-self. But while Knowing, in the sense of possessing knowledge, is an abiding-in-self on the part of the subject, nevertheless as the act of knowing, it only becomes real by a passing-beyond-self of the subject, and in this sense, it is a Doing. As regards Feeling, on the other hand, it is not only in its duration as a result of stimulation that it is an abiding-in-self; even as the process of being stimulated, it is not effected by the subject, but simply takes place in the subject, and thus, since it belongs altogether to the realm of receptivity, it is entirely an abiding-in-self; and in this sense it stands alone in antithesis to the other two—Knowing and Doing" (3, 3). Knowing and Doing, then, represent the active side of life, whereas Feeling distinctly represents the passive and receptive side. Furthermore, Schleiermacher is quite certain that, while piety (or religion) is not to be excluded from all connection with Knowing and Doing, it belongs peculiarly to the area of Feeling (3, 4-5). But how may one distinguish true piety from false piety or even from another feeling altogether? Schleiermacher answers: "The common element in all howsoever diverse expressions of piety, by which these are conjointly distinguished from all other feelings, or, in other words, the self-identical essence of piety, is this: the consciousness of being absolutely dependent, or, which is the same thing, of being in relation with God" (4, 1-2). And "in the first instance God signifies for us simply that which is the co-determinant in this feeling" of absolute dependence (4, 4). In other words, for Schleiermacher that to which a man feels related in absolute dependence and in such a way that he can in no way affect it and to which he traces his being in such a state is God, and that feeling is piety or true religion. This piety works itself out in the area of Doing as religious ethics (3, 4) and in the area of Knowing as doctrines or dogmatics. Since this is not a work on ethics, we shall concentrate for a moment only on the latter—dogmatics as the expression of the feeling of absolute dependence in the area of Knowing. Schleiermacher writes: "Christian doctrines are accounts of the Christian religious affections set forth in speech" (15). And "doctrines in all their forms have their ultimate ground so exclusively in the emotions of the religious self-consciousness, that where these do not exist the doctrines cannot arise" (15, 2). From these statements it is clear that, for Schleiermacher, no longer is the theologian ultimately dependent upon the Scriptures as the sourcebook of theology for his doctrinal statements. Rather, doctrine is anthropocentric, being grounded in the religious self-consciousness.

Schleiermacher was quite aware that one might deduce from this position a radical relativism, there being the possibility of as many "systematic theologies" as there are religious communities or even dogmaticians. But this he sought to avoid. Schleiermacher insists that the dogmatician, as one who shares the beliefs of his religious community, will purpose to make his dogmatic declarations pertaining to the beliefs of the community a true reading of the matter. For the dogmatician to do otherwise is inconceivable to him. "All who busy themselves [with dogmatic procedure] must be assumed to possess the relevant faith, if they are to offer anything profitable, because otherwise it would be a case of a professed reference and relation without any real congruity. The thing, however, is inconceivable except on the supposition that the exponent was not conscious of any religious emotions, even of a different variety. For otherwise no one could, without doing violence to himself, conceal the contradiction between the position which he expounds as internally coherent and derived from the Christian consciousness, and the position which he himself accepts" (19, 1).[10] But what of the relativism implicit in the existence of a great number of religious communities? Schleiermacher replies that the development of religious form from fetishism through polytheism to monotheism is a development from lower to higher. "Those forms of piety in which all religious affections express the dependence of everything finite upon one Supreme and Infinite Being, i.e. the monotheistic forms, occupy the highest level; and all others are related to them as subordinate forms, from which men are destined to pass to those higher ones" (8). And since, of the three great monotheistic communities, "Judaism, by its limitation of the love of Jehovah to the race of Abraham, betrays a lingering affinity with Fetishism," and "Islam, on the other hand, with its passionate character, and the strongly sensuous content of its ideas, betrays, in spite of its strict Monotheism, a large measure of that influence of the sensible upon the character of the religious emotions which elsewhere keeps men on the level of Polytheism," Christianity, "because it remains free from both these weaknesses, stands higher than either of those other two forms, and takes its place as the purest form of Monotheism which has appeared in history" (8, 4). But what of the several religious communities within Christendom? Here Schleiermacher conceives Protestantism as more favorable to the feeling of piety than Roman Catholicism, because "the former makes the individual's relation to the Church dependent on his relation to Christ, while the latter contrariwise makes the individual's relation to Christ dependent on his relation to the Church" (24). Schleiermacher's approach, then, is an instance of Cobb's observation that "in the nineteenth century much of the energy that had previously been devoted to showing that Christian beliefs are true was transferred to the task of showing that Christianity is the highest or final religion." [11] Of course, the true Christian, who has trusted Jesus Christ as his personal Savior from sin and guilt, can never be satisfied with a portrayal of Christianity as a live, or even the most viable, option. He is convinced that it is the only remedy for man's plight. As Neve, the Lutheran scholar, writes, "A positive Christianity cannot accept a theology which does not make the testimony of Scripture, God's revelation to us, in a special sense the primary source of truth and its authority." [12] Consequently, some scholars feel that, with all of his good intentions, Schleiermacher's greatest contribution to theological discipline may have been his defense of religion as such rather than his vindication of Christianity and systematic Protestant theology.[13] One influence, however, is unde-niable: by grounding religious affirmations in human self-con-sciousness, Schleiermacher laid the basis for modern Liberalism.

Albrecht Ritschl (1822-1889)

Religion has its place for Ritschl, as a Neo-Kantian, in the realm of practical values; his entire emphasis is upon will and not upon feeling, emotion, or mystery. Thus he concerned himself with a moral Christianity.

Reacting against Hegelianism, Ritschl was opposed to meta-physics. Following Kant, in dealing with the metaphysical aspect of theology, Ritschl eliminated completely the "judgments of being," restricting theology to "judgments of value." In other words, although Ritschl did not reject the metaphysical nature of God, he did deny to human reason the possibility of a theoretical knowledge of God. As a result, Christianity is to be regarded as a "morality" or system of ethics, and Christian theology is a series of ethical "value-judgments." Even with regard to Christ, as Neve writes, Ritschl "never denied the metaphysical sonship of Christ; he only claimed that it cannot be an object of theological inquiry." [14] The intention of the revelation of Christ then becomes to reveal to man the never-changing attitude of divine love, not to establish a new relationship between God and man. With this Christological con-struction, the result of his opposition to metaphysics, Ritschl trans-forms Christ into the ideal man who becomes the perfect revealer of God's love.

The task of the theologian, then, in Ritschl's opinion, is to deal not with the mysteries of "natures" and "persons" in their onto-logical relationships but with *Jesus as historically given*. For Ritschl, "theology's object could not be God understood as a metaphysical first principle or a supreme cosmological entity. Theology's object could only be God as revealed in history, which means, Jesus Christ." [15]

Ritschl's emphasis upon the historical Jesus as the proper area for theological inquiry was his main immediate contribution to his theological successors. One of them, Wilhelm Herrmann (1846-1922), developed an even more anti-metaphysical idea of Chris-tianity than did Ritschl. For Herrmann, Christianity is still bound up intrinsically with the "historical Jesus," but since Biblical criticism (he believed) has rendered the tradition about Jesus suspect, Herrmann singled out the "inner life of Jesus" as the domain of theological work, because therein is the essential content of the universal ideal of a spiritual personality and the founding of a spiritual brotherhood. When a man unites his own imperfect moral life with the moral, inner life of Jesus, he receives the ability to do good. In this way, Herrmann reduced Christianity to a subjective system.[16]

Adolf von Harnack (1851-1930), the great Ritschlian church historian, likewise shared Ritschl's anti-metaphysical tendency, fearing that Church dogma would supplant religious faith. Consequently, he felt that the stress of theology should be confessional in nature and centered in Jesus' *consciousness* of God the Father, his providence, the divine sonship of man, and the infinite value of the human soul.

This anti-metaphysical frame of reference in Ritschl's theology and then in the "Ritschlian" theologians had a far-reaching effect in its contribution toward the neo-orthodox effort to dissociate theology from cosmological and metaphysical inquiry, although it is true that Neo-orthodoxy would not follow Ritschl's judgment on the value of the historical Jesus for theological work.

Søren Kierkegaard (1813-1855)

Søren Kierkegaard, the "Danish gadfly," was born, according to some authorities (T. Haeker and A. Dru), a hunchback, to a father who believed himself cursed by God and to a mother with whom his father had had premarital relations. He inherited a deeply melancholic nature from his father, who burdened his young son with the knowledge of his own somber religious experiences and profligate tendencies. In 1840 Kierkegaard became engaged to Regina Olson, a virtuous young lady, but feeling great guilt for his own youthful debauchery, he soon broke the engagement. Throughout the literary period of his life he was the target of a weekly newspaper in Copenhagen, while he in turn relentlessly attacked Danish Christendom until his death at the age of forty-two. Yet in the short span of his life he established in Denmark a literature so original and so rich that it is absolutely without parallel in that country. Because of his incalculable influence on neo-orthodox theology, Kierkegaard's thought must be treated more extensively than any other.

To understand Kierkegaard's theology, one must first understand his enemies.[17] First, having studied Hegelian philosophy with Schelling in Berlin, Kierkegaard waged relentless war against the Hegelian system, which viewed the truth of Christianity as the necessary part of an absolute system whose content is determined by pure rationality. According to Cobb, Kierkegaard distinguished three errors which Hegelianism makes.[18] The first is its attribution to pure, impersonal rationality a power of construction which in fact it does not have. Its second flaw is its inability to account for the concrete individual in his passionate concern. In other words, Hegelianism really fails to take into account life's contingencies and problems; life just does not flow as unhesitatingly smooth as the Hegelian dialectic would assume. Against this error Kierkegaard heaps clever sarcasm, portraying, for example, the Hegelian philosopher being interrupted in the middle of a lecture on the glories of the "System" by an impulse to sneeze! Its third mistake is its profound misunderstanding of the nature of Christian faith, in identifying this faith with *rational* conviction that certain affirmations are true. If it is sarcasm which he heaped upon the second error of Hegelianism, it is a vehement hatred which Kierkegaard expressed toward any interpretation of faith which would involve rational belief. It is because of this attitude toward human reason that Kierkegaard's position is classified with Tertullian's "I believe because it is absurd," and Blaise Pascal's "The heart has its reasons which reason cannot know," that is, with the tradition that views faith as superseding reason.

Kierkegaard's second enemy was the pervasive Romanticism of his day.[19] He felt that the Romanticist takes too easy a view of the problems of human existence. He represents a life of no disorder and no decision, no inwardness and no suffering. In his *Stages of Life's Way* Kierkegaard describes life as subsisting in three levels: the aesthetic, the ethical, and the religious, moving from lower to higher. And the Romanticist, Kierkegaard describes as being on the lowest or aesthetic level, never passing beyond the mere desire for pleasure and the immediate gratification of want.

Finally, Kierkegaard deplored the apathy of Danish Christendom. In his day to be born a Dane was tantamount to being born a Christian. Baptism was equivalent to conversion. But such Christianity meant neither cross-bearing nor discipleship. For Kierkegaard, such "orthodoxy" was only playing the game of Christianity. His *Attack on Christendom,* containing his most severe diatribe, is one of his best known works today.

A knowledge of Kierkegaard's views of God, man, truth, faith, and the Christian life are absolutely vital to a proper understanding of contemporary autopistic systems. Space permits only a word about each.

For Kierkegaard, God is a hidden God *(Deus absconditus)* and existentially transcendent, that is, absolutely different from man. Man does not find God by searching for him; it is God who determines the condition of the "Moment" or the "Encounter." Also, God is always *Subject,* never object. This means for Kierkegaard that, although there is an ontological objectivity about God, God is never the object of man's knowledge like a tree can be. God is always known as a person is known. Ramm comments on Kierkegaard's thought here: "If God were known as objects were known, one could know God and remain the same sinful, selfish creature. Unless knowing transforms, it is irreligious. . . . If God is Subject, he is Person, and therefore is known by 'subjectivity in inwardness,' or in more prosaic language, existentially." [20] Such a conception of God obviously repudiates all natural theology, with which Kierkegaard had no patience.

Kierkegaard grants to man a freedom concerning "inwardness"; that is, man is capable of *inward* action. This places *man as individual* above *humanity as class.* Against Hegelian categories which classified particulars into general classes, thus losing the *individual* man in the *class* of humanity, Kierkegaard protests that inward human existence is higher than any philosophical category of humanity.[21] As an individual, however, man is infinitely different from God, according to Kierkegaard, and therefore is sinful.[22] In addition, as an individual, man is an existent, involved in existence and in need of finding Truth and the true form of existence. Man is not a detached observer, sitting on the "balcony" of some philosophical vantage point (as the Hegelian philosopher supposes) and observing the universe below as the rational outworking of Absolute Mind.

Kierkegaard's understanding of Truth is a radical departure from the philosopher's concept of Truth. For him, real truth is *existential* truth; that is, it is personal and religious, not philosophical and scientific. Real truth is "truth for me." Furthermore, existential truth is *paradoxical*. Hegel had said that thought (principles of logic) and being (reality) are one. Kierkegaard however, claims that thought is free from any metaphysical significance; therefore, a view of Being different from Hegel's is necessary. Now if the principles of thought are not the principles of reality (and Kierkegaard obviously thought so), then Reality or Truth will appear to man the existent as a paradox. And this paradox, Kierkegaard believed, will never resolve itself by the Hegelian three-term dialectic into a synthesis. Truth will always remain dipolar in nature to the existent, and no amount of intellectual mediation will remove the contradiction. Only faith can relieve the illogical "logic" of religious or existential truth. Finally, Kierkegaard contends that real truth, if it is to exist at all for the individual, must be subjectively appropriated. "Truth is Subjectivity," is his famous by-word, developed most fully in his *Concluding Unscientific Postscript*. Truth does not exist for the individual until he as a human existent existentially responds to it in existential confrontation. Although God is Truth, *statements* about God are not truths in and of themselves. They are only formulas for action or calls for decision. They become truths-in-subjectivity when the existent responds to them. Clark explains Kierkegaard's thought at this point in this way: "For Kierkegaard God is truth; but truth exists only for a believer who inwardly experiences the tension between himself and God. If an actually existing person is an unbeliever, then for him God does not exist. God exists only in subjectivity." [23]

The human response to paradox Kierkegaard regards as faith. Faith is not rational; it is not an act of the mind. It is a personal leap, a venture, a risk, a "not-knowing." The responding existent can neither be accompanied nor counselled in his leap; he must venture all upon objective uncertainty. Furthermore, he may expect no objective certainty after the faith-response. Faith is the decision to *live* in objective uncertainty and subjective certitude. Kierkegaard is well aware that this position is reprehensible to the philosopher, but the man of faith, he is assured, knows subjectively that he has been *transformed* by the paradox and that is enough "proof" for him that he is *in truth*.

Of the paradoxes of faith, the most crucial is the Incarnation of God. Consequently, for Kierkegaard, faith, aroused by this particular paradox—the Absolute Paradox—will have for its object solely a Person—Jesus Christ—and not doctrines about Jesus Christ. Or, as Ramm succinctly states Kierkegaard's position on this point: "The object of faith is not a truth to be communicated but a person to be chosen." [24]

If Kierkegaard's understanding of the Christian life was one of loneliness, subjectivity, and suffering, it was also a personal life in contemporaneity with Christ. The Christian man is unconcerned with the span of time between the Absolute Paradox and himself. In fact, he is unconcerned with the historical as far as Jesus Christ is concerned. By faith he mediates the distance between them and recovers Christ for himself. In existential terms, by faith he mediates Time and Eternity.

There is no doubt that Kierkegaard's theology was a reaction against an overpowering philosophical system and a stagnant formalism in Danish Christendom. Though he may agree with Kierkegaard that there was certainly proper provocation for a staunch reaction, the student of Orthodoxy today, nevertheless, cannot follow him for several reasons: (1) his radical stress upon the transcendence of God to the exclusion of a Biblical doctrine of creation and divine immanence; (2) his conception of the sin of man in psychological and metaphysical terms rather than in historical and Biblical terms; (3) his rejection of objective truth, which in effect denies the objective historicity of the Atonement and the validity of the stated truths of Scripture; and (4) his construction of faith as an irrational venture without any objective certainty. The writer to the Hebrews (11:6) makes it absolutely clear that Biblical faith includes objective factual content: "He who comes to God must believe that he is, and that he is a rewarder of those who seek him."

In spite of these heresies, however, Kierkegaard's contributions toward the methodology employed in the autopistic systems of the twentieth century are unequaled. Cobb distinguishes three: (1) his stress upon God as being radically beyond the grasp of reason and knowable only in faith; (2) his stress upon (a) absolute paradox as being the basis for Christian faith and (b) the task of the theologian as being only to point to the paradox, showing how it affects the human situation, rather than to explain or to justify it; and (3) his stress upon (a) the dissociation of faith from the communal life of the empirical church and (b) the affirmation of faith as a relation between God and the believer.[25] To these may be added a fourth: he coined for Neo-orthodoxy a theological vocabulary—existence, existential, incognito, encounter, contemporaneity, anxiety, and decision, to name just a few.

Friedrich Nietzsche (1844-1900)

Friedrich Nietzsche "completed the nineteenth century's atheistic, materialistic, anti-hegelian world view."[26] He saw three traditional strains in the world of his day. First, there was Greek rationalism and Apollonian art and aesthetics, of which, Nietzsche believed, only the Dionysian desirability to move beyond mere good and evil to the life of pure instinct should be retained. Second, there was the early Roman will to power, which should be given primacy once again. And third, there was the Christian tradition, which, because of its teaching on a lost humanity and the virtues of humility, meekness, and pity (termed "slave morality"), ought to be destroyed. Antichrist should be made the ideal of man. His *Thus Spake Zarathustra* and *Beyond Good and Evil* are of special significance in this connection.

Nietzsche is of primary interest to us because of his dictum— "Gott ist tot." Van Riessen writes, "Jasper correctly comments that Nietzsche does not say here that God does not exist, or that he does not believe in God; he is simply stating a fact in Western civilization."[27] Since the lives of both churchmen and laity in his day denied in practice the existence of God, Nietzsche concluded that men should simply face honestly and fearlessly the consequences of their atheism.[26] From this, Nietzsche drew a further conclusion that if God is dead, then there is no objective law over man. Such standards as moral law, concern for the weak, and equal rights for all need to be transformed to bring man to honest admission of his true instinctive urges and to free him from any and all traditional levelling tendencies. In short, man must become a true existent; he must make himself God and lay down for himself his destiny, even if that destiny is nihilism.

Nietzsche's influence on the twentieth-century theological scene is threefold. First, many theologians have reacted negatively to Nietzsche's thought as they learned from him what it really means to deny Christianity and God. Second, some contemporary theologians have utilized the profound meaning of Nietzsche's "Gott ist tot" to refer to the present "post-Christian era," and, as does Martin Buber, to the "eclipse of God" in the Western world. Finally, Nietzsche's nihilism and "freedom" element have primary appeal to contemporary philosophical existentialism. This philosophy in turn has influenced modern existentialist theologians such as Bultmann and Tillich.

Our summary of this chapter may be brief. Schleiermacher and Ritschl laid the groundwork for modern Liberalism, by the former stressing the view that religion is the feeling of absolute dependence, while dogmatics is the expression of this feeling in speech, and the latter, building upon a Kantian idealism, stressing a moral Christianity centered in the historical Jesus. Against these systems, Neo-orthodoxy in the present day has reacted, as we shall see. Both Barth and Brunner have inveighed against them. Barth, for example, speaks of Schleiermacher's theology as *Bewusstseintheologie*— a "consciousness theology," beginning with the fact of man's self-consciousness as something given and proceeding from this consciousness to inquiry about the possibility of knowing anything about God. And as early as 1928 Brunner wrote a criticism of Schleiermacher, entitled *Die Mystik und das Wort*.

Kierkegaard and Nietzsche, universally owned today as the most important existentialists of the nineteenth century although neither was so recognized in his own day, laid the groundwork for theological and philosophical existentialism respectively. Both rejected an easy-going popular Christianity, Kierkegaard affirming the unknowability and hiddenness of God and Nietzsche proclaiming the death of God. But whereas the former saw the religious crisis of his day as a challenge to recover true faith, the latter felt the situation demanded men to live as atheists. The twentieth century saw the autopistic systems responding favorably to Kierkegaard's theology and negatively to Nietzsche's theology.

1. John B. Cobb, Jr., *Living Options in Protestant Theology* (Philadelphia: The Westminster Press, 1962), p. 121.

2. Bernard Ramm, *Types of Apologetic Systems* (Wheaton, Illinois: Van Kampen Press, 1953), p. 7.

3. Bernard Ramm, *Varieties of Christian Apologetics* (Grand Rapids: Baker Book House, 1961), pp. 15-16.

4. Cf. Bernard Ramm, "The Apologetics of the OT: The Basis of a Biblical and Christian Apologetics," *Bulletin* of the Evangelical Theological Society, I, 4.

5. Cobb, *op. cit.*, pp. 122-124.

6. Nominalism is the view that universal concepts (in the case before us, human reason) are reducible to names without any objective existence corresponding to them. Luther could not elevate the questionable concept over the unquestioned fact of revelation.

7. Cobb, *op. cit.*, pp. 124-125.

8. Herman Dooyeweerd, *A New Critique of Theoretical Thought* (Philadelphia: The Presbyterian and Reformed Publishing Company, 1953), I, 517.

9. Cobb, *op. cit.*, p. 126.

10. One cannot help being overcome with amazement at Schleiermacher's extremely naïve doctrine of the goodness of man implicit in this description of the dogmatician's intentions.

11. Cobb, *op. cit.*, p. 130.

12. J. L. Neve, *A History of Christian Thought* (Philadelphia: The Muhlenberg Press, 1946), II, 116.

13. Cobb, *op. cit.*, p. 130.

14. Neve, *op. cit.*, II, 152.

15. Cobb, *op. cit.*, p. 132.

16. Neve, *op. cit.*, II, 153.

17. I am indebted to Bernard Ramm, *Varieties of Christian Apologetics*, pp. 49-65, for the major ideas of this treatment of Kierkegaard's theology.

18. Cobb, *op. cit.*, p. 133.

19. Hugh Ross Mackintosh, in *Types of Modern Theology* (London: James Nisbet & Co., Ltd., 1937), p. 33, defines the Romanticism of the nineteenth century as follows: "Romanticism, which is more a mood or temper than a creed, was a reaction against the predominance of classical norms in literature and art, as well as a revolt against the arid intellectuality of eighteenth-century rationalism. It may be defined as an impassioned return to natural instincts, to life, to freedom, to individual predilection, to the spontaneity of the creative fancy. It looked upon nature and man with eyes full of wonder, and pointed anew to the mystery of life. In its less prudent representatives it appeared to proclaim that the individual was absolute and that the liberated soul must stand for the defiance of authority,

the glorification of mere wish." In some respects Kierkegaard is a Romanticist, but in its easy view of life Kierkegaard repudiated it.

20. Ramm, *Varieties of Christian Apologetics,* p. 53.

21. By taking this position, Kierkegaard anticipates the modern existential cliché: "Existence precedes essence."

22. If there is a fall of man at all in Kierkegaard's theology, it is this infinite qualitative difference between God and man. In other words, man's sinfulness is psychologically understood in terms of his finitude.

23. Gordon H. Clark, *Thales to Dewey* (Boston: Houghton Mifflin Company, 1957), p. 488.

24. Ramm, *op. cit.,* p. 63.

25. Cobb, *op. cit.,* pp. 137-38.

26. Gordon H. Clark, *Religion, Reason and Revelation* (Philadelphia: The Presbyterian and Reformed Publishing Company, 1961), p. 79.

27. H. Van Riessen, *Nietzsche* (Philadelphia: The Presbyterian and Reformed Publishing Company, 1960), p. 25.

28. Cobb, *op. cit.,* p. 201.

CHAPTER V

BRUNNER'S DIALECTICAL ENCOUNTER

ABOUT EMIL BRUNNER

Emil Brunner (1889-1966) attended the Universities of Berlin and Zürich, taking a Th.D. from the latter, researching in the writings of Kant and Husserl. He made a trip to America in 1919 and taught at Union Theological Seminary, New York City. In 1924 he was appointed to the Chair of Systematic and Practical Theology at the University of Zürich, which post he held until his retirement from active teaching in 1955, with brief visits in the meantime to America again in 1938 to fill a guest professorship at Princeton Theological Seminary and to Japan in 1953 as Lecturer at the new International Christian University at Tokyo. In recent years, prior to his death, in spite of failing health he worked on and completed his *magnum opus,* a three-volume *Dogmatics.* Brunner's major works include *Revelation and Reason, Divine-Human Encounter, Man in Revolt, The Divine Imperative, The Mediator,* and the previously mentioned twelve-hundred-page *Dogmatics.*

Works about Brunner of interest to the American reader are Cornelius Van Til's *The New Modernism,* Paul King Jewett's *Emil Brunner's Concept of Revelation,* and *The Theology of Emil Brunner,* a collection of essays edited by Charles W. Kegley.

*　　*　　*　　*　　*

The emergence of Neo-orthodoxy in the 1920's was a protest against several widely-held theological viewpoints. Among these were the romantic idealism of Schleiermacher, the Neo-Kantianism of Ritschl, an immanentistic Hegelian pantheism, the "comparative religions school" of Troeltsch, and Biblical Orthodoxy. The two theologians who spearheaded this new theological expression were Karl Barth and Emil Brunner. And though Emil Brunner is regarded as the secondary figure, it was he, through his visits to America, and not Karl Barth who introduced Neo-orthodox thought to the American student. Furthermore, in comparison with Barth's still unfinished *Church Dogmatics,* Brunner's writings are a model of brevity and clarity. For these reasons, as John B. Cobb, Jr., observes, ". . . when [the American] undertakes to state the position in question, it is more likely to sound like that of Emil Brunner." [1] A knowledge of Brunner's basic theological thought is absolutely essential, therefore, to an intelligent understanding of the contemporary theological scene in America, for even though his ideas have lost much of the excitement they fostered thirty years ago simply because of the Church's familiarity with them, they have done much to determine the direction of American theology today.

Brunner's "Corrective" Theology

Throughout his writings Brunner discerns what, in his opinion, are misconceptions of true Christianity by prejudiced theologians.[2] Religion in general, as to its essence, has been wrongly viewed by anthropology as the simple outgrowth of a basic human trait such as fear or as the result of sociological development. Also, Liberalism had sought to ground religion in some basic structure of mankind such as the feeling of dependence (Schleiermacher) or valuational judgments (Ritschl). Brunner is convinced that Schleiermacher and Ritschl laid the groundwork for modern theological liberalism, by the former stressing the view that religion is the feeling of absolute dependence, with dogmatics being the expression of this feeling in speech, and the latter, building upon a Kantian idealism, stressing a moral Christianity centered in the historical Jesus.

Furthermore, Brunner laments, theologians for too long have used the methodologies of philosophy and science, failing to work out and employ their own special methodology. The danger of alien methodology is the abstracting of God which such a procedure invariably produces.

Roman Catholicism also suffers from misconceptions. Its type of authoritarianism degenerates the conscience and produces religious serfs rather than free men in Jesus Christ. It reduced dogma to rationalization when it wed theology to Aristotelian Thomism, and it wrongly defines faith as intellectual assent to authority and a body of dogma.

The worst misconceptions of all, however, are those of Orthodoxy; ignoring the "unimpeachable" results of Biblical criticism, it conceives of revelation as the communication of doctrinal disclosure and imposes upon Scripture a doctrine of mechanical inspiration; applying a false hermeneutic of literalism, it forces Scripture into head-on collision with modern science, with the result that Orthodoxy has lost the day in the areas of Copernican astronomy, Lyellian geology, and Darwinian evolution. To all of the foregoing misconceptions Brunner offers his theology as a corrective.

Brunner's Concept of Revelation

The heart of Brunner's theology is his concept of revelation. An understanding of it, therefore, is absolutely essential for progress into his religious thought. He regards revelation as essentially *God's activity in salvation*: ". . . 'divine revelation' always [means] the whole of the divine activity for the salvation of the world, the whole story of God's saving acts, of the 'acts of God' which reveal God's nature and His will, above all, Him in whom the preceding revelation gains its meaning, and who therefore is its fulfillment: Jesus Christ. He Himself is the Revelation. Divine revelation is not a book or a doctrine; the Revelation is God Himself in His self-manifestation within history. Revelation is something that *happens,* the living history of God in His dealings with the human race: the history of revelation is the history of salvation, and the history of salvation is the history of revelation." [3] He continues: "The real content of revelation in the Bible is not 'something,' but *God* Himself. Revelation is the self-manifestation of God. The real revelation, that is, the revelation with which the whole Bible is concerned, is God's self-manifestation." [4] And still further: ". . . by 'revelation' [the Bible] does not mean a supernaturally revealed doctrine; nor does it equate 'revelation' either with a collection of books or with one particular Book; in the Bible 'revelation' means God's mighty acts for man's salvation." [5] Thus Brunner refuses to identify revelation with the words of the Bible as such, gaining thereby (so he says elsewhere) a dynamic, moving "accomplishing" revelation, rather than the "static" revelation of Orthodoxy which is bound to the Bible.

93

But these mighty acts which comprise Brunner's concept of revelation are always personal acts, for revelation is the personal encounter of two subjects in the "I-Thou" relation. God meets man in a truth-encounter; thus revelation is never one-way communication, never a monologue, but always a dialogue. ". . . revelation actually consists," so Brunner writes, "in the meeting of two subjects, the divine and the human, the self-communication of God to man. Jesus Christ is not 'revelation' when He is not recognized by anyone as the Christ, just as He is not the Redeemer if He does not redeem anyone. The Biblical doctrine of revelation means this transition from the divine to the human subject." [6] The point should be simply noted at this juncture that, for Brunner, for the act of revelation to actually occur, man is as essential in his role of recipient to the "possibility" of revelation as is God in the role of revealer.

Since revelation is conceived as a personal divine-human encounter, it is unique (*Einmalige*), absolute, transcendent, non-repeatable, and unverifiable by logic or science. "Revelation has always and everywhere the character of a sudden event. . . . But in the Bible alone is this sudden happening understood in an absolute sense, as the unique, as that which can never be repeated." [7]

Is this revelation historical? Does it occur in history in the same sense in which Napoleon's defeat at Waterloo took place in history? Brunner is convinced that revelation must not be so understood, for should revelation be so related to history, it would imbibe of all the relativity of the historian's history. Rather, Brunner explains the relation of revelation to history tangentially, that is, revelation *touches* history but does not enter into it. He writes: "When we have discovered what history really is, we realize that we cannot seek for the decisive within history." [8] "It is impossible to introduce the eternal into the chain of historical events as though it were a specially precious and magnificent pearl. The eternal as an event, the revelation, as such, *possesses no historical extension*." [9] "The eternal in history, the revelation as the absolutely unique, *cannot be perceived in terms of historical extension*. Revelation is not the actual fact which is made known through history: the life of Jesus and the historical personality of Jesus—but the invisible secret of the Person of Jesus, hidden behind the veils of history and of human life, not the Christ after the flesh but the Christ after the Spirit, the 'Word made

94

flesh.' " [10] "The revelation of Christ is therefore absolutely decisive, for in it the non-historical, the eternal, breaks through into time at one point, and in so doing makes it a place of decision." [11] Now lest from this last quotation one conclude that he does allow revelation to "enter into" time and thereby become historical, Brunner explains what he means by this "breaking through": "The 'breaking through' would be in reality . . . 'Supranaturalism' if we were here concerned with the insertion of a new supernatural 'section.' But in so far as the 'breaking through' does not in any way result in any visible historical phenomenon, but only in the mystery of the Person of Christ on the one hand and in faith in this mystery on the other, it does not lead to the isolation of a 'section' of eternity in the midst of time, which indeed would be supranaturalism in the bad sense. Hence it is so important to distinguish between the Christ *in* the flesh and the Christ *after* the flesh." [12]

If revelation is not the actual fact which is made known through history, but still it does "break through" and touch time, where does revelation actually occur and what is the precise relation of revelation to history? Brunner's answer is "primal history" (*Urgeschichte*), which he regards as actual occurrence which is related to our space-time world but yet does not lie within it. "The general character of our history as a whole is to be recognized only from the perspective of 'primal history.' The kernel of all history is this 'primal history,' the time-space manifestation of which is that which the historian narrates for us as 'history.' " [13] He further declares that the historian never sees real history, that is, primal history, but only the "after-history" (*Nachgeschichte*), which has primal history as its prius. It is as when "he sees the tree that is struck by lightning, . . . never the stroke of lightning itself." [14] In the light of these remarks, it is clear that Brunner sees revelation as a personal encounter of God with man which lies not in history but rather behind and touching history, and which determines history.

The foregoing may be regarded as Brunner's fundamental conception of revelation. This notion will now be placed in sharper relief by a discussion of the "Christ event." In his analysis of Brunner's Christ event Cobb writes: "Revelation is the all-inclusive category for God's saving work; this work always takes place in the self-disclosure of personal encounter; and this encounter never occurs except through the person of Jesus Christ." [15] In other words, as Cobb has correctly perceived, Jesus Christ is for Brunner the point of contact in the divine-human encounter: God meets man in the act of revelation in Jesus Christ and, in a "saving" way, nowhere else. Since revelation is dynamic and not static, for Brunner the revelational encounter between God and man in Christ in a very real sense is an "event," hence the term "Christ event." Thus revelation, viewed most sharply, is "God's action in Jesus Christ." [16]

But what is the relationship of this Christ in Brunner's Christ event with Jesus of Nazareth? When Brunner talks of God's revealing himself to man in Jesus Christ, does he mean by that what Orthodoxy has traditionally meant by that expression? In the light of what has been said earlier regarding the relationship (as Brunner sees it) of revelation to history, it should be obvious that he does *not* equate the Christ event with Jesus of Nazareth or with the Jesus Christ of Orthodoxy. In fact, Brunner declares: "The question whether Jesus ever existed will always hover upon the margin of history as a possibility, in spite of the protests of the theologians. . . . Even the bare fact of the existence of Christ as an historical person is not assured. It would be a good thing once for all to admit this consequence of (necessary) historical relativism." [17] And in a footnote to this remark, he continues: "That [the existence of Jesus of Nazareth] is less certain historically, than that of Caesar, for instance, is in no wise accidental. It is only attested by those whom it actually concerns, and this means: the believers." [18]

With regard to the Virgin Birth narratives, Brunner devotes two long sections in *The Mediator* (pp. 322-327) and his *Dogmatics* (II, 352-356) to a denial of this "theory," contending that the New Testament's affirmation of it "has . . . helped to 'mingle unwisely with one another' the historical and pneumatical elements." [19] Besides, "if the idea of a Virgin Birth had really meant anything to the Apostle Paul he would hardly have laid so much stress on the fact that Christ was 'born of a woman' as an element which He shared with all other human beings, and on His origin from the 'seed of David.' " [20]

Then perhaps the revelation in the Christ event should be identified with Jesus' teaching? No, says Brunner: "What Jesus said if it be taken by itself, is just as far from being the revelation, the Gospel, as His historical personality, the picture of His life and of His inner life taken by itself is the revelation." [21]

Perhaps then the revelatory act is the atonement? Not so, says Brunner: "The atonement is not history [*Historie*]. The Atonement, the expiation of human guilt, the covering of sin through His sacrifice, is not anything which can be conceived from the point of view of history. This does not belong to the historical plane. It is super-history; it lies in the dimension which no historian knows in so far as he is merely an historian. It is an 'event' which is only an 'event' for faith. That it actually happened faith alone knows. It is not a fact which has its place in world history. It would be absurd to say: in the year 30 the Atonement of the world took place. But we can say: This event, which those who know history tell us probably took place about the year 30, is the same as that which we know through faith as the Divine Act of Atonement." [22]

Then perhaps the resurrection? To this query, Brunner rejoins: ". . . we cannot imagine what the Resurrection of Jesus means. It is as invisible, as unthinkable, as the Incarnation." [23] Assuming this attitude because of what he imagines as inconsistencies in the New Testament reporting of this event, he contends: "Whoever asserts that the New Testament gives us a definite consistent account of the Resurrection is either ignorant or unconscientious." [24] And on Brunner goes, denying the historicity of the post-resurrection ministry of Jesus Christ [25] and his bodily ascension into heaven.[26] Thus with no specific event in the life of Jesus of Nazareth will Brunner equate the revelatory act of God. This seems very strange and yet it is no misrepresentation of Brunner. He simply refuses to identify the Christ event, or the divine-human encounter between God and the individual, with the historical as such. Rather he insists that the *actual* event itself be consistently kept outside the range of history [*Historie*] in primal history [*Urgeschichte*], a relationship which Brunner expresses by the phrase "Christ *in* the flesh" but not "Christ *after* the flesh."

As primal history Christ touches time but does not extend into time. ". . . He can be known only 'in the flesh' but not 'after the flesh.' This distinction is only another way of expressing this unique fact, which, while it is really and truly historical, yet transcends all historical barriers. Historical actuality is the way in which the Eternal Divine Word, as the Eternal Son, touches the historical world. This actuality means a real entrance into the historical mode of existence, but so far as its significance is concerned this entrance merely touches the fringe of existence." [27]

With such a construction of the relation of the Christ event to Jesus of Nazareth, Brunner actually sees a sharp disjunction between, and rigidly applies an unbending dichotomous attitude toward, eternity and time and God and man. *Urgeschichte* is absolute; *Historie* is relative.

Since this is so, Brunner contends, the Christ must be viewed as *incognito* in Jesus. And this, it may now be seen, is the real relationship, as Brunner conceives it, existing between the Christ event and Jesus of Nazareth. The Christ event is there all right; there is no denying it. But Christ is there *incognito*. With nothing in the life of Jesus may he be identified. He is there but not in history; rather he is there *behind* the historical Jesus in primal history. Only by this manner of viewing things is Brunner convinced that room is made for faith; only by this manner of viewing things is Brunner convinced that the absoluteness of the revelation can be retained and spared the relativity of our earthly existence. He writes: "The personality of God is 'most hidden yet most manifest,' that is, it is revealed to faith alone in the disguise [*Inkognito*] of an historical personality, which as such, as a phenomenon which can be recognized within the sphere of history, is precisely not the true personality, namely, the personality divine." [28] He continues: "The Person is . . . the Word, the Revelation, the personal Presence. . . . But this Person is not the historical personality who can be perceived as such. The historical personality who can be perceived is the incognito under which the Person is concealed." [29] And again: "Jesus Christ has not imparted Himself directly, in order that the decision to which He calls us may be really the decision of faith. The category of this life—in contrast with every other life—is mystery, in the essential fundamental meaning of the word, the 'incognito.' Only because the deity of Christ appears in the incognito of His humanity is it possible to have a relation of faith toward Him, a real decision." [30] Thus the Christ event is, for Brunner, a Paradox: it is at one and the same instant a complete revelation and a complete veiling. "As a revelation it is complete because a real personal approach can only take place through a real person whom we meet personally. As a veiling, however, it is complete, because to us there is nothing more ordinary, less striking, more familiar, than a human person like ourselves, thus the very opposite of something which must first of all be given unto us." [31]

At this point the reader perhaps is baffled by what appears to be contradictory: a Christ *in* the flesh but not *after* the flesh, a Christ event which wholly reveals God yet wholly conceals him, a Christ which touches time yet does not actually enter time. And all this is in the interest of real decision? It is difficult, when one remembers that Brunner has drunk deeply at the metaphysical spring of Kantian thought, not to simply see here a Kantian interpretaton of Christianity. Has he not simply followed Kant and even for some of the same reasons made a distinction between reality (the noumenal world) and appearance (the phenomenal world), positing all of the so-called events of redemption in the former? One may seriously question whether this is the *Biblical* representation of the matter! But before any real criticism is made of Brunner's thought, the analysis must continue with Brunner's view of the relationship in which the Bible stands to this Christ event. Does he think he is being Biblical? What is his view of the Bible?

Brunner's View of the Bible

Throughout his writings Brunner heaps disdain upon Orthodoxy for its verbal plenary view of inspiration. The equation of the words of the Bible with the words of God is "actually a breach of the Second Commandment: it is the deification of a creature, bibliolatry." [32]

Because Orthodoxy will not admit the validity of the "assured results" of Biblical criticism, it fails to see what is so clear to Brunner, namely (among other things) that Genesis 1-11 is a late Priestly production, the creation story, the fall of man, the flood, and the Babel incident being myths or representations of religious truths under the inadequate form of historical events; that Wellhausen's view—first the Prophets and then the Law—as a whole is true; that Isaiah is not a unity but the work of several writers; that the Virgin Birth stories are legendary; that the resurrection narratives are hopelessly in conflict; that the Gospel of John is not an historical source; and that the Pauline Pastorals are late. Such results in the fields of higher and lower criticism constitute the main reason, contends Brunner, that, regardless of where they may go in the future, theologians can never return to Orthodoxy.

On Biblical doctrine Brunner writes the following: "[Revelation] is not a doctrine which is the object of faith, but Jesus Christ Himself. The doctrine is only a means which serves to lead us to Him, and therefore it is never infallible." [33] "Doctrine is only a pointer, though it may be a clear and useful pointer. Therefore faith is not directed to it, but it skims past it, as it were, like a ball from the barrel of a gun, toward a goal." [34] "God's Word is not a doctrine, but it is the self-manifestation of Christ which is accomplished through the instrument of the doctrinal message." [35] And finally, "The revelation of God must be *told*, not *taught*; the doctrine only has validity as a means of serving the 'telling' of the Good News. Where narrative is replaced by doctrine, Greek thought triumphs over the thought of the Bible." [36]

Brunner discerns not just one system of doctrine but several within the covers of the Bible, which serve to correct each other. "There is a Synoptic, a Pauline, and a Johannine type of doctrine; each differs considerably from the other, and no theological art reduces them to the same common denominator. What they all have in common is this: He Himself, Jesus Christ, is the Word of God; He is the center of their testimony; but their witness to Him, their particular doctrines, whether according to Matthew, or Paul, or John, are like radii which point toward this center from different angles, while none of them actually reaches the goal." [37] "Between the Synoptic Gospels and the Fourth Gospel, as well as between the teaching of Jesus and that of the Apostles, there is a great, and indeed, a radical difference. In my opinion, this is the most important result of the whole work of Biblical criticism." [38] He continues: ". . . the Epistle of James contributes something to our knowledge of Christ that we should not gain from Paul alone, and which, so far as Paul is concerned, is not only complementary, but also acts as a corrective. Every Apostle needs to be complemented and corrected by the others. . . ." [39] He sees, similarly, many "theologies" in the Old Testament as well.[40]

If all this is so, and Brunner thinks it is, then one may well wonder just what value Brunner places on the Bible. Just what is the relationship between this badly confused body of writing and the Christ event? Orthodoxy in the past believed, and still so believes, that all which one knows authoritatively about Christ must be gathered from Scripture. But if the Scriptures are hopelessly uncertain about what did actually happen during a specific period of thirty or so years approximately two millennia ago, can one then be certain about the truth-content of the Christ event? Brunner replies in the affirmative, averring that the resolution of the imagined problem lies in an understanding of the real value of the Bible and of faith itself.

Brunner never tires of quoting Luther's remark to the effect that the Scriptures are the crib in which Christ is laid. The Scriptures are, in a remote or secondary form, revelation.[41] Though it is not, itself, the primary revelation, the Bible is a trustworthy "pointer" to the primary revelation or Christ event. "The Bible is the word of God because in it, so far as He chooses, God makes known the mystery of His will, of His saving purpose in Jesus Christ." [42] The Bible is the Word of God in those places where it bears witness to the Word, that is, where it is a Word-bearer, but "we cannot maintain that everything that is Biblical—not even everything in the New Testament—is in the same way, or to the same extent, the 'bearer' of the word of God." [43] But in spite of all the Bible's inadequacies, Brunner is still prepared to affirm (and it must be in the light of such remarks as these just quoted that one must understand his affirmation): "Just as no one can come to the Father save through the Son, so also it is true that no one can come to the Son save through the Holy Scriptures."[44] This is so because the Scriptures, and only the Scriptures, are the crib wherein the Christ is laid.

If his mere affirmation that the Bible is a trustworthy witness to the Christ event is not convincing to his reader, Brunner is quite sure that with a proper understanding of faith, any lingering doubts which his reader might still entertain will be dispelled.

Brunner's Concept of Faith

The divine side of the divine-human encounter Brunner certainly sees as the Word of God to man in the Person of Jesus Christ. But what is its correlate on the human side? If the human side is essential to the encounter (and Brunner thinks it is), how is the encounter effected or appropriated by the human element? With these questions we are brought to Brunner's discussion of faith. *In nuce,* the human response to the revelatory Word on the divine side is faith.

How faith arises Brunner admits is an impossible proposition to answer fully. "How the heart of man opens to receive the Word of

God, and *how* the reason receives and understands the Word, is as mysterious as the incarnation of the Son of God." [45] However, this realization should not, Brunner feels, exempt the theologian from the necessity of making an effort to understand as much of it as he can. Therefore, he feels some analysis is in order.[46]

When the eternal in the form of the divine Word in the Person of Jesus Christ confronts man, that historical moment is thereby raised, Brunner declares, to the moment of decision. The man who has been confronted knows in that moment nothing of a "still-having-time, of not yet." He knows he must decide in that moment. (This *necessity* on the part of the human element to decide is the basis of Brunner's ethics.) And the instant in which he, confronted with the divine Word, decides, is the *moment* [*Augenblick*], or as Jewett writes, the place where an "atom of eternity" has pierced time.[47]

But this is only descriptive; what is faith's (or decision's) explanation? Brunner is sure that in that moment of decision, man has not simply made an affirmative choice; rather he hears of *Krisis*, that is, he learns that his whole existence stands under the judgment of God. The subjective side of *Krisis* is *Angst* (dread), or the feeling of not being at home in the universe. *Angst* leads him to the moment in which man must make a decision [*Entscheidung*]. Of course, men may accept or reject the voice of God (Brunner unequivocally rejects any doctrine of predestination that denies to man the final authority and responsibility for how he reacts to God's offer), but by *faith* some men become willing to cast aside all assurance of sense perception, mathematical proof, and logical consistency, and to *decide* for the Word to them in free venture, risking all on the personal revelation which has come to them, of course, individually.

Brunner is perfectly aware, as are all of the "encounter theologians," that such a construction of things offers no objective certitude, but he cannot see how it can be otherwise, if true faith is to actually occur. "Where personal truth is concerned, proof is neither possible nor fitting. For this truth is both trust and decision: we must decide either for proof or for trust, either for rational evidence or for the evidence of personal encounter." [48] But just to the degree that there is no objective certitude, to the same degree the divine-human encounter gives subjective certitude. The experience itself is its own best and only proof. It is credible in itself (autopistic), suprarationalistic (not capable of rational analysis), and unique, not to be confused with any other human action. In short, the only proof for this Word-faith encounter is the encounter itself: "Truth is encounter; encounter is truth." ". . . when a believer is asked: Why do you believe that Jesus is the Christ? he can only answer: Why should I not believe, since Jesus confronts me as the Christ, when He meets me. . . ." [49]

Faith, then, can have only one proper object—a Person which ever remains Subject, Jesus Christ. ". . . faith is not a relation to 'something,' to an idea, a truth, or a doctrine—not even a 'divinely revealed' doctrine—but it is wholly a personal relationship. . . ." [50] "The sole object of faith is Jesus Christ, God in His personal revelation. The 'object of faith is not a general truth, not a timeless and nonhistorical metaphysic, but the Person of Christ; . . . .' Faith, therefore, 'has one sole aim, not a variety of doctrines, but one only, which faith, in its universal application, apprehends, with increasing clarity.' Faith is 'solely our relation to Jesus.' " [51]

What are the "results" of the Word-faith encounter? First, the individual is transformed, which faith as intellectual assent fails to do. Second, he acknowledges the paradox of both the guilt and the forgiveness of sin. [52] "Man is far too profoundly a sinner to be able to admit his sin. That is the dialectic [paradox] of repentance: that man admits his true and vital need, the need which lies in himself, and which he could know himself only when he is no longer in this distress." [53] Third, he becomes a "contemporary" of Christ. "The revelation in Jesus Christ produces the *illumination* in my heart and mind, so that I can now see what I could not see before, and what so many are unable to see: that this man is the Christ. Suddenly, all the barriers of time and space have faded away; I have become 'contemporary' with Christ, as much His 'contemporary' as Peter was, though Caiaphas, who cross-examined Him, was never His contemporary (in this sense)." [54] And fourth, for him the scandal and offense of the Cross is removed. For an understanding of the Cross "the historical imagination is no help at all; for the better it functions, the more clearly do we perceive the 'scandal and folly.' Sympathetic 'feeling' and deep human understanding do not help us here, for I cannot understand the message of the Cross, as the Bible means it, from my point of view. . . . For the Cross and its meaning . . . is unique, never to be repeated, and therefore far above all human analogies; it can never be understood along the lines of intellectual argument." [55] But when faith has occurred, "at that moment when man's sense of autonomous independence vanishes there dawns upon him the meaning of God's self-revelation and self-giving in Jesus Christ; at the moment when the pride of self breaks down, the message of Christ ceases to be 'folly' and 'scandal.' " [56]

Brunner's entire thought is grounded in this divine-human encounter. God acts in a redemptive way by revealing himself to man in the Person of Jesus Christ. Man responds in faith to this voice from God, thereby "completing the circuit." Though he cannot (and would not if he could) offer any objective evidence for the truth-content of the encounter, the involved individual is nonetheless certain of the encounter, for "encounter is truth." Faith works transformation, the confession of guilt and forgiveness, contemporaneity with Christ, and the removal of the "scandal" of Christianity in the believer. All else that Brunner has to say is grounded in this dialectical relationship between God and man.

Criticism

In his construction of the revelational problem, Brunner obviously sees the theologian's main task as that of successfully grappling with the relation of eternity to time. [57] "Brunner's basic assumptions . . . are the following. History, as such, is the sphere of the relative. Revelation on the other hand is the communication of absolute truth. The problem is, how to preserve the Christian concept of an historic revelation against a mystical or idealistic negation of history, without involving oneself in historical relativism." [58] The answer, as Brunner conceives it, is the Kierkegaardian dialectic of eternity and time in which no direct identity between revelation and history, that is, no predication of absolute significance to any event in time and space, is permitted. Like a tangent to a circle, revelation *touches* time but does not *enter* it in an extension.

Jewett makes several telling criticisms of Brunner at this juncture, for after an impeccably sound discussion in which he demonstrates that Brunner is unable to carry this approach out in practice, [59] he then demonstrates that Brunner is unable to carry it out even in thesis. [60] To this demonstration we now turn.

When Paul Althaus complained that Brunner "had defined the Jesus event too narrowly for the minimal interests of faith," Brunner conceded that "the picture of the story of Jesus is of fundamental importance for our faith. The line of absolute withdrawal which Kierkegaard tries to set up as one that cannot be touched lies too far behind the lines of the actual encounter with Christ to do justice to faith. [There is a definite] necessity of the stories of Jesus for leading people to the Christian faith. . . ." [61] To this concession Jewett rejoins: "If it be true that it belongs to the *essence* of the Christian concept of faith 'that the *divine* revelational presence be set in antithesis to the world . . .' then, as Brunner himself repeatedly asserted in *Der Mittler,* all discussion about the empirical extent of the Jesus event is immaterial to faith. When he subsequently concedes that Kierkegaard defined the ground of faith too narrowly and proceeds to extend the historical basis of faith, this does not constitute a *corrective* to his Kierkegaardian dialectical approach, but a repudiation of it. This much ought to be made emphatically clear, that one cannot expand the point at which a 'perpendicular from above' bifurcates the horizontal plane of history, nor the vortex of a parabola. Points are *per definitionem* without extension. An extended point is no longer a point. In trying to do the impossible, Brunner has altered the face of the whole problem." [62] He concludes, therefore, that "this leaves the issue right where it was when the dialectical theologians appeared on the scene; that is to say, either Jesus was the kind of person described in the Gospel tradition or else Christianity is a mistake. . . . the dialectical approach has not proven a successful instrument in getting above the Orthodox-Liberal antithesis. 'If history is given its right, then the dialectic must disappear. If the dialectic triumphs, however, then one can no longer talk about a historical revelation.' " [63]

But Brunner's troubles are not over simply with his inability to retain his Christianity as long as he persists in a dialectical construction of it. He cannot consistently show that even the divine-human encounter, wherein the apprehension of truth is alleged to be subjectively certain, yields truth for sure. Though he claims that "something which, to the historian is only a point of relative certainty in the historical continuum, is absolutely certain to faith in an entirely different way," [64] he cannot explain how this can be. For example, Brunner argues that "the Gospel writers did not intend to give us a scientific biography, but rather to tell us who Jesus was as seen by the eye of resurrection faith. He calls the Christ whom the historian sees 'the Christ after the flesh.' " [65] A critical problem, however, arises for Brunner when, while having to admit that if any ever did behold the Christ by faith, it was the Apostolic witness, he has to likewise admit, because of the "assured results" of Biblical criticism, that their witness was a witness with only "more or less historical fidelity." In fact, as we saw earlier, he feels he must describe the respective witnesses of Matthew, Paul, John, and the other New Testament writers as "radii which point toward this center from different angles, while none of them actually reaches the goal." In short, as Jewett states so clearly, ". . . not only is the picture of the critical historian defective, because lacking the dimension of the transcendental, but so also is the picture of faith." [66] It may be legitimately asked, where is the certainty in the Word-faith event?

Certain other attitudes of Brunner are equally problematical to the orthodox theologian. At least in the area of communication, God, according to Brunner's construction, needs man as much as man needs God in salvation. God cannot reveal himself unless man apprehends the revelation, and the decision to apprehend the revelation remains ultimately man's decision. Man has it in his power, then, to render God a deaf mute, a God who can act but who cannot reveal his act. This does away with a God-in-himself and substitutes a God-for-man. No longer is there an ontological Trinity; rather, only a functional or economical Trinity remains.

Nor can the truly Reformed Christian have anything at all to do with any theology which grants to man the final authority and responsibility for how he responds to the divine offer of salvation. He knows that the unbeliever is made a partaker of the redemption purchased by Christ by the effectual application of it to him by the Holy Spirit of God (*Westminster Shorter Catechism,* Q. 29), that the Spirit of God works faith in the unbeliever, thereby uniting him to Christ in his effectual calling (*Catechism,* Q. 30), and that effectual calling is solely the work of God's Spirit, whereby the unbeliever is persuaded and enabled to embrace Jesus Christ as he is freely offered to him in the gospel (*Catechism,* Q. 31). Moreover, the truly Reformed Christian knows that it could not be otherwise, for he is well aware that the unbeliever is spiritually dead in trespasses and sins (Eph. 2:1), that is, he is incapable, in himself, of correctly comprehending anything spiritual (Rom. 1:21-22; 3:11; I Cor. 1:20-21; 2:14; Eph. 4:17-19).

Of course, he knows, on the other hand, that Paul does not deny that all men, as men, have an innate knowledge of God's existence. Indeed, Paul affirms that all men do know God, though not in a saving way (*gnontes ton theon,* Rom. 1:21), that all men know experientially God's ordinance that the sinner is worthy of death (*epignontes dikaioma tou theou,* Rom. 1:32), and that all men "show the work of the law written in their hearts, their conscience being witness" (Rom. 2:15). Does Paul mean by these words that men may in themselves respond to God's call? The Reformed Christian is certain that Paul should not be so understood, for Paul is equally insistent that the unbeliever, although he knows all these things in the deepest recesses of his heart, cannot face this knowledge squarely, because to become genuinely *God*-conscious would require his becoming at the same moment epistemologically *self*-conscious. And since genuine self-consciousness is identical with *covenant*-consciousness, attendant upon such self-consciousness is the realization of his own creaturehood, his apostasy from the Creator, his guilt before God, and the justice of divine retribution upon his sin. Consequently, though revelation streams into man's consciousness from nature continually (Rom. 1:20, cf. Ps. 19:1) and though man, made in the image of God, is himself revelational of the Deity to himself, *since it is no longer his nature to own this revelation, the natural man suppresses* (katechonton) *this truth through his own unrighteousness* (Rom. 1:18). Why then would man respond any differently when encountered by the Christ of Brunner's Christ event unless he be *compelled* to respond, an affirmation which Brunner is not prepared to make? Would he not just as assuredly suppress this revelation as well? Beyond controversy, any revelation which comes to the unregenerate man apart from the insistent grace of God will be immediately suppressed. Thus at this point too, Brunner's theology, when compared with the teaching of Scripture, is found deficient and sub-Christian.

Finally, Brunner's refusal to identify the saving acts of God with any particular fact or event of the Incarnation should be regarded as dangerous in the extreme to the Gospel of the grace of God and must be rejected by a genuinely Christian theism. A gospel whose Christ did not actually take to himself a true body and a reasonable soul, that is, did not actually become incarnate; whose Christ did not live obediently under the law, thereby obtaining a righteousness which is peculiarly fitted to man's need and which could be imputed to man through faith; whose Christ did not actually die a vicarious death for the sins of his own on a specific calendar day on a particular hill outside of Jerusalem some two thousand years ago; whose Christ did not literally and bodily leave the tomb on the third day after death; whose Christ did not literally and bodily ascend into heaven after his resurrection, there to intercede in behalf of those for whom he died—such a gospel is no gospel at all! A gospel whose Christ is a phantom, whose cross is merely a symbol, and whose resurrection occurs only in primal history but not in our history simply has no salvation in it! As J. Gresham Machen said many years ago, even the simple Biblical statement, "Christ died for our sins," includes both history and theology. "Christ died"—that is history; "for our sins"—that is theology. And both must be retained in the fullest sense of their respective meanings if the Gospel as the life-giving channel of the grace of God is to be maintained.

Brunner's problems all stem from his refusal to admit the existence of objective truth in the inscripturated revelation of God and his correlative definition of truth in terms of subjectivity or inwardness. As we have seen, Brunner believes that the religious encounter is credible in itself, that it is so self-validating to the one involved that it is its own basis for credibility. The writers of Scripture, however, never define truth in such a manner or by such a criterion. Truth is, for them, primarily objective, coming to man *ab extra,* found ultimately in the ontological Trinity and the incarnate Son of God and derivatively in the written Word of God, the Holy Scriptures. God is, to them, no deaf mute who acts but cannot, or at least does not, speak. Quite to the contrary, the Biblical God is light in himself and His Word gives light to all. Furthermore, their conception of the nature of revelation, though not exhausted by it, clearly allows for the existence of revealed propositional truths. Revelation may take the form of declarative, imperative, interrogative, and interjectional sentences. The Bible is replete with the notion that behind the words of Scripture is the God who revealed himself to man and then superintended the recording of that revelation so closely that the written product was rendered inerrant (not liable to be false or mistaken) and infallible (not liable to the teaching of error). The alleged indisputable results of Biblical criticism, when closely examined, are not as problematical as they might seem (though admittedly problems will always remain), and the proffered lists of alleged Scriptural discrepancies are embarrassingly archaic. Most have been grappled with with a high degree of successful harmonization (in the minds of many scholars) and are consequently regarded as inconsequential. Certainly none seems so compelling that the Scripture's claim for itself must *necessarily* be relinquished. This, of course, Brunner is unable to accept. Consequently, he who would seek, above all else, to have a "theology of the Word" has, in reality, no Word from heaven at all since he rejects the objective written revelation of God, the Sacred Scriptures. Though a man of massive breadth of learning, a man of unquestionably great intellectual and literary achievement, Brunner is unable to overcome a very poorly defined and colorless Christ event, about which, as soon as he says anything at all, he must speak in Biblical terms, terms the truthfulness of which he is not at all sure. Orthodoxy is convinced that it has something far more trustworthy, pistically speaking, and satisfying, epistemologically speaking, than this in its Word become flesh, set forth in an inspired, inerrant Scripture.

NOTES

1. John B. Cobb, Jr., *Living Options in Protestant Theology* (Philadelphia: The Westminster Press, 1962), p. 143.

2. For the following brief analysis of the misconceptions of Christianity as Brunner sees them, I am indebted to Bernard Ramm, *Varieties of Christian Apologetics* (Grand Rapids: Baker Book House, 1961), pp. 67-70.

3. Emil Brunner, *Revelation and Reason* (Translated by Olive Wyon; Philadelphia: The Westminster Press, 1946), p. 8.

4. *Ibid.*, p. 25.

5. *Ibid.*, p. 118.

6. *Ibid.*, p. 33.

7. *Ibid.*, pp. 30-31.

8. Emil Brunner, *The Mediator* (Translated by Olive Wyon; Philadelphia: The Westminster Press, 1947), p. 304.

9. *Ibid.*, p. 305 (italics mine).

10. *Ibid.*, (italics mine).

11. *Ibid.*, p. 308.

12. *Ibid.*

13. Cited by Paul King Jewett, *Emil Brunner's Concept of Revelation* (London: James Clarke & Co., Ltd., 1954), p. 25.

14. Emil Brunner, *The Philosophy of Religion from the Standpoint of Protestant Theology* (Translated by Farrer and Woolf; New York: Charles Scribner's Sons, 1937), p. 121.

15. Cobb, *op. cit.*, p. 161.

16. Brunner, *Revelation and Reason*, p. 10.

17. Brunner, *The Mediator*, p. 187.

18. *Ibid.*

19. *Ibid.*, p. 329.

20. *Ibid.*, p. 361.

21. *Ibid.*, p. 429.

22. *Ibid.*, pp. 504-505.

23. *Ibid.*, p. 573.

24. *Ibid.*, 577.

25. Emil Brunner, *Dogmatics* (Philadelphia: The Westminster Press, 1956), II, 373.

26. *Ibid.*, pp. 373-376, 377.

27. Brunner, *The Mediator*, pp. 156-157.

28. *Ibid.*, p. 270.

29. *Ibid.*, p. 271.

30. *Ibid.*, p. 337.

31. *Ibid.*, pp. 333-334.

32. Brunner, *Revelation and Reason*, p. 120.

33. *Ibid.*, p. 156.

34. *Ibid.*

35. *Ibid.*, p. 150.

36. *Ibid.*, p. 201.

37. *Ibid.*, p. 129.

38. *Ibid.*, p. 288.

39. *Ibid.*, p. 290.

40. *Ibid.*, p. 291.

41. *Ibid.*, pp. 132-133.

42. *Ibid.*, p. 135.

43. *Ibid.*, p. 129.

44. *Ibid.*, p. 136.

45. *Ibid.*, p. 415.

46. *Ibid.*

47. Jewett, *op. cit.*, p. 50.

48. Brunner, *Revelation and Reason*, p. 179.

49. Brunner, *Dogmatics*, II, 255.

50. Brunner, *Revelation and Reason*, p. 36.

51. *Ibid.*, pp. 36-37.

52. Brunner, *Dogmatics*, III, 292-293.

53. Brunner, *Revelation and Reason*, p. 425.

54. *Ibid.*, p. 170.

55. *Ibid.*, p. 166.

56. *Ibid.*, p. 173.

57. For the following criticism of Brunner's concepts of the paradox of time and eternity and the truth-content in the divine-human encounter, I gladly acknowledge my great indebtedness to Jewett's monograph on Brunner's concept of revelation and heartily commend it to the reader.

58. Jewett, *Emil Brunner's Concept of Revelation,* p. 140.

59. *Ibid.*, pp. 140-142.

60. *Ibid.*, pp. 142-146.

61. Brunner, *Revelation and Reason,* p. 284, footnote 21.

62. Jewett, *op. cit.,* p. 144.

63. *Ibid.*, pp. 145-146.

64. Cited by *ibid.*, p. 151.

65. *Ibid.*, pp. 153-154.

66. *Ibid.*, p. 154.

CHAPTER VI

BARTH'S SOTERIOLOGY

ABOUT KARL BARTH

Karl Barth (1886-   ) was born in Basel, Switzerland, and educated at the Universities of Berne (under his father, a New Testament theologian), Berlin (under Adolf von Harnack, the Ritschlian church historian), and Marburg (under Wilhelm Herrmann). During the second decade of this century he pastored a church in Safenwil, Switzerland, becoming there increasingly disenchanted with his liberal theological training because of the backing which his mentors had given to the military policy of Kaiser Wilhelm II and because of the fact of World War I itself. Between 1915 and 1919 Barth and Eduard Thurneysen, an intimate friend and also a pastor, re-evaluated their theology, the result of Barth's research being his *Römerbrief*. Therein, besides the Bible, was the influence of Kierkegaard, Overbeck, and Dostoievski. During the 1920's which may be regarded as the decade of his existentialist approach to theology, Barth taught at the Universities of Göttingen and Münster. The year 1927 saw the publication of the first (and only) volume of his *Christian Dogmatics,* an effort which he later began anew and replaced with his monumental *Church Dogmatics.* From 1930 to 1934 he taught at the University of Bonn, at the end of which time he returned to his home town of Basel and taught there in the University until his retirement in 1961.

The last thirty years have witnessed an amazing literary creativity, his *Church Dogmatics* already filling thirteen large volumes in English translation. In 1962 he visited the United States for the first time under the auspices of Chicago Divinity School and Princeton Theological Seminary. Though now an octogenarian, he is still actively engaged in the completion of the final volume of his *magnum opus*.

In addition to his *Dogmatics*, he has authored some forty or fifty books and several hundred articles covering a wide range of topics, many of a non-theological nature.

Books about Barth of interest to the American reader are Gerrit C. Berkouwer's *The Triumph of Grace in the Theology of Karl Barth*, Cornelius Van Til's *The New Modernism* and *Christianity and Barthianism*, Gordon H. Clark's *Karl Barth's Theological Method*, Fred Klooster's *The Significance of Barth's Theology*, and A. D. R. Polman's *Barth*. Neo-orthodox treatments of Barth which are also valuable are those by Torrance, Weber, and Come.

NOTE

A word of explanation is deemed advisable concerning the use of the term "soteriology" in the title of this chapter. As is well known, Barth rarely uses the word, and in the few places where he does so, he for the most part rejects its traditional meaning (cf. his *Church Dogmatics*, IV/I, pp. 108, 124, 144). Barth subsumes Christology, hamartiology, and ecclesiology, along with that which has been traditionally treated as soteriology under his doctrine of reconciliation, much preferring this latter term. I use the term in its traditional sense—to indicate God's plan in relation to, and his manner of bringing about, the salvation of men—in attempting to elucidate for students who are familiar with this term Barth's understanding of God's plan and *"modus operandi"* relative to man's salvation.

*　　　*　　　*　　　*　　　*

Karl Barth, though now past eighty years of age, is regarded by many theologians today as still the foremost living voice on the theological scene. Certainly in creativity and originality his peers are few indeed. Though their opinion could be seriously debated, some qualified thinkers even see him as continuing the line of Orthodoxy extending from Paul and running through Augustine and Anselm, Luther and Calvin.

This prominence is no doubt due primarily to the fact that Barth spearheaded the theological revolt in the 1920's against classical Liberalism and to the fact that he has refused to be silent throughout his long career but has continued to speak to the world's leading theologians through his *Church Dogmatics*, the publication of which has already spanned some thirty-five years since the appearance of the first installment in 1932. This time factor has led Cobb and many others to insist that Barth "needs to be understood in terms of the development of his thought," [1] though Cobb admits that throughout Barth's literary activity lies a profound consistency. T. F. Torrance distinguishes between a critical liberal period prior to the third decade of this century, an existential period in the 1920's and since then a post-existential period in which (so he says) Barth has repudiated any and all reliance upon philosophy.[2] Of course, it is true that Barth's *Römerbrief* (1919) had refused to ground Christian faith in objective history and objective knowledge, this refusal rendering his dialectic theology wholly compatible with existential emphases and in broad early agreement with Bultmann's redirecting the dialectical approach until the latter insisted that the Christian faith demands no historical foundation other than the mere "thatness" of Jesus' existence and that the New Testament is to be understood only existentially. And it is also true, of course, that to forestall any existential takeover of his position, Barth broke with Bultmann in the late 1920's and rejected existentialism in the 1932 *Church Dogmatics*, steadily adding since then "objectifying" elements to his theological structure.[3] But there are sound reasons for feeling that this much-discussed "development" has been greatly exaggerated and that Barth is still controlled today in his methodology by the presuppositions which bound his thinking in the second edition (1921) of his *Römerbrief*. In the Preface to the second quarter-volume of Volume IV of his *Dogmatics* (E.T. published in 1956), Barth himself bears out this conclusion when he writes: ". . . at the decisive points [evangelical groups] cannot fail to hear something of the rolling thunder of the 1921 *Romans*. . . . Perspicuous readers will surely notice that there is no break with the basic view which I have adopted since my parting from Liberalism. . . ." [4] Klooster views this development in Barth as one of *emphasis* mainly: Barth's resounding divine *No* upon man in his earlier writings only prepared the way for his even more resounding and final divine *Yes* in man's behalf in his later work.[5] It would appear that Klooster's analysis is correct. Consequently, direct regard for this development will not play a prominent role in the present discussion.

According to Barth, the two doctrines which are central to all the ways and works of God are election and reconciliation, the former because it is the sum and substance of the Gospel and of all words that can be said it is the best, the latter because it is the center of all Christian knowledge. In his discussion of them, Barth reveals his understanding of soteriology. His dialectic will be clearly visible in his understanding of Jesus Christ as Electing God/Elected man and as the Reconciliation between God and man.

Barth's Doctrine of Election

Barth's doctrine of election is found in the second half-volume of Volume II of the *Dogmatics,* which volume the *Union Seminary Quarterly* suggests "may turn out to be the most important volume in Karl Barth's massive *Church Dogmatics*." [6] Klooster reports: "After Barth spoke to a ministers' conference in Germany in 1949, the response of some was that this doctrine of election gave them new joy in preaching." [7] How does Barth himself feel about his construction of this doctrine? He writes: "The work has this peculiarity, that in it I have had to leave the framework of theological tradition to a far greater extent than in the first part on the doctrine of God. I would have preferred to follow Calvin's doctrine of predestination much more closely, instead of departing from it so radically. . . . But I could not and cannot do so. As I let the Bible itself speak to me on these matters, as I meditated upon what I seemed to hear, I was driven irresistibly to reconstruction." [8] What importance does Barth place upon the doctrine of election in his "system"? He declares: "The doctrine of election is the sum of the Gospel because of all words that can be said or heard it is the best." [9] And still more to the point he affirms: "The election of grace is the sum of the Gospel—we must put it as pointedly as that. But more, the election of grace is the whole of the Gospel, the Gospel *in nuce*." [10]

The foundation of election. Barth begins his construction of election by rejecting tradition, experience, and any preconceived notion of God as proper bases for a truly Scriptural notion of election.[11] Rather, he declares: ". . . we must begin as we seek to be taught by the self-revelation of God attested by Holy Scripture." [12] Of course, he recognizes that the Reformers had sought to do the same thing: "We must not overlook the fact that these older theologians did read their Bible carefully, and that in the teaching they did intend to comment as we do on Rom. 9-11 and other passages in the scriptural witness." [13] Why then does Barth feel that he must depart from their earlier teaching? In brief, Barth disagrees with the way that the Reformers read their Bibles. On the reading of the Bible Barth writes: "The decisive point is the reading of the Bible itself. It is the question where and how we find in the Bible itself the electing God and elected man, and therefore that reality of the divine election as a whole which must shape our thinking about the election and form the object of all our individual reflection and speech concerning it." [14] How then does Barth read his Bible at this point? The Reformers read the Bible as a body of divinely revealed information about God's decrees, but this avenue of approach Barth is not willing to follow. Rather, Barth speaks of the "christological basis and starting point for the doctrine." [15] We will let Barth explain himself at this point: ". . . in the name and person of Jesus Christ we are called upon to recognize the Word of God, the decree of God and the election of God at the beginning of all things, at the beginning of our own being and thinking, at the basis of our faith in the ways and works of God." [16] And he adds: "When it is a question of the understanding and exposition of what the Bible calls predestination or election, why and on what authority are we suddenly to formulate a statement which leaves out all mention of Jesus Christ? How is it that at this point there suddenly arises the possibility of looking elsewhere?" [17]   Barth believes that there must be "a continuity between the christological centre and *telos* of the temporal work of God . . . and the eternal presupposing of that work in the divine election." [18]   What is the significance for Barth of this christological starting point for election? Klooster quite correctly answers: "Barth means to say that from the work of Jesus Christ one must be able to conclude backwards to a knowledge of the whole will of God." [19]   He continues: "Since Jesus Christ came to save men, Barth concludes that God's will is the election and not the rejection of man." [20]   Barth wonders "how could one ever deduce a doctrine of reprobation from an analysis of the crucifixion and death of Jesus Christ? Obviously this was the work of grace. . . ." [21]   And so Barth strikes his hermeneutical note of Christomonism, which asserts that at every point the theologian who would be Biblical must begin with Christ and Christ alone in the formulation of doctrine. Would the theologian wish to pronounce in the area of election? Then to be Biblical, he must view election from Jesus Christ as God's expression of all his will, ways, and works. And it is this note that Barth consciously seeks to hear in all of his theological pronouncements. What are the results for his construction of election of Barth's rigid following of this hermeneutical procedure? To answer this question, we must turn to Barth's construction itself.

The election of Jesus Christ. Barth understands election to be primarily the election of Jesus Christ,[22] the genitive "of Jesus Christ" being taken here both subjectively and objectively. Barth rejects both the "covenant of redemption" and the "covenant of works" of traditional Reformed thought. Of the former he writes: "Can we really think of the first and second persons of the triune Godhead as two divine subjects and therefore as two legal subjects who can have dealings and enter into obligations one with another? This is mythology, for which there is no place in a right understanding of the doctrine of the Trinity as the doctrine of the three modes of being of the one God. . . ."[23] Of the latter he writes: "There never was a golden age. There is no point in looking back to one. The first man was immediately the first sinner."[24] Barth is left then with only *one covenant* (and this is what he was after all along) — the covenant of grace — and *one decree* — the decree of election of Jesus Christ. "In its simplest and most comprehensive form the dogma of predestination consists . . . in the assertion that the divine predestination is the election of Jesus Christ."[25] Claiming simply to follow John 1:1-2, Barth asserts: "Jesus Christ was in the beginning with God. He was not merely so in the sense that in view of God's eternal knowing and willing all things may be said to have been in the beginning with God, in His plan and decree. . . . He was also in the beginning with God as . . . Himself the plan and decree of God, Himself the divine decision with respect to all creation and its history whose content is already determined."[26] This means, according to Barth, that *Jesus Christ is both the Electing God and the Elected Man:* ". . . of Jesus Christ we know nothing more surely and definitely than this — that in free obedience to His Father He elected to be man, and as man, to do the will of God:"[27] As the Elected Man, "Jesus Christ is not merely one object of the divine good-pleasure side by side with others. On the contrary, He is the sole object of this good-pleasure."[28] Jesus Christ, then, is *the* God who does the electing, he is *the* man who is elected. But such a construction has removed the double election of traditional Reformed theology, has it not? For where is the decree of reprobation pertaining to the non-elect? Barth agrees that the Reformers' construction of a double election is removed by this viewing of things, but he feels quite confident that a double object of election still remains, and this time the construction is a truly Biblical one. "In so far as [Jesus Christ] is the electing God, we must obviously . . . ascribe to Him the active determination of electing," that is, the electing which is "the divine determination of the existence of Jesus Christ. . . ."[29] "In so far as He is man, the passive determination of election is also and necessarily proper to Him," that is, the election (the being elected) which is "the human [determination of the existence of Jesus Christ]."[30] Thus a double election — and Barth thinks this is the only double election which Scripture will tolerate — remains, namely, that God has "elected fellowship with man for Himself," and "fellowship with Himself for man."[31] Furthermore, election has a new double content now. God has willed that he himself shall lose, that Christ will be reprobated, that the No of election concerns only himself, that for himself alone there is reprobation, perdition, and death. On the other hand, God has willed that man shall only gain, that man shall be elected, that the Yes of election concerns man, that for man there is election, salvation, and life. In short, "When we look into the innermost recesses of the divine good-pleasure," Barth writes, "predestination is the non-rejection of man. It is so because it is the rejection of the Son of God." [32]

A summary of Barth's doctrine up to this point may perhaps clarify Barth's thoughts concerning election. In his own words, ". . . the simplest form of the dogma may be divided at once into the two assertions that Jesus Christ is the electing God, and that He is also elected man." [33] "Starting from John 1:1f., we have laid down and developed two statements concerning the election of Jesus Christ. The first is that Jesus Christ is the electing God. This statement answers the question of the Subject of the eternal election of grace. And the second is that Jesus Christ is elected man. This statement answers the question of the object of the eternal election of grace. Strictly speaking, the whole dogma of predestination is contained in these two statements." [34]

Barth sees two chief values in his construction of election over that of the Reformers. *First*, the theologian is no longer dealing with unknown quantities, with abstractions; he is now dealing with the living electing God and with the living elected man. In the older interpretation of the doctrine, "ultimately and fundamentally the electing God is an unknown quantity," and "ultimately and fundamentally elected man is also an unknown quantity." [35] But now, says Barth, ". . . our thesis that the eternal will of God is the election of Jesus Christ means that we deny the existence of any such twofold mystery." [36] He continues: "The thesis does avoid this twofold obscurity. It does give a single and known form to the unknown God and unknown man. The two together acquire one name and the name of one person. . . ." [37] *Second*, the theologian is done with the Reformers' *decretum absolutum* which involves, so Barth feels, a static view of God's relation to the universe, so that God himself becomes a prisoner of his own decree. Declares Barth: "The substitution of the election of Jesus Christ for the *decretum absolutum* is . . . the decisive point in the amendment of the doctrine of predestination," [38] and, continues Barth, "It is one of the great puzzles of history that the step which we are now taking towards a true form of the electing

God and elected man was not taken long ago." [39] But with no hesitation Barth takes this very step: "There is no such thing as a *decretum absolutum*. There is no such thing as a will of God apart from the will of Jesus Christ." [40] Calvinism was "pagan rather than Christian" because "it thought of predestination as an isolated and given enactment which God had decreed from all eternity and which to some extent pledged and committed even God Himself in time." [41] Barth elaborates further: "The point that we have to make against the older doctrine is this, that while in other respects it laid too great stress upon God's freedom, in this context it came very near to thinking of this freedom in such a way that in predestination God became His own prisoner." [42] And so Barth concludes: "At root, can there be anything more unchristian or anti-christian than the horror or the peace which is given by the thought of the *decretum absolutum* as the first and last truth from which everything else proceeds?" [43]

Having disposed of the Reformers' *decretum absolutum* by replacing it with the election of Jesus Christ, Barth is now prepared to draw the full implications of his doctrine. "It is now possible and necessary for us to make the controversial assertion that predestination is the divine act of will itself and not an abstraction from or fixed and static result of it." [44] That is, Barth means to say that what we actually see Jesus Christ working out and doing in history is that which is predestinated, and not something else. "The order proclaimed in the work of revelation and atonement must be regarded and respected as also the order of the divine predestination." [45] In short, predestination is itself history, encounter, and decision,[46] which is simply another way of saying in Barthian terminology that predestination is Jesus Christ. And this in turn makes Jesus Christ an "event" or an "act." States Barth: "The fundamental significance of the character of predestination as act ought to be clear without further discussion. If it is unchanged and unchangeably the history, encounter and decision between God and man, there is in time an electing by God and an election of man, as there is also a rejecting by God and a rejection of man, but not in the sense that God Himself is bound and imprisoned by it, not as though God's decree, the first step which He took, committed Him to take a corresponding second step, and the second a third. If it is true that the predestinating God not only is free but remains

121

free, that He does not cease to make use of His freedom but continues to decide, then in the course of God's eternal deciding we have constantly to reckon with new decisions in time. As the Bible itself presents the matter, there is no election which cannot be followed by rejection, no rejection which cannot be followed by election. God continues always the Lord of all His works and ways." [47] And he concludes: "Ultimately there is only one reason that we can give for deciding in favor of an activist understanding, and that is that the predestination which we know in the person and work of Jesus Christ is undoubtedly event, the history, encounter and decision between God and man." [48]

What does this all mean? What precisely has Barth done by such a construction? *First*, he has disposed of a decreeing God who is ontologically detached from this world. Or at least we can know nothing of such a God. The only decreeing God we can know is the God who continues to decree in time and who works in time as history, encounter, and decision. As far as our knowledge of a divine decree is concerned, it must be a knowledge related far more to time than to eternity. *Second*, he has "activated" the Incarnation, that is, he conceives of the Incarnation as an ongoing process by interpreting the person of Christ as his work. Christ, then, becomes an event. Or Jesus Christ, it can be said, is predestination, and nothing is predestined outside the work which Jesus Christ accomplishes. And what is this work? It is his electing to be man, and his election of himself to be both the Elect and the Reject. Of course, Barth is aware that Christ's Incarnation has been understood traditionally in an historical sense, namely, as referring to that time in human history when the Son of God took to himself a true body and a reasonable soul in the person of Jesus of Nazareth. But with this understanding, Barth contends, the grace of God is bound to certain happenings in Palestine a good many years ago and cannot be the original relation of every man to God. But if Jesus Christ be regarded, not primarily as *Historie* (the kind of history that historians write), but primarily as *Geschichte* (revelational history which includes everything that exists and which makes human nature what it is because of its participation in *Geschichte*), then Christ's human nature will not be understood statically but as event. "In Jesus Christ it comes about that God takes time to Himself, that He Himself, the eternal One, becomes

122

temporal, that He is present for us in the form of our existence and our own world, not simply embracing our time and ruling it, but submitting Himself to it, and permitting created time to be the form of His eternity." [49] *Geschichte* takes *Historie* up into itself, and Christ as the presence of God in *Geschichte* becomes event. Christ is *Geschichte*, and man is man because he participates in this *Geschichte*. The original relation of every man to God becomes thereby one of grace, for all men are related to Christ who is in his Incarnation *Geschichte*. *Third*, in the interest of preserving God's freedom, Barth refuses to interpret the divine decreeing in any sense as inviolably fixed or unalterable. God continues to decree, new decisions actually making their appearances in time. We shall not comment upon Barth's construction at this juncture. Rather, we shall follow Barth's thought to discover what this election of Jesus Christ means for mankind.

The election of the community. Barth sees election as secondarily the election of the community.[50] "The election of grace, as the election of Jesus Christ, is simultaneously the eternal election of the one community of God." [51] Barth feels that the Reformers were too quick to deal with the election of the individual: ". . . if we keep to Holy Scripture, we find that unlike the classical doctrine of predestination it is in no hurry to busy itself with the 'many' men elected in Jesus Christ, either in the singular or plural. It does do this, of course, and we shall have to do so. But starting from the election of Jesus Christ it does not immediately envisage the election of the individual believer (and in this too we shall have to follow it), but in the first place a mediate and mediating election. The Subject of this is indeed God in Jesus Christ, and its particular object is indeed men. But it is these men as a fellowship elected by God in Jesus Christ and determined from all eternity for a peculiar service." [52]

The task of this elected community, as Barth understands it, is to attest to Jesus Christ before the whole world and to summon the world to faith in Jesus Christ.[53] It carries out this twofold task by its very *nature* and by its *message*.

What is the nature of this elected community? To answer this question, Barth turns to Romans 9-11 and, interpreting Paul existentially rather than historically as Paul intended to be understood, applies Israel and the Church to this elected community as two aspects or phases of the one community of God.

Commenting on Romans 9, Barth concludes that as Israel the community serves the representation of the divine judgment; as the Church it serves the representation of the divine mercy.[54] "The specific service for which Israel is determined within the whole of the elected community is to reflect the judgment from which God has rescued man and which He wills to endure Himself in the person of Jesus of Nazareth." [55] "The service for which the Church as the perfect form of the one elected community is determined . . . consists always in the fact that it is the reflection of the mercy in which God turns His glory to man. The community in the form of the Church is the community of the risen Lord Jesus Christ." [56] Commenting on Romans 10, Barth concludes that as Israel the community is determined (destined) to hear the promise sent to man; as the Church it is determined (destined) to believe the promise sent to man.[57] "The special service of Israel within the totality of the elected community consists . . . in the hearing, the reception and the acceptance of the divine promise." [58] "In the perfect form of the one elected community of God the service of the Church consists . . . in the fact that it secures attention for the promise heard by putting faith in it." [59] Finally, commenting on Romans 11, Barth concludes that Israel is the passing form of the community, the Church the coming form of the community.[60] "The specific service which within the whole of the elected community is Israel's determination is the praise of the mercy of God in the passing, the death, the setting aside of the old man, of the man who resists his election and therefore God." [61] ". . . the service of the Church as the perfect form of the one community of God consists in attesting, by faith in the Word heard, by laying hold of the divine mercy, the coming kingdom of God as the end of all human need, the coming of the new man and his eternal life." [62]

One thing is apparent from Barth's analysis of Israel and the Church as aspects of the one elected community. The two terms do not refer to a past and a present of the elected community in the sense that the community is not now what it once was, and was at one time in the past something that it now is not; rather, there was and never will be a time when the elected community is not both Israel and the Church, the former merely speaking of that impossible possibility which God in his grace passed by, the latter speaking of what all men are, though they perhaps realize it not.

This new understanding of Israel and the Church is brought out even more clearly in the message which, according to Barth, the elected community is to proclaim. The community in Jesus Christ is not really two but one; in Christ the elect triumph in the "gracious end" which Israel manifests and in the "new gracious beginning" which the Church reflects.[63] In this dual role the one community approaches every man with the promise that "he, too, is an elect man," [64] for although it is fully aware of man's perverted choice, fully aware of man's godlessness, it remembers that "it consists itself of godless men who were enabled to hear and believe this promise, and who still need to hear and believe it. It must and does reckon continually with the original godlessness of its members. It is fully aware, too, of the eternal condemnation of the man who is isolated over against God, which is unfailingly exhibited by the godlessness of every such man. . . . It knows the wrath and judgment and punishment of God in which the rejection of the man isolated over against God takes its course. And it also knows of the shadow into which every man does actually move because he desires and undertakes at all costs to be a man isolated, and therefore rejected, in relation to God; because he behaves and conducts himself at all costs *as though he were this rejected man.* But it knows, *above all,* about Jesus Christ. . . . It knows that God . . . has taken upon Himself the rejection merited by the man isolated in relation to Him; that on the basis of this decree of His *the only truly rejected man is His own Son.* . . . And *this is the very goal which the godless cannot reach, because it has already been taken away by the eternally decreed offering of the Son of God. . . . It testifies to them that the way in which they find themselves was . . . nullified before the world began.* They may choose as they do. They may proceed as far as they are able. But *the situation and reward of the rejected for which they stretch out their hands in their folly when they reject God, will assuredly not be secured by them. . . .* It knows supremely that Jesus Christ died and rose for [the rejected] also. And because of this it must address him without reserve. . . . *It is to say to each of them that he is the actual object of the divine election of grace.*" [65]

125

From this rather lengthy quotation it is obvious that the message of the elected community, as both Israel and the Church, is actually and purely a message of grace. Though it understands, because of its own nature as Israel, the godlessness of all men, yet it understands even better, because of its nature as the Church, that all men are the actual objects of divine grace in election, that no man is actually outside of Jesus Christ, that try as he might the godless man is unable to undo what God in Jesus Christ has graciously decreed in his behalf. In short, God's wrath is always and only penultimate; his grace is always and finally ultimate. Klooster observes that, beyond question, Barth teaches a universal election.[66] As to whether this affirmation by Barth teaches a universal salvation will be considered shortly. At this point the discussion will simply continue to follow Barth as he proceeds to the election of the individual.

The election of the individual. Barth arrives, only after treating the election of Jesus Christ and the election of the community in him, at the election of the individual,[67] an approach which he thinks is the only Biblical one. He writes: "Included in His [Jesus Christ] election there is . . . this 'other' election, the election of the many (from whom none is excluded)." [68] Indeed, "the election of the individual [is] the *telos* of the election of the community."[69] Barth is critical of the traditional Reformed doctrine of election for its "over anxious" approach to the election of the individual. As a result, its construction was more in the interest of a non-Biblical humanism than in the interest of true Biblical exposition. ". . . the doctrine [of election as the Reformers understood it] is not merely one of those factors which have paved the way for Pietism and Rationalism within the Church itself, but is also one of the presuppositions without which the further development of secular individualism would have been inconceivable (the development from J. J. Rousseau and the younger Schleiermacher through Max Stirner and Kierkegaard to Ibsen and Nietzsche)." [70] This is so because the older doctrine involved the "conviction that the beginning and end of all the ways of God, and even the essence of all divine truth, are to be recognized and honoured in individual human beings." [71]

One cannot but feel that Barth is very reluctant to deal with the non-elect in his construction of election, for still Barth refuses to deal with them separately apart from the elect. Rather, he first treats the elect and the non-elect together, avoiding the very terms "non-elect" or "reject," preferring the neutral and colorless term, the "others" (but cf. Eph. 2:3). What is the difference for Barth between the elect and these others. Answers Barth: "This, then, is how the elect and others differ from one another: the former by witnessing in their lives to the truth, the latter by lying against the same truth. *It ought to be clear that to this extent they belong together.* The elect are obviously to be found in the sphere of the divine election of grace, in the hand of the one God, under the reign whose beginning and principle are called Jesus Christ. *But the others are also to be found there.* The former are there in obedience, the latter in disobedience. . . . If the former testify by their truthful witness to what God wills, the latter no less expressively testify by their lying witness to what God does not will. Thus both serve the revelation of the divine will and decree which by nature are wholly light, but which cannot be revealed or recognized except as light and shade. Believers 'are' the elect in this service so far as they bear witness to the truth, that is, to the elect man, Jesus Christ, and manifest and reproduce and reflect the life of this one Elect. The godless 'are' the rejected in the same service so far as by their false witness to man's rejection they manifest and reproduce and reflect the death of the one Rejected, Jesus Christ. Because this One is the Elect and the Rejected, He is — attested by both — the Lord and Head of the elect and also of the rejected. Thus not only the former, but no less indispensably, in their own place and after their own totally different fashion, the latter, are His representatives, just as originally and properly He is theirs." [72] It is beyond debate that Barth still does not take seriously a group which could actually be designated the "non-elect." Rather, both the elect and the non-elect find themselves within the sphere of the grace of God, serving correlative purposes. Neither is dispensable; each needs the other to testify to opposing principles with which they have to do. Barth continues: "It is from this solidarity of the elect and the rejected in the One Jesus Christ that there arises a very definite expectation for others." [73] What is the recollection for the elect and the expectation for the "others" to which Barth refers? "The recollection for the elect is this. . . . As they work out their election, in faith in Jesus Christ, they can never think of the basis

127

of their election without thinking simultaneously of the rejection which has been diverted from them in their election. . . ." [74] "The expectation for others is this. The original and proper distinction of Jesus Christ, which alone makes possible and actual the distinction of the elect, is the truth which also transcends, comprehends and illumines their existence, but which does not appear to be theirs because . . . they are obviously involved in the evil, perilous and futile manifestation, repetition and reproduction of the life of men rejected by God. In this respect we must not forget that the distinction of the elect, which originally and properly is that of Jesus Christ alone, is also valid for these others; that they do not possess it only in so far as they do not recognize and accept it as their own distinction. . . . They can, of course, dishonour the divine election of grace; but they cannot overthrow or overturn it. They cannot prevent God from regarding them as from all eternity He has willed to regard and has actually regarded sinful men in His own Son. . . . A limit is fixed by the fact that the rejected man, who alone and truly takes and bears and bears away the wrath of God, is called Jesus Christ. They can be only potentially rejected. They may indeed conduct themselves as rejected, but even if they deserved it a thousand times they have no power to bring down on themselves a second time the sword of God's wrath now that it has fallen." [75] It would seem, then, that still for Barth there are no truly and ultimately non-elect men, but let us not be hasty in our judgment. Let us continue to let Barth speak. "Both the necessary recollection for the elect and the necessary expectation for others means, then, that we have every reason to consider the elect and others together for all their opposition. We cannot, at any rate, regard their opposition as absolute. For all its distinctive sharpness, the opposition between them can only be relative, because both are in the one absolute hand of God." [76] Barth readily affirms that according to Scripture these two lines are followed out in human history which is "the history of the continually renewed consolidation, separation and encounter of these two peoples," [77] but this contrast is clearest, declares Barth, where these two are not two but one — namely, Jesus Christ who is the Elect and the Rejected. "He is *the* Rejected, as and because He is *the* Elect. In view of His election, there is no other rejected but Himself." [78] And so Barth concludes that both groups are necessary:

"We can no more consider and understand the elect apart from the rejected than we can consider and understand the rejected apart from the elect."[79]

Only now, after he has treated the elect and the "others" together in such a way that the two groups are equally within the sphere of the divine election of grace, does Barth consider the elect separately and the non-elect separately. But still it is the elect which come in for treatment first.[80] This treatment, however, is largely repetitious of all the expressions of grace which Barth has previously written concerning the elect: no new decisions or conclusions are reached. Consequently, we are here primarily concerned with what Barth does with the "others." [81] But the suspicious reader can hardly be blamed for thinking that the decisions concerning them have already been made in preceding sections of Barth's discussion or for being less than surprised when he is confronted with Barth's actual handling of the matter. For, as we shall show, Barth does not regard the non-elect as being essentially different from the elect. In fact, he actually denies the independent existence of the unbeliever. He writes: "Because Jesus Christ takes [the rejected man's place], He takes from him the right and possibility of his own independent being and gives him His own being. With Jesus Christ the rejected can only *have been* rejected. He cannot *be rejected* anymore." [82] Thus a rejected man is not independently really actual or actually real. Barth seen man only in Jesus Christ, which means that only Jesus Christ is a person; we achieve participation in personhood only in him. Apart from believing participation in Jesus Christ there are no real persons at all. Of course, Barth does not mean by all this that the rejected man is an imaginary entity or that he would not meet empirical tests of existing. But, as Cobb has rightly observed, Barth is using "real" in a very special sense. "[Barth's sense of 'real'] can be grasped, if at all, only by imaginatively sharing in his own vision of the sole agency of God and the unlimited graciousness of that agency. From this point of view we must see by faith, and in spite of all appearances, that what resists God's grace is *really* nothing—is already negated, wholly negative. Hence those men who attempt to stand in that rejection have in fact nothing to stand upon and no being or power to oppose God's grace. Barth does, it is true, allot a certain limited and negative reality to the rejected, but this he insists is derived from the elect. One exists as rejected by virtue of being known as such by the elect. He represents man in this need for election and in that negative condition which is the only alternative to faith. As such he too exists by the will of God as the shadow of this gracious election." [83]

But what about Judas? Surely if ever there were one, here is one whom the Scriptures regard as actually and independently real and as rejected by God. Barth is not so convinced, for he devotes forty-eight pages to a demonstration that Judas may be regarded as an elect individual. He does this by arguing that the Greek word *paradidomi* does not mean "betray" with reference to Judas' actions concerning the Christ. Rather, it means "a handing over." And Judas' "handing over" was only one of three "handings-over." First, there was the "handing over" of the Son by the Father.[84] Second, the apostolic mission "handed over" the Christ in the preaching and teaching of the Gospel.[85] And third, there was Judas' "handing over" of Jesus to the religious leaders and the Roman soldiers. Now the Christian should not be too harsh with Judas, so thinks Barth, for if redemption may for the moment be compared to a huge stone, it is this stone which Judas starts rolling—but only starts rolling. ". . . this almost incidental denunciation by Judas is the first link in the chain: the smallest, but one which involves and controls all those that follow. . . . At this point it is a disciple and apostle of Jesus who makes the decisive movement. It is quite a small movement, trifling as compared with everything that follows once it has taken place. It is carried out by the kiss, which, in point of fact, attests and seals again the fellowship of the perpetrator with Jesus. Judas delivers Jesus, and in so doing he initiates the decisive movement which Jesus had to perform for the accomplishment of His work—His suffering and death." [86] ". . . the treacherous kiss by which Judas distinguishes Jesus from the surrounding disciples is . . . the sign of the gratitude of lost men for the existence of Him who now wills to intervene for him." [87] And Barth concludes: "In one sense Judas is the most important figure in the New Testament apart from Jesus. For he, and he alone of the apostles, was actively at work in this decisive situation." [88] In this manner Barth vindicates the actions of Judas and denies to him the status of the rejected. But even though it undoubtedly is true that Judas' betrayal of Jesus

130

did initiate the first movement which eventuated in Christ's death on Calvary's tree (though Barth's viewing of the kiss of betrayal as an attestation and seal of the fellowship which Judas enjoyed with Jesus stretches legitimate Biblical exegesis beyond the breaking point), is not the testimony of Scripture clear to the effect that Judas died and "went to his own place"? Is it not the clear intent of Scripture to portray Judas as a lost man? Barth answers this objection by declaring that we need not accept as true the Scripture concerning Judas' final destiny. For one thing, does not the Scripture disagree with itself regarding the manner of Judas' death, the Gospel account ascribing his death to suicide by hanging but Peter in Acts speaking of his death in far more violent terms— as a falling down followed by a bursting open in the middle and the gushing forth of his bowels? To Barth this disagreement speaks of an uncertainty within the early Church itself over what did actually happen to Judas. Consequently, he argues, from this factor, that all the disparagement of Judas found within the pages of Scripture simply reflects the early Church's effort to cover up the faithlessness of the other disciples by portraying Judas in deep shades of greed, selfishness, disloyalty, and dishonor. In this manner Barth feels he has succeeded in opening to Judas the doors of grace.

In the light of all that we have seen Barth affirming concerning the blessed position of both the elect and the "others" as objects of the divine election of grace, it cannot be denied that a universal salvation should be the logical outcome of Barth's construction of election. But Barth will neither affirm nor deny the theory of universal salvation. He writes: "If we are to respect the freedom of divine grace, we cannot venture the statement that it must and will finally be coincident with the world of man as such (as in the doctrine of the so-called *apokatastasis*). No such right or necessity can legitimately be deduced. Just as the gracious God does not need to elect or call any single man, so He does not need to elect or call all mankind. His election and calling do not give rise to any historical metaphysics, but only to the necessity of attesting them on the ground that they have taken place in Jesus Christ and His community. But, again, in grateful recognition of the grace of the divine freedom we cannot venture the opposite statement that there cannot and will not be this final opening up and enlargement of the circle of election and calling. . . . We would be developing an opposing historical metaphysics if we were to try to attribute any limits . . . to the loving-kindness of God." [89] In his book *The Humanity of God*, after describing his construction of election, Barth writes: "Does this mean universalism? I wish here to make only three short observations, in which one is to detect no position for or against that which passes among us under this term. 1. One should not surrender himself in any case to the panic which this word seems to spread abroad, before informing himself exactly concerning its possible sense or non-sense. 2. One should at least be stimulated by the passage, Colossians 1:20, which admittedly states that God has determined through His Son as His image and as the first-born of the whole Creation to 'reconcile all things (*ta panta*) to himself,' to consider whether the concept could not perhaps have a good meaning. The same can be said of parallel passages. 3. One question should for a moment be asked, in view of the 'danger' with which one may see this concept gradually surrounded. What of the 'danger' of the eternally skeptical-critical theologian who is ever and again suspiciously questioning, because fundamentally always legalistic and therefore in the main morosely gloomy? Is not his presence among us currently more threatening than that of the unbecoming cheerful indifferentism or even antinomianism, to which one with a certain understanding of universalism could in fact deliver himself? This much is certain, that we have no theological right to set any sort of limits to the loving-kindness of God which has appeared in Jesus Christ. Our theological duty is to see and understand it as being still greater than we had seen before." [90]

Thus Barth concludes his treament of election, which at every turn pointed on the surface at least toward a clear unequivocal universalism, by declaring himself an agnostic with reference to the final outcome of the divine election of grace. Only this attitude, he feels, preserves the divine freedom.

Criticism. The Bible believer will have already discerned that Barth's construction of election does, as Barth readily admits, differ at almost every point from the view which he has been taught. But just why this is so is due to several reasons. The following discussion of these reasons will form in the main our criticisms of Barth's doctrine of election.

First, Barth begins his construction of election with a very low view of the inspiration and infallibility of Scripture. The surprising thing is that he refers to Scripture as much as he does and employs its terminology as much as he does in the light of the fact that he does not believe that the Bible *is* the Word of God. For Barth the Bible only *becomes* God's Word from time to time. Writes Barth: "The Bible is God's Word so far as God lets it be His Word, so far as God speaks through it." [91] Barth assumes this position because, raised as he was in the liberal tradition, he accepts the "unimpeachable results" of the destructive Biblical criticism which arose on the Continent during the nineteenth and early twentieth centuries. He does not hesitate to speak of errors and contradictions within the pages of Holy Scripture. The Bible simply is not the Word of God for Barth. It is a book through which God may choose from time to time to reveal himself through certain of its statements, but no man has the guarantee that he will be confronted by the Word of God when he turns to its pages, and no two men have the guarantee that the same statement will be the Word of God alike to both. Gordon H. Clark has correctly perceived the end result of this position when he writes: ". . . rationality requires that each Scriptural statement be true permanently or untrue permanently. Ambiguous sentences, such as the favorite Stoic example 'It is daytime now,' can change from true to false as the meaning of 'now' is changed. But if unambiguous sentences can become true and then become false, if they are true only from time to time, there is no defense against skepticism." [92] Yet Barth continues to claim that "we do the Bible a poor honour, and one unwelcome to itself, when we directly identify it with . . . revelation itself." [93] Thus in spite of all his claims to the effect that he seeks above all else to let the Bible speak to him in all matters, Barth in actuality sits in judgment, as the autonomous man, on what the Bible can and cannot say. This must be true from the very nature of the case. By denying to the words of Scripture any inherent infallibility and viewing God's Word as "God's Word to me" in the moment of revelation, Barth has removed all objectivity from God's Word and has subjectivized all religious truth. The Biblical writers, however, never subjectivized truth in such a manner. For them truth is primarily objective, coming to man *ab extra*, found ultimately in the ontological Trinity and the incarnate Son of God and derivatively in the written Word of God, the Holy Scriptures. Nevertheless, in "proof-text" fashion, Barth quotes those Scriptures that "speak" to him (that is, aid him) in his construction of his doctrine whereas those Scripture statements which contradict his construction he rejects. A clear case in point is his treatment of the passages relating to Judas. He does not hesitate to affirm that Scripture contradicts itself in the matter of Judas' death, for this "fact" allows him to interpret Judas' actions in the manner he deems will best aid his construction of election. And this reading into Scripture that which he wishes to see there Barth extends throughout his writing. Thus there can be no controversy that over the question of whether or not the Bible is the inspired, infallible Word of the living God Barth remains ever an unbeliever. And it is this unbelief that gives rise to and shapes all of the other errors in his doctrine.

Second, his christomonistic principle of interpretation, that is, his effort to view all of the decreed ways and works of God only from the work of Jesus Christ is simply unbiblical. Barth rejects the orthodox understanding of the Trinity, that is, that there are three Persons in the Godhead, the Father, the Son, and the Holy Spirit, and that these three are one God, the same in substance, equal in power and glory. Rather, though he rejects likewise the formulation of historic Modalism, Barth describes the three Persons as simply "three modes of being of the one God." He is adamant in his insistence that the only God man can know is the God who reveals himself in Jesus Christ; therefore, he will not speak of the God "behind" Jesus Christ, for then, he declares, he would be no better off than the Reformers who spoke about a decreeing God other than Jesus Christ and his *decretum absolutum*. For Barth, then, though he will refer to the election of the Father and the Holy Spirit, God for all practical purposes is simply and solely Jesus Christ.

Because of his practical Unitarianism of the Second Person Barth must twist the clear meaning of many passages of Scripture in order to speak of Jesus Christ as being the pre-existent God-man who decreed to become both the Elect and the Reject. In fallacious proof-text fashion Barth affirms on the basis of John 1:1ff. "two statements concerning the election of Jesus Christ. The first is that Jesus Christ is the electing God. . . . And the second is that Jesus Christ is elected man." [94] Now it just simply is not Biblical to speak of Jesus Christ alone as the electing God. For while Scripture certainly speaks of the eternal pre-existence, prior to his Incarnation, of the Second Person of the Holy Trinity as the Logos of God, who did participate in the decisions of the covenant of redemption, who later in our time and in our history took to himself a true body and a reasonable soul in a genuine Incarnation, who bore his humanity through the tomb and to heaven at his ascension, and who will continue to bear his assumed humanity forever in behalf of his elect, Scripture nowhere ascribes election solely to Jesus Christ. Eternal pre-existence applies only to Christ's deity, and to speak of the eternal pre-existence of Jesus Christ rather than the eternal pre-existence of the Logos of God is simply fallacious exegesis. The very compound name, Jesus Christ, refers to his human and divine natures in his Incarnation.

Furthermore, it just is not Biblical to conclude backward from the earthly work of Jesus Christ to a knowledge of the whole decretive will of God. The work of Jesus Christ pertains in its redemptive aspect only to his elect; this means that with reference to the non-elect the triune God has decreed to regard them as outside of Jesus Christ and to leave them to their ordained perdition. But, of course, it is this very teaching of Scripture which Barth refuses to hear, preferring his own construction which, if carried to its logical end, leads to an unqualified universalism.

Third, it is actually Barth's view of election that involves an unknown God.[95] For in Barth's opinion, although all men are elect in Jesus Christ, so that what Jesus Christ has done has been done for all men, in the interest of preserving God's freedom in his sovereignty, Barth leaves open the question of a possible universalism, affirming that "the gracious God does not need to elect or call any single man," [96] and that "there is no election which cannot be followed by rejection, no rejection which cannot be followed by election." [97] In short, Barth is prepared to affirm that "if it is true that the predestinating God not only is free but remains free, that He does not cease to make use of His freedom but continues to decide, then in the course of God's eternal deciding we have constantly to reckon with new decisions in time." [98] But if a man can never be sure at any moment what God is going to decide about his election or rejection, does this not mean that God is unpredictable? And an unpredictable God can never become a God who can be irrevocably known. He remains forever an unknown God.

But does God's eternal decree which must necessarily "bind" him to his word deny to him his freedom? Who forced this binding upon him? No one. Whose will is being done? His own. The Christian is grateful that God eternally wills to bind himself even by oath to an eternal covenant of grace with those whom he fore-loved before the world was made. In the eyes of the Christian such a God is not less than free; indeed, it is through his eternal willing that as the Sovereign of the Universe, he has, according to the counsel of his own will and for his own glory, foreordained whatsoever comes to pass. It is by his eternal willing that, as far as man is concerned, his sovereignty is established. And this is simply to say that it is *his* freedom of choice which is working itself out in our history. Indeed, as Klooster declares, "Scripture indicates that the unchangeable God never desires to change his decree. It is because he eternally wills that he is never the prisoner of the decree laid before the foundation of the world." [99]

Fourth, though Barth admittedly does not affirm in so many words universal salvation, it would appear that he does not do so simply because he does not choose to do so. His voiced fear that such an affirmation would deny to God his freedom is groundless if it is universal salvation that the Scriptures teach. It would seem that this is just another example of the irrationalism which pervades his whole theological construction—the unwillingness to assume a position which is the only logical result of his methodology. Everything in his methodology and treatment points as straight as the arrow's flight to a universalism, but then, having advanced to the very threshold of this affirmation, he is unwilling to step across the threshold, but haltingly affirms that he is not sure what God will do. "The frontier from election to rejection and vice versa can be repeatedly crossed and crisscrossed." [100] The Christian, of course, rejoices that Barth does not affirm a universalism; in this Barth is right. But the Christian must always have strong objections to a construction which leads beyond doubt to a universalism.

Finally, it is clear from his description of the message of the elect community that for Barth it is not one primarily of warning and crying out against sin; it is not one primarily of beseeching men in Christ's stead to be reconciled to God. Rather, it is an informing them that all men are already elected in Jesus Christ, that even the "others," choose as they may, "can be only potentially rejected. They may conduct themselves as rejected, but even if they deserved it a thousand times they have no power to bring down on themselves a second time the sword of God's wrath now that it has fallen" [101] on *the* rejected Man, Jesus Christ. With such a message, the Scriptural warning against apostasy as well as the Church's call to conversion is minimized if not completely aborted. Barth's construction of election cuts the very heart out of all true evangelism.

Barth's Doctrine of Reconciliation

Barth's doctrine of reconciliation, found in Volume IV of his *Church Dogmatics*, includes what theologians have usually distinguished as Christology, hamartiology, soteriology, and ecclesiology. Barth himself describes this area as the "centre of all Christian knowledge," and attaches such importance to it that he exclaims: ". . . to fail here is to fail everywhere. To be on the right track here makes it impossible to be completely mistaken in the whole." [102]

The schema of Barth's construction. Traditionally, the Biblical message has been schematized under the three terms of creation, fall, and redemption. Barth is quite familiar with this fact, of course: "Between the doctrine of creation and that of atonement it was and is customary (and logically it is very instructive and didactically most illuminating) to interpose a special section *De peccato*: a doctrine of the fall, of original sin and its consequences, of the state and constitution of sinful man, of individual or actual sins." [103] But Barth feels compelled to substitute for the traditional schema the "dialectic of covenant, sin and reconciliation." [104] Barth does not speak first of creation but of covenant. This is due, first, to Barth's contention that one must begin with John 1 rather than Genesis 1 if a genuinely christological starting point is to be made. (For this reason Barth is regarded as a supralapsarian by many of his readers, the decree to create being subordinated to the covenant.) Second, the fact that he rejects the historical authenticity of the first chapters of Genesis, viewing them as *Saga*, that is, as description of events having to do with Adam as representative man, and as such, events that happen again and again, quite probably contributes to his aversion to begin with the creation of man.

137

Barth regards the covenant of grace as the first presupposition of reconciliation. As we saw earlier, Barth rejects Orthodoxy's traditional handling of the covenant program, failing to see either its "covenant of redemption" or its "covenant of work." Consequently, he posits the one covenant of grace, after assuming an original gulf between God and man which may be bridged only by God's reconciling action. It is true that Barth speaks of an "original fellowship" between God and man, but it should be carefully noted that this original fellowship between God and man is described as the fellowship of the *covenant of grace*: "The fellowship which originally existed between God and man, which was then disturbed and jeopardised, the purpose of which is now fulfilled in Jesus Christ and in the work of reconciliation, we describe as the covenant." [105] Consequently, Barth regards the first man as "immediately the first sinner," [106] standing in need of the grace of the covenant. It may be legitimately asked, where is the golden age of Eden, where is the fall of man from his created position of holiness in all of this? Of course, Barth removes both, insisting that only in this way may one actually be able to begin from a genuinely christological starting point. It may be said in passing that one can hardly be blamed for seriously questioning the validity of Barth's christological starting point that necessitates the setting aside of the teaching of entire blocks of Scripture.

Barth looks upon the doctrine of sin as the second presupposition of reconciliation. But what is sin in Barth's system? It is essentially a breaking of the covenant of grace which asks that man be thankful for God's grace! ". . . man is called to hold to the grace of his Creator, to be thankful for it, to bow to it and adapt himself to it, to honour it as the truth. And the essence of sin is that he does not do this." [107] This definition is certainly a far cry from the definition of sin in even the *Westminster Shorter Catechism*: "Sin is any want of conformity unto, or transgression of, the law of God." What is the relation of sin, as Barth sees it, to grace? Traditionally, God's grace has been viewed against the backdrop of sin since the Bible always represents grace as God's response to man's sin; consider, for example, "Where sin abounded, grace did much more abound" (Rom. 5:20), and "God commendeth his love toward us, in that, while we were yet sinners, Christ died for us" (Rom. 5:8). But Barth reverses this order and maintains that sin can only be seen in the light of grace, otherwise sin is an abstraction. ". . . we cannot with a good conscience," writes Barth, "follow the procedure which would give [sin] a treatment which is independent, self-originating and self-contained." [108] ". . . there can be no place in dogmatics for an autonomous section *De peccato* constructed in a vacuum between the doctrine of creation and that of reconciliation." [109] "If it takes place as a breach of one covenant [of grace], and not in any other way [and this is the burden of Barth's entire discussion to this point], it can be known only in the light of the covenant. But since man has broken the covenant, that can mean only in the light of the covenant fulfilled and restored in Jesus Christ and therefore in the light of the atonement made in Him." [110] And this is simply saying that sin must be seen as already regarded by God in the light of the covenant of grace and hence negated. "In all its forms it exists and is only as that which negates and therefore as that which is itself negated, on the left hand of God, where God in saying Yes has already said No, where in electing He has rejected, where in willing He has not willed. But the divine Yes in which sin negates and by which it is negated is the Yes of God's covenant with man. . . ." [111] Barth continues: ". . . we have no option but to consider and answer the question of sin in the light of the Gospel and therefore within the doctrine of reconciliation, to take it up into that doctrine instead of giving it precedence over it as though it were an autonomous question. In this context we shall find a natural place for it immediately after the Christology. It is in the knowledge of Jesus Christ as the revelation of the grace of God that we shall necessarily perceive step by step both the fact that man is a transgressor, and the nature of the transgression in which he contradicts the grace of God and for the sake of which he is decisively contradicted by that grace." [112] The result of this christological approach to sin is really the viewing of sin as an "impossible possibility." Barth has terrible pictures of sin to paint and he does so, but he can afford to in his thought because he sees this sin, no matter how black and hideous, as already taken up into and dealt with in reconciliation.

The "christological aspects" of reconciliation. With this background we come now to the "christological aspects" of Barth's construction of reconciliation. The sections on Christology in IV/1, IV/2, and IV/3 of the *Church Dogmatics* will provide one with an adequate amount of material in order to understand Barth's christo-monistic construction of the doctrine of reconciliation. He himself avers that the christological sections stand "at the head and contain the whole *in nuce*." [113] In these sections "the decisions are made." [114] Barth writes further: "We have to develop the whole doctrine of reconciliation in accordance with our Christology and the three basic christological aspects. . . . The Christology is the key to the whole. From each of the three aspects suggested it will be our starting point and will necessarily control all the detailed developments." [115]

As at so many other points, Barth replaces with his own view the traditional view of Christology. Traditionally, theologians have distinguished between Christ's person and Christ's work. This was done not out of scholastic necessity but because it was regarded as Scriptural and for facility of handling all of the material. In connection with his person, his natures were distinguished. As an example, the *Westminster Shorter Catechism* declares: "The only Redeemer of God's elect is the Lord Jesus Christ, who, being the eternal Son of God, became man, and so was, and continueth to be, God and man, in two distinct natures, and one person, forever." In regard to his work, theologians treated both the threefold office of prophet, priest, and king, and the two states of humiliation and exaltation within which he exercised his threefold office. Barth, of course, is aware of these facts. "It was," he writes, "and is customary to have a single complete and self-contained chapter on Jesus Christ, the so-called 'Christology,' as the climax in the whole presentation. This includes (1) a special doctrine of the 'person' of Christ, i.e., the incarnation of the Word of God, and also His Godhead and manhood in their relationship the one to the other, (2) a special doctrine of His work (following the *munus triplex* arrangement of the Reformation period), and usually (3) a special doctrine of the two 'states' of Christ, His humiliation and exaltation." [116] Feeling that such a treatment tends only to abstractionism, Barth, however, brings together into intimate relationship the doctrines of the two natures and the two states, together with the three offices: "An abstract doctrine of the person of Christ may have its own apparent importance, but it is always an empty form, in which what we have to say concerning Jesus Christ can never be said. Again, it is almost inevitable that a doctrine of the work of

Christ separated from that of His person will sooner or later give rise to the question, and perhaps even impose it, whether this work cannot be understood as that of someone other than that divine-human person." [117] Barth then wants to view Christ's work as his person and his person as his work. "It is in the particular fact and the particular way that Jesus Christ is very God, very man, and very God-man that He works, and He works in the fact and only in the fact that He is this One and not another. His being as this One is His history [Geschichte], and His history [Geschichte] is His being. This is the truth which must light up the doctrine of reconciliation as Christology." [118] From this it is apparent that for Barth *reconciliation is Christology and Christology is reconciliation.*

We then see that Barth has substituted for the traditional view his own Christology. But of what details does his Christology consist? We shall look at his Christology (which the reader should keep constantly in mind is for Barth equivalent to reconciliation) in greater detail, but a summary of Barth's Christology at this point will stand the reader in good stead in his effort to comprehend the intricate thought of Barth on this matter.

First, Jesus Christ as very God corresponds to the humiliation of God and to the priestly office.[119] Second, Jesus Christ as very man corresponds to the exaltation of man and to the kingly office.[120] Third, Jesus Christ as the God-man corresponds to no specific state but does speak of the prophetic office.[121] These then are Barth's three "christological aspects," and a careful study of them will reveal that Barth does seek to relate the person of Christ to his work and his work to his person. Each of these aspects will now be discussed in greater detail.

What is involved for Barth in his affirmation that Jesus Christ is very God? Barth responds: "The content of the doctrine of reconciliation is the knowledge of Jesus Christ who is . . . very God, that is, the God who humbles Himself, and therefore the reconciling God. . . ." [122] Barth further elucidates: "God became man. That is what is, i.e., what has taken place, in Jesus Christ. He is very God acting for us men, God Himself become man. He is the authentic Revealer of God as Himself God. Again, He is the effective proof of the power of God as Himself God. Yet again, He is the fulfiller of the covenant as Himself God. He is nothing less or other than God Himself, but God as man. When we say God we say honour and glory and eternity and power, in short, a regnant freedom as it is proper to Him who is distinct from and superior to everything else that is. When we say God we say the Creator and Lord of all things. And we can say all that without reservation or diminution of Jesus Christ. . . ." [123]

At first blush the unwary reader might conclude that Barth has certainly listened to Scripture in his description of Jesus Christ as very God. But there is sound reason to believe that Barth, in spite of all that is good and holy in what he says about Christ, is not talking about the Scriptural Christ at all. For, to Barth, the deity of Jesus Christ is not a self-contained, ontological deity, but rather *it is the nature of this God to humble himself and to turn himself into his opposite, namely, the creature.* Scripture speaks of God as a Spirit, infinite, eternal, and unchangeable, in his being, wisdom, power, holiness, justice, goodness, and truth. There are three persons in this Godhead, and this Trinity is ontologically independent, self-contained, and self-subsisting. Any turning on the part of the triune God to his creation is done, not out of necessity, but out of loving interest and concern. In truth, God does not need anything (Acts 17:24-25). But Barth does not have an ontological Trinity in his theology at all. For Barth the Trinity is a modal revelational representation and essentially functional in nature. Barth himself describes Jesus Christ as "the One whose eternity . . . commands Him to be in time and Himself to be temporal. . . ." [124] He continues: "He, the true God, is the one whose Godhead . . . plainly consists in essence in the fact that . . . He . . . wills this condescension. . . ." [125] And finally, "He is God in that He takes [the fallen] creature to Himself. . . . He is God in the fact that He can give Himself up and does give Himself up not merely to the creaturely limitations but to the suffering of the human creature, becoming one of these men, Himself bearing the judgment under which they stand, willing to die, and, in fact, dying the death they have deserved. *That is the nature and essence of the true God as He has intervened actively and manifestly in Jesus Christ."* [126] This simply means, as Van Til has seen, that Jesus Christ is God *because* he turns himself completely into the creature. This means in turn for Christianity that it no longer has a God-in-himself. It has only a God-for-man, with all the correlativity between Creator and creature which this implies.

God needs the creature in order to be God just as much as the creature needs God in order to be saved. Only a functional Trinity remains for the needy creature. All of this must be clearly kept in mind if one is to comprehend what Barth means when he speaks of Jesus Christ as very God.

Corresponding to Jesus Christ as very God, in Barth's Christology, is what traditionally has been termed the state of humiliation. Traditionally, it has been said that "Christ's humiliation consisted in his being born, and that in a low condition, made under the law, undergoing the miseries of this life, the wrath of God, and the cursed death of the cross, in being buried and continuing under the power of death for a time (*Westminster Shorter Catechism*, Q. 27). That is, Christ's state of humiliation pertains to the time of his Incarnation, extending up to and including his burial in the tomb. Christ's humiliation, then, necessarily included and refers to the atoning deeds of both his active and passive obedience, that is, his *atoning work*. But in the interest of relating Christ's work to his person, Barth refuses to speak of Christ's humiliation as that specific time of his earthly career extending from his birth to his enclosure in Joseph's tomb. Rather, he relates the state of humiliation to Jesus Christ's *divine* nature. ". . . what is the humiliation of Jesus Christ? To say that He is lowly as a man is tautology which does not help us in the least to explain His humiliation," [127] "The humiliation, therefore, is the humiliation of God." [128] Christ's divine nature, then, corresponds to the work included in his state of humiliation. And it is to this aspect that Barth relates Christ's priestly office.

Barth's second "christological aspect" refers to Jesus Christ as very man. "The content of the doctrine of reconciliation is the knowledge of Jesus Christ who is . . . very man, that is, man exalted and therefore reconciled by God. [129] He elaborates: "The second christological aspect is that in Jesus Christ we have to do with a true man. The reconciliation of the world with God takes place in the person of a man in whom, because He is also true God, the conversion of all men to God is an actual event. It is the person of a true man, like all other men in every respect, subjected without exception to all the limitations of the human situation. The conditions in which other men exist and their suffering are also His conditions and His suffering. He is altogether man just as He is altogether God. . . . To say man is to say creature and sin, and

143

this means limitation and suffering. Both these have to be said of Jesus Christ." [130]

Corresponding to Jesus Christ as very man, in Barth's Christology, is what traditionally has been termed his state of exaltation. Traditionally, Christ's exaltation has referred to "his rising again from the dead on the third day, in ascending up into heaven, in sitting at the right hand of God the Father, and in coming to judge the world at the last day (*Westminster Shorter Catechism*, Q. 28). In other words, his exaltation has been regarded as having followed temporally his humiliation, and this certainly is the Scriptural representation (cf. Phil. 2:6-11). But again in the interest of relating Christ's work to his person, Barth speaks of exaltation in reference to Christ's *human* nature. ". . . what is the exaltation of Jesus Christ? To say that as God He is transcendent, free, sovereign, above the world, and therefore above the limitation and suffering of the human situation is again tautology which does not help us to understand His exaltation." [131] Christ's exaltation is the exaltation of man,[132] because it is of the nature of this man to exalt mankind. "What has happened in Him as the one true man is the conversion of all of us to God, the realisation of true humanity. It is anticipated in Him, but it is in fact accomplished and revealed. As in Him God became like man, so too in Him man has become like God. . . . That is the atonement made in Jesus Christ in this second aspect. *In Him humanity is exalted humanity, just as Godhead is humiliated Godhead.*" [133] Christ's humanity, then, corresponds to the work included in the state of exaltation. And it is to this aspect that Barth relates Christ's kingly office.

Barth's third "christological aspect" pertains to Jesus Christ as the God-man. "The content of the doctrine of reconciliation is the knowledge of Jesus Christ who is . . . in the unity of the two [natures] the guarantor and witness of our atonement." [134] This aspect, however, does not add materially to our understanding of reconciliation in Jesus Christ. "There can be no question," writes Barth, "of our trying to see a third thing in what we have called the third christological aspect. Everything that can be said materially concerning Jesus Christ and the atonement made in Him has been said exhaustively in the twofold fact . . . that He is very God and very man, i.e., the Lord who became a servant and the servant who became Lord, the reconciling God and the reconciled man. [Only the bringing together of these two things historically] is the new thing in the third christological aspect. Jesus Christ is the actuality of the atonement." [135]

While there is no specific corresponding state to this union of natures, it is to this aspect that Barth relates Christ's prophetic office.

The results of this construction. What are the results of Barth's relating Christ's person to his work? In a word, Barth has again "actualized" the Incarnation and resultingly has interpreted Christology as the work of reconciliation. For Barth, as we have seen, Christ's two states (which he regards as equivalent to his work) cannot be separated from his two natures. Jesus Christ, then, as the God-man was never humiliated apart from being exalted or exalted apart from being humiliated. "Where and when is He not both humiliated and exalted, already exalted in His humiliation, and humiliated in His exaltation?" [136] "Both aspects force themselves upon us. We have to do with the being of the one and entire Jesus Christ whose humiliation detracts nothing and whose exaltation adds nothing. And in this His *being* we have to do with His action, the work and event of atonement." [137]

By seeing in the work of Christ also the person of Christ, Barth declares that the Incarnation is "actualized," that is, made into an ongoing process. This is done in the interest of interpreting Jesus Christ as "event." By this event which contains both the person and work of Christ, "the being of Jesus Christ, the unity of being of the living God and this living man, takes place in the event of the concrete existence of this man. It is a being, but a being in history. The gracious God is in this history, so is reconciled man, so both are in their unity. And what takes place in this history [*Geschichte*], and therefore in the being of Jesus Christ as such, is atonement. *Jesus Christ is not what He is—very God, very man, very God-man —in order as such to mean and do and accomplish something else which is atonement. But His being as God and man and God-man consists in the completed act of the reconciliation of man with God.*" [138] For Barth the Incarnation itself is unquestionably *the reconciling act!*

We conclude this survey of Barth's christological construction of reconciliation with his summary of the atonement. "The atonement as it took place in Jesus Christ is the one inclusive event of this going out of the Son of God and coming in of the Son of Man. In its literal and original sense the word *apokatallassein* ('to reconcile') means 'to exchange.' The reconstitution and renewal of the covenant between God and man consists in this interchange— the *exinanitio*, the abasement, of God, and the *exaltatio*, the exaltation, of man. It was God who went into the far country, and it is man who returns home. Both took place in the one Jesus Christ. It is not, therefore, a matter of two different and successive actions, but of a single action in which each of the two elements is related to the other and can be known and understood only in this relationship: the going out of God only as it aims at the coming in of man; the coming in of man only as the reach and outworking of the going out of God; and the whole in its original and proper form only as the being and history of the one Jesus Christ." [139]

Criticism. There can be no doubt that Barth's doctrine of reconciliation, taking up into itself Christology, hamartiology, soteriology, and ecclesiology as it does, is a new doctrine in which older traditions and themes have been thoroughly recast. Yet it is from the older traditional (and we believe Biblical) position that we make the following criticisms.

First, because of his low view of the historicity of Genesis, Barth fails to adopt the Biblical view of the origin of man, his original state, and the origin and nature of sin. This is the seed-bed of all of Barth's erroneous thinking; because unless one takes seriously a genuine creation of man in a state of original knowledge, righteousness, and holiness, he will never understand the Biblical teaching of the fall of man, he will never understand the nature of sin as any want of conformity unto, or transgression of, the law of God or understand the present desperate estate of man as one of sin and misery. And unless one takes seriously the Biblical teaching of man's present estate of sin and misery, he will never understand the Bible's unique doctrine of redemption. In any construction of the atonement, it will invariably be deficient and sub-Christian unless a genuine creation and a genuine fall are affirmed. For this reason, the traditional schema of the Biblical message was summarized under the three terms of creation, fall, and redemption. Regardless of what he may feel about this traditional schema, the honest interpreter must admit that Barth's construction, whatever else it may be, certainly is not Biblically oriented in this regard.

In the interest of an acceptable affirmation of the universality of sin, it might be objected, why not accept Barth's view of Adam as representative man? For Barth's view of Adam as representative man standing in the need of the grace of God universalizes sin, does it not? To this objection it must be pointed out that such an interpretation of the Adam of Genesis, though on the surface appearing to make sin universal, actually denies other important doctrines, not the least of which, as we have already seen, is the Genesis account of the fall of man from a state of created holiness, not to mention the exceedingly important doctrine of the imputation of Adam's guilt to all those who have descended from him by ordinary generation as set˙forth by Paul in Romans 5:12ff. Now there is a legitimate sense in which Adam represented every man, that sense being as the covenant head of his race and his obedience or disobedience under the covenant of works being imputed to his natural progeny. As the *Westminster Shorter Catechism* (Q. 16) states: "The covenant being made with Adam, not only for himself, but for his posterity, all mankind descending from him by ordinary generation, sinned in him, and fell with him, in his first transgression." And it is through a similar principle of imputation of Christ's righteousness that the redeemed are made acceptable in God's sight. But Barth wants nothing to do with such a view of Adam. For him Adam depicts the essential state and attitude of every man. Every man sins like Adam. Of course, this view denies the Biblical doctrine of original sin, for it just is not true that all men sin like Adam. Adam had a choice; there was nothing within him that inclined him toward evil. Indeed, his created state inclined him toward good. But that is not the condition in which men, according to Scripture, now enter this world. Adam's descendants now begin life with a propensity toward evil. They are born in sin. They are dead in trespasses and sins by nature. Hence, Barth's understanding of Adam can hardly be regarded as Biblical, and for this reason it is unacceptable to a Christian.

Second, Barth's failure to distinguish between the person and work of Christ is unbiblical. Scripture makes this distinction: the Second Person of the Trinity existed prior to his Incarnation and birth by the Virgin. Furthermore, his mediatorial work of redemption was performed, according to the Scriptures, once and for all (*epha-pax*) in history and is now a complete work, a redemption accomplished and remaining only to be applied historically to God's elect.[140]

Third, in spite of all his talk about their unity, Barth destroys the unity of Christ's two natures when he ascribes the humiliation of Jesus Christ only to his divine nature and the exaltation of Jesus Christ only to his human nature. Chalcedon's description of the union included the terms, "indivisibly" and "inseparably": ". . . one and the same Christ, Son, Lord, Only-begotten, to be acknowledged in two natures inconfusedly, unchangeably, indivisibly, inseparably. . . ."[141] A similar unscriptural division of Christ's nature results from Barth's ascription of Christ's priestly office to his divine nature and his kingly office to his human nature.

Fourth, in Barth's view the Incarnation is the really crucial event in man's reconciliation to God. Jesus' suffering and death on the cross are little more than revelatory of the depth of the humiliation resulting from God turning into his opposite, namely the creature. The resurrection is essentially only revelatory of the exaltation of man that occurs in the Incarnation.[142] But this understanding of reconciliation by no means does justice to the Biblical doctrine of reconciliation. Again and again at various stages in his earthly ministry, Christ declared: "Mine hour has not yet come." But standing in the shadow of the cross, he exclaimed: "For this hour came I into the world." Paul nowhere speaks of our being reconciled by the mere event of the Incarnation, but rather proclaims our reconciliation to God through the death of his Son (Rom. 5:10; Col. 1:22) and Christ's having made peace through the blood of his cross (Col. 1:20; Eph. 2:16). Barth is completely incapable of harmonizing the teaching of these Scripture passages with his construction.[143]

Finally, and this criticism applies equally both to his construction of election and to his construction of reconciliation, Barth has, as Berkouwer has so aptly declared, no transition for the sinner from wrath to grace in history. The sinner has always stood under both the wrath and the grace of God. But the wrath of God is always and only penultimate; the grace of God is always and finally ultimate. Though man has always been rejected in

148

Jesus Christ as *the* one rejected Man, he has also and ultimately always been elected and therefore exalted in Jesus Christ as *the* one elected Man. Barth cannot avert an ultimate universalism.

Because of the shattered liberal dogmas of man's inherent goodness, the breakdown of confidence in humanistic man, and the discredited assumptions of the optimism of the Enlightenment, modern culture has drifted toward despair. Because of his inability to explain his own history logically, modern man has sought his salvation in mysticism and irrationalism.

Instead of challenging this nihilistic culture to face its despair squarely and pressing upon it the rationality to be found in the Christian Gospel, Barth, in dependence upon a Kantian metaphysics and a destructive Biblical criticism, has followed his culture into the same mood of irrationalism by substituting his own plan of salvation and a reconstructed gospel for the Biblical plan of salvation and the only Gospel (Gal. 1:6-9) which can meet the real need of "modern" man. For Barth, the words of the Bible may ever remain fallible and human as long as the Word of God in *Geschichte* is believed; creation may be affirmed as long as it has no relation to the Genesis account of a *creatio ex nihilo* of the Universe or to man in an original state of righteousness and holiness; the fall of man may be believed as long as Adam's personal existence as the first man is denied; the figure of Jesus of Nazareth may remain shrouded in mystery as long as the Christ of faith is proclaimed; the Cross may be proclaimed as long as the sacrificial blood of Christ is neglected; and the resurrection of Christ may be spoken of as long as it is understood that this "event" is for believers only. But, of course, such a gospel is no gospel at all, certainly not the Biblical Gospel.

The only answer to man's need is to be found in the Gospel of historic Christianity, which rejects all of the ambiguity and theological doubletalk of modern Neo-orthodoxy and projects a message that is rationally and historically true. Only a Christian theism that is grounded in the authority of the infallible Bible, in a genuine creation and real historical fall, and in the atonement wrought out by the God of the Incarnation—only this will supply the cures for the spiritual ills of mankind.

149

NOTES

1. John B. Cobb, Jr., *Living Options in Protestant Theology* (Philadelphia: The Westminster Press, 1962), p. 171.

2. T. F. Torrance, "Karl Barth," *Ten Makers of Modern Protestant Thought* (Edited by George Hunt; New York: Association Press, 1958), pp. 59-63.

3. Carl F. H. Henry, "Cross-currents in Contemporary Theology," *Jesus of Nazareth: Saviour and Lord* (Edited by Carl F. H. Henry; Grand Rapids: Wm. B. Eerdmans Publishing Company, 1966), pp. 5-6.

4. Karl Barth, *Church Dogmatics* (Edited and translated by G. T. Thomson, G. W. Bromiley, T. F. Torrance; Edinburgh: T. & T. Clark, 1956), IV/2, x.

5. Fred Klooster, *The Significance of Barth's Theology* (Grand Rapids: Baker Book House, 1961), p. 20.

6. *Union Seminary Quarterly* (May, 1959), p. 55; cited by Klooster, *ibid.*, p. 39.

7. Klooster, *ibid.*, p. 41, fn.

8. Barth, *op. cit.*, II/2, x.

9. *Ibid.*, p. 3.

10. *Ibid.*, pp. 13-14.

11. *Ibid.*, pp. 35, 38, 44.

12. *Ibid.*, p. 52.

13. *Ibid.*, p. 148.

14. *Ibid.*

15. *Ibid.*, p. 145.

16. *Ibid.*, p. 99.

17. *Ibid.*, p. 153.

18. *Ibid.*, p. 149.

19. Klooster, *op. cit.*, p. 45.

20. *Ibid.*

21. *Ibid.*, p. 46.

22. Cf. Barth, *op. cit.*, II/2, 94-194.

23. *Ibid.*, IV/1, 65.

24. *Ibid.*, p. 508.

25. *Ibid.*, II/2, 103.

26. *Ibid.*, p. 104.

27. *Ibid.*, p. 105.

28. *Ibid.*, p. 104.

29. *Ibid.*, p. 103.

30. *Ibid.*

31. *Ibid.*, p. 162.

32. *Ibid.*, p. 167.

33. *Ibid.*, p. 103.

34. *Ibid.*, p. 145.

35. *Ibid.*, p. 146.
36. *Ibid.*
37. *Ibid.*, p. 147.
38. *Ibid.*, p. 161.
39. *Ibid.*, p. 147.
40. *Ibid.*, p. 115.
41. *Ibid.*, p. 181.
42. *Ibid.*, p. 184.
43. *Ibid.*, p. 158.
44. *Ibid.*, p. 181.
45. *Ibid.*, p. 174.
46. *Ibid.*, p. 184.
47. *Ibid.*, p. 186.
48. *Ibid.*, p. 187.
49. *Ibid.*, II/1, 616.
50. Cf. *ibid.*, II/2, 195-305.
51. *Ibid.*, p. 195.
52. *Ibid.*, pp. 195-196.
53. *Ibid.*, p. 195.
54. *Ibid.*
55. *Ibid.*, p. 206.
56. *Ibid.*, p. 210.
57. *Ibid.*, p. 195.
58. *Ibid.*, p. 233.
59. *Ibid.*, p. 237.
60. *Ibid.*, p. 195.
61. *Ibid.*, p. 260.
62. *Ibid.*, p. 264.
63. *Ibid.*, p. 259.
64. *Ibid.*, p. 318.
65. *Ibid.*, pp. 318-320 (italics mine).
66. Klooster, *op. cit.*, p. 59.
67. Cf. Barth, *Dogmatics,* II/2, 306-506.
68. *Ibid.*, p. 195.
69. *Ibid.*, p. 311.
70. *Ibid.*, p. 308.
71. *Ibid.*
72. *Ibid.*, pp. 346-347 (italics mine).
73. *Ibid.*, p. 347.
74. *Ibid.*, pp. 347-348.
75. *Ibid.*, p. 349.
76. *Ibid.*, p. 350.
77. *Ibid.*, p. 351.
78. *Ibid.*, p. 353.
79. *Ibid.*

80. Cf. *ibid.*, pp. 410-449.

81. Cf. *ibid.*, pp. 449-506.

82. *Ibid.*, p. 453.

83. Cobb, *op. cit.*, pp. 187-188.

84. Barth, *Dogmatics,* II/2, 488; cf. Rom. 4:25; 8:32; Gal. 2:20; Eph. 5:2, 25.

85. *Ibid.*, p. 482; cf. II Thess. 2:15; I Cor. 11:2, 23; 15:3.

86. *Ibid.*, p. 460.

87. *Ibid.*, p. 502.

88. *Ibid.*

89. *Ibid.*, pp. 417-418.

90. Karl Barth, *The Humanity of God* (Richmond: John Knox Press, 1960), pp. 61-62.

91. Barth, *Dogmatics,* I/1, 123.

92. Gordon H. Clark, *Karl Barth's Theological Method* (Philadelphia: Presbyterian and Reformed Publishing Company, 1963), p. 164.

93. Barth, *op. cit.,* I/1, 126.

94. *Ibid.*, II/2, 145.

95. I am indebted to Klooster for this criticism of Barth. Indeed, I must acknowledge the profound debt I owe to his *The Significance of Barth's Theology.*

96. Barth, *Dogmatics,* II/2, 417.

97. *Ibid.*, p. 186.

98. *Ibid.*

99. Klooster, *op. cit.*, p. 68.

100. *Ibid.*, p. 70.

101. Barth, *Dogmatics,* II/2, 349.

102. *Ibid.*, IV/1, ix.

103. *Ibid.*, p. 139.

104. *Ibid.*, p. 80.

105. *Ibid.*, p. 22.

106. *Ibid.*, p. 508.

107. *Ibid.*, p. 140.

108. *Ibid.*, p. 139.

109. *Ibid.*, p. 141.

110. *Ibid.*, pp. 140-141.

111. *Ibid.*, p. 140.

112. *Ibid.*, 142.

113. *Ibid.*, IV/2, x.

114. *Ibid.*

115. *Ibid.*, IV/1, p. 138.

116. *Ibid.*, p. 123.

117. *Ibid.*, p. 127.

118. *Ibid.*, p. 128.

119. Cf. *ibid.*, pp. 128-130 and IV/1 — "Jesus Christ, the Lord as Servant."

120. Cf. *ibid.*, pp. 130-135 and IV/2 — "Jesus Christ, the Servant as Lord."

121. Cf. *ibid.*, pp. 135-138 and IV/3 — "Jesus Christ the Guarantor."

122. *Ibid.*, p. 79.

123. *Ibid.*, pp. 128-129.

124. *Ibid.*, p. 129.

125. *Ibid.*, p. 130.

126. *Ibid.* (italics mine).

127. *Ibid.*, p. 134.

128. *Ibid.*

129. *Ibid.*, 79.

130. *Ibid.*, pp. 130-131.

131. *Ibid.*, p. 134.

132. *Ibid.*

133. *Ibid.*, p. 131 (italics mine).

134. *Ibid.*, p. 79.

135. *Ibid.*, p. 136.

136. *Ibid.*, p. 133.

137. *Ibid.*

138. *Ibid.*, pp. 126-127 (italics mine).

139. *Ibid.*, IV/2, 20-21.

140. Cf. Klooster, *op. cit.*, p. 94.

141. *Ibid.*, pp. 94-95.

142. Cf. Barth, *Dogmatics in Outline* (New York: Harper & Row, 1959), pp. 101-102.

143. Klooster, *op. cit.*, pp. 95-96.

PART III. THEOLOGICAL SYSTEMS STRESSING EXISTENTIALISTIC THEMES

CHAPTER VII

PHILOSOPHICAL EXISTENTIALISM

On the contemporary theological scene in both Europe and here in America, several theologians of stature, for example, the two to be treated in Chapters VIII and IX—Rudolf Bultmann and Paul Tillich, have attempted to develop a Christian theology relevant to this age of scientific achievement and radical religious doubt by bringing Christian themes into conjunction with several dominant motifs in philosophical existentialism. In a very real sense, the end of this effort constitutes a natural theology. Inasmuch, however, as philosophical existentialism projects a marked hostility toward traditional philosophy because of what it regards in the latter as naive uncritical assumptions and beginnings, the theological systems utilizing existential motives appear to be more sophisticated and more closely reasoned than the systems examined in Part I. For this reason these systems in Part III are treated as a separate theological "type," although a genuinely Christian analysis will reveal that the (so-called) novel turns taken in these systems are reflections of the old irrationalism and the old humanism.

Some knowledge of philosophical existentialism is essential to an understanding of these modern existential theologies. Therefore, the purpose in these pages is to discuss the rise and major characteristics of philosophical existentialism.

The roots of existentialism have been traced back as far as the New Testament and some of the Greek and Latin fathers, particularly Augustine. The Christian themes of the dignity, freedom, and responsibility of the individual human being are alleged to reflect existential themes. Even the natural theology of Thomas

Aquinas, in which God's existence is treated prior to his essence, is said to anticipate the existential cliché: "Existence precedes essence." But although these supposed relations are suspect inasmuch as the *content* of the ancient concepts is in every case of a different nature from their modern counterparts, it is universally acknowledged that Kierkegaard and Nietzsche, the two nineteenth-century thinkers, are the immediate forerunners of *modern* philosophical existentialism.

Summaries of Kierkegaard and Nietzsche have been given in Chapter IV. Nothing more needs to be added here beyond the fact that these two men had in common a thoroughgoing animosity toward the comfortable religion of their times, a recognition of the futility of a Christian apologetic grounded in a speculative prolegomenon, and a realization that the lives of Christians denied, in practice, God's reality. However, they responded differently to the religious crises confronting them. Kierkegaard sought to recover a true concept of God and of the Christian life for the Church whereas Nietzsche concluded that men should accept their evident atheism and live lives in accord with that view. Theological existentialism has been more inclined to the insights of Kierkegaard; contemporary philosophical existentialism, accepting the Nietzschean theme of the death of God, is characteristically *nihilistic*. Yet Bultmann and Tillich have attempted to come to terms with philosophical existentialism.

Edmund Husserl (1859-1938)

Any adequate treatment of contemporary philosophical existentialism must begin with Edmund Husserl, the Jewish philosopher, who gave to existentialism its method of inquiry. About Husserl, H. J. Blackham writes: "His influence upon existentialist philosophers is incalculable, and it is safe to say that existentialism in its modern phase would not have been developed without him." [1] Fernando Molina, in fact, characterizes contemporary existentialism in general as "the product of the application of a methodology based on Husserl's phenomenology to thematic material introduced into Western thinking (and feeling) by the reflections of Kierkegaard and Nietzsche." [2]

Husserl was interested in the investigation of the structure of being (ontology), but he was convinced that unless philosophy found a critical, scientific method of inquiry, it could never achieve scientific precision. He desired more than simply *adequate* evidence in experience on the basis of which the existence of an object is posited; he wanted *apodictic,* or absolutely certain, evidence. But how can this be achieved? Husserl was convinced that the method of pure *description* is the only means whereby apodictic evidence is attainable. The method which he developed—"a more accurate and modern version of Cartesianism," he called "phenomenology," and he regarded its chief task as being the establishment of the foundations of both the *regional ontologies* of, for example, material things and animated things and the *formal ontology* that investigates the principles common to all regional ontologies.[3] In other words, phenomenology may be defined as the science of describing, apart from epistemological and metaphysical postulates, what is given to human experience in order to arrive at a true theory of being. His views were elaborated first in his *Ideas Toward A Pure Phenomenology* (1913) and later in his *Cartesian Meditations* (1929).

Cobb distinguishes four ways in which phenomenological description differs from ordinary empirical description.[4] First, whereas ordinary empirical description is affected by an interpretive framework based on earlier experience, phenomenological description "brackets" or sets aside all extraneous information or theory and sees the object just as it presents itself apart from all interpretation. Second, whereas ordinary empirical description understands itself as describing *existent* entities, phenomenological description insists that even the existence of the object being described must be bracketed and the object then be described in only those terms of objectivity with which it presents itself. Third, whereas ordinary empirical description takes its objects to be particulars and proceeds to generalizations about them, phenomenological description takes its objects to be forms, meanings, or ideas. And fourth, whereas ordinary empirical description ignores the process of consciousness by which the object being described is experienced, phenomenological description understands each object as the intentional object of consciousness and must describe also the process of intending that constitutes the object as such. Molina describes the place occupied by common sense during phenomenological investigation in this way: "Common sense is not doubted by the phenomenologist. . . . Common sense is simply *held in suspense* in phenomenology; what is usually admitted into the real world with full-blown status is now asked to present its credentials. Human experience of the world, to state the matter from a radically different angle, is no longer treated as a means for analyzing the contents and laws of the world, but is now *itself* an object for analysis." [5]

Husserl teaches that consciousness, or our way of perceiving an object, "constitutes" or structures the object of experience as its correlate. The most universal aspects of consciousness comprise *pure* or "transcendental" consciousness, which is never objectified but which always remains the absolute subject of experience, that is, it always points *beyond* itself to the objects of consciousness. The unifying subject of transcendental consciousness is the transcendental Ego. Husserl makes an important distinction between the human Ego and the transcendental Ego. The human Ego, or observable object that wills and thinks, is an entity within the natural order. It is one object among many, phenomenologically speaking; it is immersed in the world. The transcendental Ego, on the other hand, is disembodied pure consciousness; it transcends all regional ontologies and is never objectified but rather constitutes the whole world of objects as its correlate. By taking this step, Husserl removes the absolute existence of the transcendental Ego from phenomenological analysis, a step which none of the leading existentialists today are willing to take. Rather, they regard human existence in every aspect as "constituted" object and therefore an object of phenomenological analysis. Indeed, it is primarily on the strength of this distinction made by Husserl between the human and transcendental Egos that Husserl failed to bridge the gap between phenomenology and modern existentialism. Nevertheless, his method has profoundly influenced contemporary existentialism.

The Christian student of philosophy, of course, can take little, if anything, in Husserl's phenomenology seriously. He knows, first of all, that not one of the four goals of the phenomenological method, as spelled out by Cobb, is humanly capable of being achieved. No man is able to "bracket" all of his pre-scientific (presuppositional) judgments in order to work within a frame of reference free from all metaphysical postulates. Second, he recognizes that Husserl's concept of pure consciousness is indefinable apart from the Christian God. Husserl himself cannot define it. And third, he understands Husserl's "transcendental Ego" as simply a poor substitute for the existence of the true and living God whom Husserl has already "bracketed" out of existence. Unless the ontological Trinity of Christian theism is made the ultimate reference point for all human predication, nothing ultimately meaningful can be said about anything. Without the triune God, there is no "Archimedean point" upon which to stand to build a theory of being. These facts alone make any philosophy constructed through the use of the phenomenological method suspect at the outset.

With this background, we are now ready to offer a definition of existentialism and to analyze one major expression of it in order to set forth its major characteristics. Existentialism may be defined as a philosophy that "confronts the human situation *in its totality* to ask what the basic conditions of human existence are and how man can establish his own meaning out of these conditions. Its method is phenomenological: it begins with human existence as a fact without any ready-made preconceptions about the essence of man, as far as this is possible. There is no prefabricated human nature that freezes human possibilities into a preordained mold; on the contrary, man exists first and makes himself what he is out of the conditions into which he is thrown."[6]

Inasmuch as our present purpose is simply to introduce the reader to the major themes of contemporary existentialism, we shall treat only the early Heidegger, a one-time follower of Husserl and the dominant figure in German existentialism in the second quarter of this century. He is the most appropriate choice here because it is his analysis of human existence that shapes to a great extent Bultmann's anthropology and (to a lesser extent) Tillich's ontology.

Martin Heidegger (1889-   )

When Husserl retired from the chair of philosophy at the University of Freiberg in 1928, Martin Heidegger, his student, succeeded him. Heidegger had developed his existential views in a published work entitled *Sein und Zeit* (*Being and Time*) the preceding year.[7]

Remaining faithful to the phenomenological method, Heidegger, it can be seen even from the title of his major work, attempts to arrive at a universal theory of being, particularly in relation to temporality. But whereas Husserl denied to phenomenological analysis the existence of pure or transcendental consciousness, Heidegger believes that a universal ontology must be preceded by an existential theory of human existence inasmuch as human existence is in the world and is part of Being. In fact, Heidegger conceives of human existence as the fundamental ontology underlying all other regional ontologies.

For Heidegger the main distinction in Being is that which belongs to the regional ontology of the *Dasein* ("[human] being there") and that which does not belong to the *Dasein*. What is this *Dasein* and how does one learn to know it? *Dasein* is Heidegger's technical term for human existence—that which characterizes man. As such, the *Dasein* signifies the individual's self-transcending tendency: to exist is to exceed onself. In other words, the *Dasein* is never being but always becoming. Spier elucidates Heidegger's thought in this way: "All human *Existence* or *Dasein* is, in essence, Existence. That is to say, it is *self-determination, self-projection,* or *self-transcendence.* . . . The *Dasein* is never identical with itself. *Dasein* is not static. It is always something different than it was. It is always becoming itself. . . ." [8] How may one learn to know the *Dasein*? Since the *Dasein* can never be an object of empirical thought because of its nature of becoming, the meaning of the *Dasein* is inaccessible to man until it reveals itself through its "existentialia"—the essential attributes of the *Dasein*. And even this revelation from the *Dasein* is only understood in the phenomenological analysis.

The existentialia of the *Dasein* shall be taken up presently, but first, one important distinction which Heidegger makes within the *Dasein* must be noted: unauthentic and authentic existence. Authentic existence stands as a mode or manner of being of unauthentic existence, but unauthentic existence is always prior. *Unauthentic* existence is existence fallen away from true existence. Furthermore, as Spier notes, "unauthentic Existence is the general attitude toward life of the large masses of people. The masses flee from their own responsibility and voluntarily abandon their own freedom. They are resolved or absorbed in the world. . . . Unauthentic *Dasein* is preoccupied with the *externals* of humanity. It loses itself in society and the masses (*Das Man*). It listens to an hypostatized *Mankind,* the One like the many, *the Man.* The average, common, everyday man does not act independently and freely. He acts as *Man* acts. He behaves as the One (*Das Man*) does and avoids doing anything

162

that is not done by everyone else. The mass-man is no longer himself; he does not dare to live. Public opinion is his norm. A person who is lost in the *One* does not reflect on authentic Existence of being. He is driven about with each passing tide and is tossed upon the waves of society and the world. He runs away from himself. He is *fallen* from his true self and no longer understands what real *Dasein* is. . . . He is occupied with the many things which are in the world and the countless people that surround him." [9] In addition, losing himself in the world, he is unconcerned with death and lives as though his life were endless.

Authentic existence is existence which has overcome the fallen attitude of unauthentic existence. It has attained unto existence which really *is,* by becoming individual existence in freedom.

Now what are the existentialia of the *Dasein?* First, the *Dasein* is always *being-in-the-world* (*Sein und Zeit,* Subsection 12). This means that *Dasein* is not an entity that has being in itself and *in addition* also stands related to other beings. *Dasein, as Dasein,* is already *in the world.* But what is the meaning of "world" here? The world is not the empirical world; it is not the totality of things open to scientific investigation. Rather, it is the *experienced* world *as organized in relation to Dasein.* Since unauthentic *Dasein* construes the experienced world one way and authentic existence construes it another, the ends at which *Dasein* as being-in-the-world aims, as Cobb writes, "may be either possibilities manifested in the entities in its world or possibilities which it finds in its own distinctive being." [10] To unauthentic existence the world is only environment, the totality of all objects. The real world is foreign to the unauthentic existence of the everyday man. The mass-man is concerned with objects. Authentic existence transcends the pragmatic attitude of unauthentic existence toward the objects of the world. It refuses to be exclusively concerned with the utility of things, even though it is in the world, for the world of authentic existence is broader than the environment and more than all objects.

Another essential characteristic of the *Dasein* is *being-together,* that is, existing together with other beings within *Dasein.*[11] Here *Dasein* constitutes the *public* world. But whereas the person in unauthentic existence conceives of the public world as an environment to which he subjects himself, the person living authentically refuses to lose himself and his autonomy, and thus experiences this relation to others in full freedom.

The *One* (*Das Man*) is another of the essential characteristics of the *Dasein*. But whereas unauthentic existence accepts a heteronomy from its environment and relegates its responsibility and freedom to the environmental *One*, thus ending in cultural slavery, authentic existence refuses to "feel at home" in its environment. It maintains its autonomy and self-determination.

The last two characteristics of *Dasein* are the "thrown-ness" (*ibid.*, Subsection 29) and the "understanding" (*ibid.*, Subsection 31) of existence. By "thrown-ness," Heidegger refers to the fact that man is not self-caused. He has been "thrown" into existence. He cannot help it that he is in *Dasein*. He simply must accept the fact that something has occurred outside of his will. "Understanding" refers to the projection (self-transcendence) of *Dasein* into the future for the purpose of realizing its possibilities. But it always understands that the world in which it finds itself is the *final* context of all realized possibilities. This understanding supports in a very special sense the "being-in-the-*world*-ness" of *Dasein*.

How can a man pass from unauthentic to authentic existence? Spier declares this to be the cardinal question in the philosophy of Heidegger. And Heidegger's existential answer is forthcoming: through *Angst* or Dread. But this *Angst* is not simply fear. Fear is fear of something; *Angst* is unspecified with regard to an object. It constitutes a threat which one cannot quite "put his finger on." *Angst* suddenly arises out of the depth of *Dasein*. Precisely what does *Angst* perform or produce? In a word, *Angst breaks through the delusions of unauthentic existence.* Unauthentic existence, we have seen, losing itself in its environment, fails to grasp the real essence of human existence. It shows no concern over the fact of death. But *Angst* can enter a life and cause human existence really to confront itself *in its totality,* including the impossibility of escaping death. As a result, authentic existence discovers itself in a threefold manner.

First, *Angst* reveals to man the "thrown-ness" of his existence. He is not self-caused. He is here and cannot help it.

Second, *Angst* reveals to man that his is a being-toward-death. His life is permeated by death and determined by it. "Death can never be overcome. It is never to be replaced by any other possibility. Death and the grave are unavoidable. To think that death can be overcome is an idle illusion. Death dominates all the other possibilities of human existence. Its shadow falls as a deceptive destiny over the whole of life and marks it as *nullity*." [12] Whoever wishes to live authentically must face death directly and not seek to camouflage the fact that he is going to die.

Third, *Angst* reveals to man his freedom to choose and to produce his own possibilities. Because he knows he is going to die, he lives today and takes seriously today his possibilities. But he understands that all of his realized possibilities are related temporally to this world. In other words he exercises his freedom to choose his own course, to fulfill his own temporally-related destiny, but even here, through *Angst,* man learns that he is free to choose, along with this possibility for his life, also freedom toward death. The authentic man is conscious of the vanity of the realized possibilities of existence and freely accepts death.

As a result of this threefold revelation from *Angst,* man, if he accepts his "thrown-ness" and being-toward-death, will recognize the nullity of human existence. This nullity arises first from the fact that now he knows himself to be finite, and second, from his cognition that he can choose and realize with his life only one of many possibilities. He can never realize all possibilities at the same time. In other words, "what is our crowning achievement, namely, self-projection and self-transcendence, is at the same time our poverty, our privation, our nullity." [13]

In the light of his pessimistic outlook, Heidegger's view of *Dasein* ends quite remarkably. He affirms that after a person who has attained authenticity sees the meaninglessness of pragmatic existence, he may return to it and accept it for what it is. "Since a person who is authentic knows that he is *free-toward-death,* he possesses an inexhaustible tolerance and endless patience. He can, therefore, return to the world of his environment and take part in the activity of the masses. The only difference is that he has seen through the delusion of life, is certain of the nullity of Existence and bears it as an inalienable possession." [14]

Family Characteristics [15]

Although Heidegger's existential views certainly do not represent the views of all of the leading existentialists today, enough similarity still exists between them that a number of family characteristics of existentialism in general may now be derived from him by way of summary.

1. Existentialism is based upon the freedom of man and is dominated by the ideal of autonomous human personality.

2. Existentialism is irrational in its view of the essence of man as lying not in reason but above reason.

3. Existentialism is subjectivistic in its teaching that human existence is not subject to any ordinances or laws extrinsic to man. In the final analysis, existence is considered a law unto itself.

4. Existentialism is anthropocentric in its attempt to find true existence in human existence apart from its true relation to Christian theism.

5. Existentialism is pessimistic in its dark and dreary view of life. Temporality and life are nullity and meaningless.

6. Existentialism is individualistic both in its rejection of the Biblical unity of the human race and in its placing the individual above society. This attitude is expressed in the existentialist's cliché: "Existence precedes essence."

7. Existentialism is aristocratic in its affirmation that authentic existence is the possession of only a few exceptional people; it never becomes the common possession of all.

8. Existentialism is abnormalistic in its view towards man. All existential philosophies set forth the antithesis between authentic and unauthentic existence and affirm that man has "fallen" away from his true or authentic existence.

9. Existentialism is temporalistic in its affirmation that human existence is being-in-the-world and that realized possibilities have for their final context this world.

10. Existentialism is fatalistic in its view that death can never be overcome and nihilistic in its view that death is the most proper possibility of human existence.

11. Existentialism is activistic in its protest against the attitude of detached reflection, in which man insulates himself against the realities of life.

A truly Christian philosophy cannot tolerate the life- and world-view of modern existentialism. Modern existentialism's concept of human existence, though including a "fall," is not Biblical. Man is made the measure of all things; God, for the most part, is denied. Any and all meaning in life, which for the Christian is grounded in the Creator-creature relationship and the realization that God has a will for every life, is destroyed. Existentialism leaves men precisely where it finds them—lost, and without a Savior. While it is long on diagnosis, it is short on cure. Nor can the existentialist's view of life and death be reconciled with the Biblical view of life and death, particularly the Christian's life and death. The Apostle Paul writes in Romans 8:38-39: "For I am convinced that neither death, nor life, nor angels, nor principalities, nor things present, nor things to come, nor powers, nor height, nor depth, nor any other created thing, shall be able to separate us from the love of God, which is in Christ Jesus our Lord." And in I Corinthians 3:21-23 he writes: "For all things belong to you, whether Paul or Apollos or Cephas or the world or life or death or things present or things to come, all things belong to you, and you belong to Christ; and Christ belongs to God." Here is no pessimism, no fatalism, no nihilism. Here is only humble admission that all things are God's. Here is glorious confidence that this world is not the end but rather that a rest awaits the child of God. Yet in spite of the anti-Christian philosophy of existentialism, some theologians have attempted to relate Christian themes to certain of its dominant motifs. For the most part, this task has been undertaken by men who unabashedly reject the Orthodoxy of the Reformation such as the two theologians discussed in the following pages.

NOTES

1. H. J. Blackham, *Six Existentialist Thinkers* (New York: Harper & Row, Publishers, 1959), p. 87.

2. Fernando Molina, *Existentialism As Philosophy* (Englewood Cliffs, New Jersey: Prentice-Hall, Inc., 1962), p. 33.

3. John B. Cobb, Jr., *Living Options in Protestant Theology* (Philadelphia: The Westminster Press, 1962), p. 206.

4. *Ibid.,* pp. 203-04.

5. Molina, *op. cit.,* p. 40.

6. I am indebted to William Barrett, *Philosophy in the Twentieth Century* (New York: Random House, 1962), III, 143, for this definition.

7. This treatment of Heidegger follows the analysis of J. M. Spier, *Christianity and Existentialism* (Philadelphia: The Presbyterian and Reformed

Publishing Company, 1953), pp. 27-37.

8. *Ibid.*, p. 30.

9. *Ibid.*, pp. 29-30.

10. Cobb, *op. cit.*, p. 211.

11. Spier writes, "Because of his absolute subjectivism, Sartre differs with [Heidegger] and does not have room in his thought for an authentic *living-together*. The essence of society for Sartre is conflict and struggle." *Op. cit.*, pp. 65-66.

12. *Ibid.*, p. 36.

13. *Ibid.*, p. 35.

14. *Ibid.*, p. 36.

15. *Ibid.*, pp. 110-119. A selection has been made here from Spier's more complete listing.

CHAPTER VIII

BULTMANN'S DEMYTHOLOGIZED KERYGMA

ABOUT RUDOLF BULTMANN

Rudolf Bultmann was born in Oldenburg, Germany, in 1884 and received his theological education under Karl Müller at Tübingen, Hermann Gunkel and Adolph von Harnack at Berlin, and Adolf Jülicher, Johannes Weiss, and Wilhelm Herrmann at Marburg. He served as Professor of New Testament at Marburg from the autumn of 1921 until his retirement from active teaching in 1951. During the time of Nazi domination, he took part in the opposition to Nazism which the "confessing church" built up. Bultmann's prominence in Continental theology is usually dated from his programmatic essay of 1941 entitled *New Testament and Mythology* in which he outlined a felt need to "demythologize" the New Testament in order to discover the pure New Testament *kerygma*. Since that time his thought has even gained the ascendancy over Barth's thought, though recent years have seen a "revolt" among his students toward more "objectivity" in the construction of a New Testament theology. Since his retirement he has lectured in Sweden, Holland, Denmark, Scotland, and the United States. He has been ill and feeble in recent times; however, the choicest theological chairs in Europe are filled by his pupils or disciples, for example, Günther Bornkamm at Heidelberg, Hans Conzelmann at Göttingen, and Ernst Käsemann at Tübingen.

Important works by Bultmann are *Jesus and the Word, Jesus Christ and Mythology, The Presence of Eternity*, and a two-volume *Theology of the New Testament*.

Works about Bultmann or Bultmannism are *Kerygma and Myth*, edited by H. W. Bartsch, *Christ Without Myth* by Shubert Ogden,

Myth in the New Testament by Ian Henderson, *The New Testament in Current Study* by Reginald Fuller, *A New Quest of the Historical Jesus* by James Robinson, *The Theology of Rudolf Bultmann*, edited by Charles W. Kegley, *Bultmann* by H. Ridderbos, and *Jesus of Nazareth: Saviour and Lord*, edited by Carl F. H. Henry.

* * * * *

In the early years of Neo-orthodoxy's revolt against classic Liberalism, Karl Barth and Rudolf Bultmann were the chief exponents of an existential Christianity. Gradually, the former became disenchanted with any and all efforts to construct a theology in conjunction with any philosophy and since around 1930 has endeavored to purge theology of alien elements. Bultmann, however, has remained unwaveringly convinced that Christianity must be interpreted existentially and has devoted his entire academic career to the development of a program and a methodology of a truly existential Christianity. His program is popularly described by the phrase, "demythologization of the New Testament," and his methodology, aiming at a "positive" (existential) construction of the Christian faith, has been "borrowed" from the school of form criticism and the existential philosophy of Martin Heidegger.

Bultmann claims that his entire program is simply a consistent following through of the Reformation principle of *sola fide*. As Bornkamm correctly discerns: "Bultmann cannot accept any 'objective' revelatory realm of being that can be recognized, established, and understood in and by itself prior to its relation to faith." [1]

Bultmann's Modern Scientific World-View

Bultmann begins by taking very seriously the modern scientific world-view. Cobb views Bultmann's attitude here as a major key to Bultmann's thought: ". . . one must begin with [Bultmann's] understanding of the relation between God and the world. He understands the world as the totality of spatio-temporal phenomena, the whole object of human knowledge. It may be approached both externally, in an objectifying way that is appropriate to the physical sciences, and internally, in the way that is appropriate to the study of man and human history. In either case, we find a closed system of cause and effect—objective causal relations in the former instance, subjective motivations and human decisions in the latter. In so far as our knowledge is concerned, any failure to find a cause simply means that we do not yet have adequate tools at our command. We always properly presuppose that the causes of this-worldly phenomena are this-worldly. This means that God can never be introduced as a factor into the explanation of this-worldly events." [2] And to this axiom there are no exceptions. Bultmann himself declares: ". . . modern man acknowledges as reality only such phenomena or events as are comprehensible within the framework of the rational order of the universe. . . . When a strange or marvelous accident occurs, he does not rest until he has found a rational cause." [3] Furthermore, ". . . there are still many superstitions among modern men, but they are exceptions or even anomalies. Modern men take it for granted that the course of nature and of history, like their own inner life and their practical life, is nowhere interrupted by the intervention of supernatural powers." [4] And finally: "Although modern physical theories take account of chance in the chain of cause and effect in subatomic phenomena, our daily living, purposes and actions are not affected. In any case, modern science does not believe that the course of nature can be interrupted or, so to speak, perforated, by supernatural powers." [5] Bultmann frankly admits that his program "takes the modern world-view as a criterion." [6]

What are the results for one's understanding of the New Testament of this acceptance of the world-view of modern science? Simply this: the New Testament becomes to a large degree "mythological." Bultmann declares: ". . . the world-view of Scripture is mythological and is therefore unacceptable to modern man whose thinking has been shaped by science and is therefore no longer mythological." [7]

By "myth" Bultmann, of course, does not mean fiction or fairy tale. He has reference to the use of imagery to express the other-worldly in terms of this world, the divine in terms of human life, and the "other side" in terms of "this side." [8] But it must be noted here that such description or imagery is anthropological and not specifically cosmological. In other words, Bultmann means that though in a myth man appears to be describing the world, he is actually describing his own existence. (This demythologization of the New Testament, as we shall see, does not consist merely in eliminating what one concludes is mythology. Rather, it involves interpreting the New Testament anthropologically, or, as Bultmann prefers to

171

say, existentially.) Understood in this way, mythology constitutes, in Bultmann's opinion, a great amount of New Testament teaching.

To illustrate this understanding of the so-called mythological teaching of the New Testament, one could do no better than to turn to his 1941 essay, *New Testament and Mythology*, wherein he specifies what he feels are distinct mythological elements surrounding the New Testament kerygma: "The cosmology of the New Testament is essentially mythical in character. The world is viewed as a three-storied structure, with the earth in the centre, the heaven above, and the underworld beneath. Heaven is the abode of God and of celestial beings—the angels. The underworld is hell, the place of torment. Even the earth is more than the scene of natural, everyday events, of the trivial round and common task. It is the scene of the supernatural activity of God and his angels on the one hand, and of Satan and his deamons on the other. These supernatural forces intervene in the course of nature and in all that men think and will and do. Miracles are by no means rare. . . . *This then is the mythical view of the world which the New Testament presupposes when it presents the event of redemption which is the subject of its preaching.* It proclaims in the language of mythology that the last time has now come. 'In the fulness of time' God sent forth his Son, a pre-existent divine Being, who appears on earth as a man. He dies the death of a sinner on the cross and makes atonement for the sins of men. His resurrection marks the beginning of the cosmic catastrophe. . . . The risen Christ is exalted to the right hand of God in heaven and made 'Lord' and 'King.' He will come again on the clouds of heaven to complete the work of redemption, and the resurrection and judgment of men will follow. . . . All this is the language of mythology, and the origin of the various themes can be easily traced in the contemporary mythology of Jewish Apocalyptic and in the redemption myths of Gnosticism. To this extent *the kerygma is incredible to modern man, for he is convinced that the mythical view of the world is obsolete.* We are therefore bound to ask whether, when we preach the Gospel to-day, we expect our converts to accept not only the Gospel message, but also the mythical view of the world in which it is set. If not, does the New Testament embody a truth which is quite independent of its mythical setting? If it does, theology must undertake the task of stripping the Kerygma from its mythical framework, of 'demythologizing' it. Can Christian preaching expect modern man

172

to accept the mythical view of the world as true? . . . Man's knowl-edge and mastery of the world have advanced to such an extent through science and technology that it is no longer possible for any-one to hold the New Testament view of the world. . . . Now that the forces and the laws of nature have been discovered, we can no longer believe in *spirits, whether good or evil.* . . . The *miracles of the New Testament* have ceased to be miraculous. . . . *The mythical eschatology* is untenable for the simple reason that the parousia of Christ never took place as the New Testament expected [sic]. His-tory did not come to an end, and, as every schoolboy knows, it will continue to run its course. [Whether modern man regards himself as pure nature or as pure spirit], he finds *what the New Testament has to say about the 'Spirit (pneuma) and the sacraments utterly strange and incomprehensible.* . . . Again, the biblical doctrine that *death is the punishment of sin* is equally abhorrent to naturalism and ideal-ism. . . . The same objections apply to *the doctrine of the atonement.* How can the guilt of one man be expiated by the death of another who is sinless—if indeed one may speak of a sinless man at all? What primitive notions of guilt and righteousness does this imply? And what primitive idea of God? . . . What a primitive mythology it is, that a divine Being should become incarnate, and atone for the sins of man through his own blood! . . . The *resurrection of Jesus* is just as difficult for modern man. . . . It is only with effort that modern man can think himself back into such an intellectual atmosphere. . . ." [9] So it is beyond debate that, though Bultmann (as we shall see more fully later) recognizes the existence of a gen-uine New Testament proclamation which is relevant to today's "modern man," this New Testament kerygma is couched in and covered over with a great amount of first-century mythology. The New Testament writers were definitely attempting to tell us some-thing of a meaningful nature, but they related this message in exis-tential terminology. That is, seeped as they were in a pre-scientific understanding of the world and spirits, they could not avoid relating their message in mythological terms. But the modern man, in-structed as he is in the scientific world-view of the twentieth century, must now face the realization that he lives in a closed cause-and-effect cosmic system. He is not afforded the "luxury" of falling back upon explanations of a supernatural nature to account for mys-terious enigmas. God can never be introduced as a factor into the explanation of any this-worldly phenomenon! This acceptance of the modern scientific world-view is basic to Bultmann's theology.

Bultmann's Understanding of Faith and Its Task

In the light of the foregoing summary of Bultmann's scientific world-view, one might easily conclude that the theological task was ruled out at the outset prior to any statement about God. But for Bultmann the way has only now been cleared for a truly Biblical faith relationship between man and God. For Bultmann faith is a "nevertheless" perception. In other words, although an event may be fully and correctly understood in terms of this-worldly causes, "nevertheless" by faith it may be seen as having an essentially different meaning. To support his view Bultmann delights in referring to such passages as Psalm 73:22-23: "So foolish was I, and ignorant; I was like a beast before thee. Nevertheless, I am continually with thee! thou has held me by my right hand," and I Corinthians 7: 29-31: "But this I say, brethren, The time is short; it remaineth that both they that have wives be as though they had none; And they that weep, as though they wept not; and they that rejoice, as though they rejoiced not; and they that buy, as though they possessed not; And they that use this world, as not abusing it, for the fashion of this world passeth away." Illustrations of his use of these rather uncommon verses to support his construction of faith as a *nevertheless* concept are the following: "In faith I deny the closed connection of the worldly events, the chain of cause and effect as it presents itself to the neutral observer. . . . This is the paradox of faith, that faith 'nevertheless' understands as God's action here and now an event which is completely intelligible in the natural or historical connection of events. This 'nevertheless' (the German *dennoch* of Psalm 73:23; and Paul Tillich's *in spite of*) is inseparable from faith. Only this is real faith . . .," [10] and ". . . our relation to the world as believers is paradoxical. As Paul puts it in I Cor. 7:29-31, 'Let those who have wives live as though they had none, and those who mourn as though they were not mourning, and those who rejoice as though they were not rejoicing, and those who buy as though they had no goods, and those who deal with the world as though they had no dealings with it.' In terms of this book [*Jesus Christ and Mythology*], we may say, 'Let those who have the modern world-view live as though they had none.' " [11] Ridderbos correctly interprets Bultmann at this point: "In Bultmann's theology, the world and human personality retain their own independence and are completely shut off from God. At the very most, only something which occurs within this closed order can be *understood* by faith as an act of God."[12] In short, then, for Bultmann a given event or phenomenon, though no doubt having a this-worldly explanation, can be for the believer, but *only* for the believer, an act of God. By faith, God is made real and effective in relation to human existence.

It might be well if at this point a word is said concerning Bultmann's understanding of God. Just who is this one who is made real and effective by faith. Bultmann declares that God is the "absolutely transcendent One," "the Wholly Other"; therefore, we cannot say what God is like. We can only say what God does for us. Hence to speak of God means to speak of man. Theology, then, for Bultmann is the explanation of the self-understanding which man achieves when God speaks to him through the kerygma. In other words, God and all talk about him, if genuine, can never be understood as mere abstractions. If God is genuinely apprehended by faith's "nevertheless" perception, it transforms the way in which the individual understands his own existence. ". . . faith is a new understanding of personal existence. In other words, God's action bestows upon us a new understanding of ourselves." [13] And further, ". . . the most important thing is that basic insight that the theological thoughts of the New Testament are the unfolding of faith itself growing out of that new understanding of God, the world, and man which is conferred in and by faith—or, as it can also be phrased: *out of one's new self-understanding*. For by the believer's new understanding of himself we, of course, do not mean 'understanding' as in a scientific anthropology which objectifies man into a phenomenon of the world, but we do mean an existential understanding of myself which is at one with and inseparable from my understanding of God and the world." [14] In other words, an apprehension of God's action for me by faith is actually at the same time an acquisition of a new existential understanding of myself. Furthermore, not only do I have a new *self*-understanding, but also by faith all of nature and existence is viewed in its boundedness by and radical dependence upon that which altogether transcends it, that is, God.

175

Thus far we have determined that, for Bultmann, we live in a closed world-system, free from all supernatural intrusion, but by faith we may nevertheless perceive that God acts in our behalf, this perception resulting in a new understanding of ourselves, which is the *telos* of the faith perception. Immediately, it may justly be asked, is this the Bible's understanding of God, the world, faith, and faith's *telos* or task? If one understands the Bible as a trustworthy document respecting its cosmology, eschatology, and historicity, then, of course, Bultmann's understanding of these items is incorrect. But Bultmann is convinced that the Bible, specifically the New Testament as it is this which concerns him as a New Testament scholar, is on the face of it, for the most part, outdated mythology. Yet underlying this mythology is something else with deep meaning—namely, the New Testament proclamation of the act of God, or, in short, the *kerygma.* For instance, Jesus' disciples, say Matthew, for example, were convinced that through their association with Jesus of Nazareth they had by faith perceived God acting in Jesus Christ for them, giving them a new understanding of themselves and the world in which they lived. Being "children of their age," they naturally and unconsciously expressed this new self-understanding derived from their apprehension of God's action for them in pre-scientific mythological terms. Bultmann is convinced that the New Testament kerygma is absolutely essential to modern man's own self-understanding, but it can only be made relevant to him if the New Testament is stripped of the mythological shell which surrounds the true New Testament kerygma. "This method of interpretation of the New Testament which tries to recover the deeper meaning behind the mythological conceptions," affirms Bultmann, "I call *de-mythologizing.*" [15] By demythologizing the New Testament, Bultmann declares that the true proclamation of the act of God may be seen and understood for what it is and not taken as itself a bit of outdated mythology. How does he propose to carry out this program?

Before his actual methodology is considered, it must be made clear that Bultmann views demythologization as neither an attempt to discover certain New Testament passages which are not mythological and to regard these as the gospel for our day, nor is it an effort to go behind the form of the New Testament to the teaching of Jesus, for this too is mythological, made more so by the interpretation which the faith of the early Church placed upon his words and deeds. Rather it is a program to *identify* the existential intention of myth and to *reaffirm* this intention in non-mythological categories, that is, in categories devoid of the cosmological and eschatological categories of the New Testament.[16] The result of such a program is our hearing "in the Bible authoritative words about our existence." [17]

To arrive at a proper comprehension of the true kerygma, Bultmann follows a basic twofold methodology: first, the "form-historical" (*Form-Geschichtliche*) method, expressed in a highly detailed, voluminous work entitled *Die Geschichte der synoptischen Tradition* (1921), and second, what may be termed for lack of a more precise designation, the "presuppositional-existentialist" method, developed in his *Glauben und Verstehen* (I, 1933; II, 1952) and *Theologie des Neuen Testaments* (1953).

Bultmann's form-historical method. "Form history," more popularly known as "form criticism," endeavors to "get behind the written Gospels and their literary sources to the oral stage of the Gospel tradition, and to classify and examine the various 'forms' or types of story, utterance, etc., represented in that oral tradition." [18] "These [oral] forms are supposed to have provided material for the Gospels and are also thought to have been so thoroughly shaped by the needs of the early Church as to preclude a full historical basis for all the events recorded in the Gospels." [19] Hence, though for him Jesus is nothing other than a man whom the later faith of the Church made a deity, Bultmann is well aware that, contrary to Liberalism's efforts to free the "life of Jesus" of all supernaturalism, the history of Jesus as recorded in the Gospels is very definitely a *super*natural history which at the same time is freighted with the character of preaching. But according to Bultmann, "this preaching does not give us a trustworthy account of what occurred; it represents only the faith of the later church." [20] Moreover, "this faith of the later church (and its accompanying 'theology') has taken such a thorough hold of what was originally said by Jesus that it is extremely difficult to derive, from this proclamation of faith, a clear picture of what Jesus actually said and did." [21] (It is for this reason that one rarely hears the Bultmannian scholar declare, "Jesus said"; rather, he prefers to say, "Jesus is purported to have said," or "It

177

has been put into the mouth of Jesus that 'such and such' is the case.") Bultmann is willing to concede that the words and sayings ascribed to Jesus actually have historical kernels, but these sayings are no longer to be taken with any certainty. For example, whether Jesus ever regarded himself as the Messiah cannot be determined by any information presently available to us. Actually, the Gospels, so declares Bultmann, are not concerned with Jesus but with the faith and the preaching of the Church with respect to Jesus. By going behind the Gospels as simple expressions of the faith of the early Church to the original forms of the Gospel tradition (insofar as they are capable of determination) before they were brought together into the unity exhibited in the present Gospel records, Bultmann is convinced that the *Sitz im Leben* (the life-setting) of these oral traditions may be in many instances readily grasped, thus enabling the New Testament interpreter to more easily determine the precise influences —whether Jewish apocalyptic, whether Gnostic—which bore upon the original saying. Such a determination in turn will aid the interpreter in his demythologization of a given narrative or saying. Herein resides the value of the form-critical method for Bultmann's *Entmythologisierungsprogram*.

Bultmann's presuppositional-existentialist method. Bultmann maintains that if one would demythologize the New Testament writer's expression of his self-understanding in order to understand his theology, he must come to the New Testament with some kind of question or previous understanding (*Vorverständnis*). Herein lies Bultmann's presuppositionalism. He declares: ". . . it is important to remember that every interpretation is actuated by the framing of specific questions, and without this there could be no interpretation at all. Of course these questions need not be framed explicitly or consciously, but unless they are framed the texts have nothing to say to us." [22] When the objection is raised that the presuppositional approach to the text inevitably colors one's findings, Bultmann's argument, while readily admitting this to be the case, presses for the recognition that there is no interpretation of any document without preconceived concepts: ". . . it would be a fallacy to suppose that exegesis can ever be pursued independently of profane terminology. Every exegete is dependent upon a terminology which has come down to him by tradition. . . ." [23] Thus having cleared the way for the framing of a certain question to be directed to the New Testament text in his approach to it, Bultmann declares what this question should be: "I think I may take for granted that the right question to frame with regard to the Bible—at any rate within the Church—is the question of human existence. I am driven to that by the urge to inquire existentially about my own existence. But that is a question which at bottom determines our approach to and interpretation of all historical documents. For the ultimate purpose in the study of history is to realize consciously the possibilities it affords for the understanding of human existence." [24] In another place Bultmann affirms: "Our task . . . is to discover the hermeneutical principle by which we can understand what is said in the Bible. . . . In other words, the question of the 'right' philosophy arises. . . . Our question is simply which philosophy today offers the most adequate perspective and conceptions for understanding human existence. Here it seems to me that we should learn from existentialist philosophy, because in this philosophical school human existence is directly the object of attention." [25] In particular, Bultmann feels that Martin Heidegger's existentialist construction of human existence, as a philosophical anthropology, provides a sound basis for asking sensitive questions. Writes Bultmann: ". . . Heidegger's existentialist analysis of the ontological structure of being would seem to be no more than a secularized, philosophical version of the New Testament view of human life. For him the chief characteristic of man's Being in history is anxiety. Man exists in a permanent tension between the past and the future. At every moment he is confronted with an alternative. Either he must immerse himself in the concrete world of nature, and thus inevitably lose his individuality, or he must abandon all security and commit himself unreservedly to the future, and thus alone achieve his authentic Being. Is not that exactly the New Testament understanding of human life? Some critics have objected that I am borrowing Heidegger's categories and forcing them upon the New Testament. I am afraid this only shows that they are blinding their eyes to the real problem. I mean, one should rather be startled that philosophy is saying the same thing as the New Testament and saying it quite independently." [26] Bultmann is confident that this existentialist methodology as *phenomenology* seeks to be objective and as *ontology* limits itself to the sphere of what is universal to human existence as such and omits the variety of actual forms which human existence can take.

The Results of Bultmann's Demythologizing Program

The form-critical, existentialist analysis of the New Testament, declares Bultmann, demythologizes the texts and results in the New Testament's untrammeled proclamation of the Christian message that God, the wholly transcendent, has acted decisively for man's salvation in Jesus Christ. As proclamation of God's past act in Jesus Christ, the kerygma is likewise promise of God's act in the here-and-now as it functions as a call to the radical decision of faith (total surrender of self to God). Faith, as the authentic response to the kerygma, is at the same time God's act in the present in the believer's "death" to self and "resurrection" to the life of freedom. All this sounds, of course, on the surface something like the traditional message of the Church, but Bultmann's program actually alters the traditional message in nearly every feature. Specifically, how has Bultmann's construction altered the Church's traditional understanding of man, his world, and God?

In his interpretation of man, Bultmann treats Paul's antithesis of flesh and spirit. Here, for Bultmann, Paul is speaking of two modes of human existence; however, in Bultmann's opinion, Paul's terminology leads to confusion. But informed by Heidegger's analysis of *Dasein*, Paul's two modes are seen to be respectively unauthentic and authentic existence, the former alluding to the way of understanding one's self from the world of things and which leads to a care for that world that prevents man from being truly himself, the latter describing life lived in terms of the real potentialities of the existent personality, free from past ancestry, achievement, and failure, and open to the future and responsible decision.[27] The transition from the former to the latter mode of existence occurs when the existent responds in faith to the kerygma.

Bultmann's reinterpretation of the New Testament message replaces New Testament cosmology and eschatology with a new understanding of nature and history. In the sphere of nature, the New Testament confronts us with a three-tiered cosmology, the *supra*-worldly (God's world) being treated, for example, as an objectively real world alongside of the spatio-temporal world. But interpreting this aspect of the New Testament cosmology existentially, Bultmann asserts that the conception of heaven as the abode of God is simply the conception by means of the category of space of the transcendence of God. In the sphere of history, the New Testament sets forth an eschatology in which a new kind of world will in the chronological future replace this one. But again, his methodology leads Bultmann to view this "mythology" similarly as simply the conception by means of the category of time of the transcendence of God, but in the special sense of God's transcendence in judgment over finite man.[28] In short, Bultmann completely disposes with the traditional understanding of New Testament cosmology and eschatology.

Bultmann's understanding of God was seen earlier to involve a conception of him as the absolutely transcendent, wholly other One who is hidden to every eye except the eye of faith. It is through faith alone that God becomes relevant to our existence, for apart from faith we live in a closed world-system of cause and effect. Yet it is this God, Bultmann insists, who reveals himself in Jesus Christ for man's salvation, this affirmation being in a unique sense *the* New Testament proclamation. With this we are brought to Bultmann's Christology.

At the outset it must be understood that Bultmann's view of the *relationship* between God's act in Christ and Jesus of Nazareth is paradoxical. Because of his form-critical approach to the Gospels, Bultmann is sure that we possess today exceedingly little real information about Jesus of Nazareth: "I do indeed think that we can know almost nothing concerning the life and personality of Jesus." [29] Furthermore, because of his modern scientfic world-view with its corollary—the rejection of the New Testament world-view, Bultmann is equally insistent that knowledge about Jesus is of little or no interest to him. For him, the Christian faith is essentially indifferent to what Jesus said or did or how he understood himself. He writes: "The facts which historical criticism can verify cannot exhaust, indeed they cannot adequately indicate, all that Jesus means to me. How he actually originated matters little, indeed we can appreciate his significance only when we cease to worry about such questions. Our interest in the events of his life, and above all in the cross, is more than an academic concern with the history of the past. We can see meaning in them only when we ask what God is trying to say to each one of us through them." [30] In another context he states: "If I desire an encounter with the Jesus of history, it is true that I must rely on certain historical documents. Yet the study of these documents can bring us to an encounter with the historical phenomenon 'Jesus' only on the basis of one phenomenon of past history. Yet we can hope, by means of this study, to recognize the historical phenomenon 'Jesus' only on the basis of one's own historic [geschichtlich] encounter. That was the aim and method of my *Jesus and the Word*. The Jesus of history is not kerygma, any more than my book was. For in the kerygma Jesus encounters us as the Christ—that is, as the eschatological phenomenon *par excellence*. Neither St Paul nor St John mediate an historic encounter with the historic Jesus. Even if the synoptic gospels appear to do so, that is only when they are read in the light of the historical problems which have arisen since their day, not when they are read in their original sense. . . . So far, then, from running away from *Historie* and taking refuge in *Geschichte*, I am deliberately renouncing any form of encounter with a phenomenon of past history, including an encounter with the Christ after the flesh, in order to encounter the Christ proclaimed in the kerygma, which confronts me in my historic situation." [31] From these remarks it is evident that Bultmann is unconcerned, apart from the mere "thatness" of Jesus, with Jesus of Nazareth, simply because Jesus of Nazareth is not *the* subject of the kerygma. Right here appears the paradox to rationality. Bultmann believes that God acts only with human existence here and now (which act is revelation) and this act can never become an event of the past.[32] Yet the kerygma is the proclamation that God acted in the historical Jesus of Nazareth, although we can know little about and should be interested even less in this Jesus "after the flesh." (The mere "thatness" but not the "whatness" of Jesus is all that is essential to the kerygma.) Certainly, knowledge about this one in whom God acted for man's salvation would seem on this construction to be reduced too much for even the barest interests of faith; certainly, any *proof* of this act is rendered impossible. Nevertheless, Bultmann is positive that God did "speak" in the historical Jesus and that this "Word" demands decision. In fact, this is the only way, in Bultmann's opinion, to preserve the *skandalon* of Christianity, for it is only in this manner that all objectivity, upon which the interests of faith might rest (which would in turn rend the true nature of faith), is removed.

Bultmann's attitude toward faith as decision apart from all objectivity may at this juncture be related to his view of this world. As we saw earlier, Bultmann views the objective world as closed to divine causality. We will miss a fine nuance in his thought if we assume here that his view of the world as a closed system is due *solely* to his scientific *Weltanshauung*. This is one but not the main factor.[33] For behind his view of the objective world is an even more basic commitment, namely, his view of faith. In his opinion it is only the scientific world-view with its view of the world as a closed system which does justice to or allows for a proper understanding of faith. Cobb explains Bultmann's point in this way: "Faith knows that what is seen apart from faith is always explicable in categories that make no reference to the act of God and that no kind of historical event points more clearly to God than any other. But faith sees that *nevertheless* precisely these events are the act of God for the believer. Hence, *for faith*, the events that for the historian are the historical Jesus are the act of God. Faith connects the act of God to the historical event, not on the basis of historical evidence that such a connection is warranted, but precisely *by faith* in spite of the lack of objective reason of any kind." [34] Thus Bultmann does not demythogize the New Testament primarily in order to harmonize with his world-view; his most basic motivation is to do justice to faith itself.[35] For Bultmann, faith understands itself as a leap, as pure risk; it does not understand itself as based upon any objective evidence. Moreover, Bultmann claims that only this view of faith is consonant with Paul's principle of justification by faith alone. In order to do full justice to faith, then, the principle of justification *sola fide* applied by Paul against seeking security in good works must be applied also against seeking security in objective facts of history. For to fail to do so, that is, to base faith on certain objective events of history, is a salvation by works! True faith is believing *in spite of* the absence of all objective evidence. Herein and only here is the *skandalon* of Christianity.

Regarding the *person* of Jesus of Nazareth, Bultmann does not hesitate to affirm that he was born like every other member of the race; and he denies that Jesus possessed any nature other than that common to all men. In fact, he sees a discrepancy between the doctrine of Christ's pre-existence as given by Paul and John and the "legend" of the Virgin Birth in Matthew and Luke.[36] Bultmann finds it extremely difficult to harmonize in Jesus a concept of eternal pre-existence on the one hand and a beginning in time through human birth on the other. This is due, of course, to his denial of Christ's two natures. He explains the doctrine of Christ's pre-existence and the accounts of the Virgin Birth as merely attempts of the early Church to explain the meaning of the person of Christ for faith.[37]

As for the redemptive acts of God in Jesus Christ, that is, Christ's *work*, Bultmann demythologizes both the cross and the resurrection of Jesus and interprets them existentially.[38] He declares that the idea of an incarnate God-man who vicariously atones for man's sin by enduring man's punishment and death is a mythological interpretation of the crucifixion of Jesus consisting of "a mixture of sacrificial and juridical analogies, which have ceased to be tenable for us to-day." [39] And as for the resurrection of Jesus, it is a mythical event pure and simple, not an objective event of past history at all.[40] What then are these "events" intended to convey if they do not indicate a vicarious atonement and an objective event of past history? When one recalls that for Bultmann mythology is essentially anthropological and not cosmological, that is, that in myth, though he appears to be describing the world and certain events in the world, man is really describing his own existence, he is not surprised when Bultmann interprets the redemptive acts of God as set forth in the New Testament anthropologically, or perhaps better, existentially. The cross becomes then a symbol of human self-mastery over the passions, and the resurrection becomes an attempt to explain the significance of the cross to faith.

Concerning the cross, Bultmann writes: "To believe in the cross of Christ does not mean to concern ourselves with a mythical process wrought outside of us and our world, with an objective event turned by God to our advantage, but rather to make the cross of Christ our own, to undergo crucifixion with him." [41] By thus entering by the leap and risk of faith into Christ's sufferings, the "flesh with the passions and lusts thereof" (Gal. 5:24) is crucified, which means existentially "the overcoming of our natural dread of suffering and the perfection of our detachment from the world." [42] In so far as man is judged and delivered from his passions and concern for the world by his understanding of the cross, so far is Christ crucified "for us," but not in the sense of any theory of sacrifice or satisfaction.[43] And the proclamation of the cross as the event of redemption from these things challenges all who hear it to appropriate this significance for themselves. Existentially, this all means simply a challenge to modern man to abandon unauthentic living, to surrender himself to the invisible and to freedom to face the future with individual responsibility.

Concerning the resurrection, Bultmann insists that it must be viewed with the cross in an inseparable unity as a faith affirmation that the cross is actually the salvation of the world. ". . . the cross and the resurrection form a single, indivisible cosmic event. . . . The cross is not an isolated event, as though it were the end of Jesus, which needed the resurrection subsequently to reverse it. . . . Cross and resurrection form a single, indivisible cosmic event which brings judgment to the world and opens up for men the possibility of authentic life." [44] This means that the resurrection itself is not an event of past history. Rather, it means that the affirmation of faith in the resurrection is simply the affirmation of faith that the salvation of God works itself out in the cross.[45] Bultmann avers: "The resurrection itself is not an event of past history. All that historical criticism can establish is the fact that the first disciples came to believe in the resurrection. The historian can perhaps to some extent account for that faith from the personal intimacy which the disciples had enjoyed with Jesus during his earthly life, and so reduce the resurrection appearances to a series of subjective visions. But the historical problem is not of interest to Christian belief in the resurrection. For the historical event of the rise of the Easter faith means for us what it meant for the first disciples—namely, . . . the act of God in which the redemptive event of the cross is completed." [46] Existentially, this means the affirmation, by faith, that the cross has "saving" efficacy. And these events—the cross and resurrection—when proclaimed constitute the New Testament kerygma—a message of deliverance from unauthentic living and translation into authentic living.

A summary at this point of the kerygma which Bultmann feels needs to be proclaimed to modern man may aid in solidifying what has just been said. Bultmann is asking the modern preacher to proclaim that God acted in Jesus Christ in his death and resurrection. Of course, he is to make it clear to his hearers that this death and this resurrection are expressed in the New Testament in mythological, that is, in existential language—in language of a pre-scientific age intended to express and to explain the New Testament writers' own existence, how their lives were shaped by this man Jesus. As intimate followers of Jesus, by the crucifixion of their friend, the disciples entered into his suffering, no longer fearing the same, and thus became open to what God had for them. In faith (which was God's act in them) they believed that somehow God had acted in this one for the forgiveness of their sins. They expressed this faith in this act of God for them in Christ by picturing him as on the third day rising from the dead. Finally, by believing the same *in spite of* the evidence of modern science to support the view of this world as a closed system of cause and effect, modern man too may know God's act for him, no longer fearing the past and opening up to the future. In short, he may know the meaning of authentic existence as freedom in love and as freedom toward responsible decision.

As for Bultmann's understanding of the Holy Spirit, his de-mythologized concept of that divine person consists in his being the "factual possibility of the new life" which the modern man can acquire through faith.[47]

Christian Theology or Heideggerian Philosophy?

For many interpreters of Bultmann, his understanding of New Testament theology is, as Cobb puts it, simply "baptizing" Heidegger's philosophy as Christian theology. Bultmann emphatically denies that he has done such, *since* Heidegger's existentialism tells us only *that* we should live authentically and not *what* constitutes authentic existence, *since* Heidegger's existentialism, though insisting on the attainment of authentic existence, cannot prescribe how it is to be attained, and *since* Heidegger's existentialism assigns a decisive place to "being-toward-death," whereas Christian thought assigns the decisive place to the encounter with a "Thou." [48] The Christian faith provides in the kerygma the call to decision and the content of authentic existence. The Christian faith places before the religious existent an encounter with God in Jesus Christ and opens up the possibility of authentic *freedom* from one's past and the *experience* of faith, love, hope, and joy which characterizes Christian experience.

Viewing the relationship between Heidegger's philosophy and Christian theology in this manner, Bultmann, as we have seen, simply allows existentialism to frame the sensitive questions of and for

186

modern man, but the New Testament "act of God in Christ," he insists, must give the answers. In short, Bultmann begins with and builds his theology upon existentialist philosophy.

Has Bultmann's *Entmythologisierungsprogram* removed the scandal of Christianity for modern man? Bultmann vehemently denies this, insisting that there is still a scandal—indeed, a scandal of even greater moment than the scandal of traditional Christianity since he has removed the latter's objective basis of faith—namely Christianity's continuing insistence that it is only faith in the decisive act of God in Jesus Christ that transforms man and delivers him up to true authenticity.

Criticism

George E. Ladd is certainly correct when he writes: "The most superficial reading of [Bultmann's] writings would show that he is not and does not desire to be an orthodox theologian." [49] When Bultmann rejects all of the cardinal articles of the orthodox Christian faith, he certainly places himself beyond the confines of Orthodoxy. Indeed, it would seem that only in the sense that Bultmann continues to insist that God acts in *Jesus Christ* for man's salvation and not, say, in Buddha that he may be considered a *Christian* theologian at all. He rejects the infallibility and inerrancy of the Old and New Testaments; he denies the orthodox understanding of God as subsisting eternally in three persons, the Father, the Son, and the Holy Spirit, all three possessing the same essential deity and equality in power and glory; he repudiates the eternal pre-existence of the divine nature of Jesus Christ, averring that Jesus was only a man, born like all other men. Though willing to speak of Jesus' cross as an event of past history, Bultmann rejects all ideas of his death as in any sense a vicarious atonement for the sins of the world. Jesus' resurrection is pure mythology as is his ascension into heaven. At best, from the point of view of Orthodoxy, the most that can be said for Bultmann's view of God is that it is absolutely deistic, with God and the world as two independent, mutually exclusive, non-intervening entities.

When Bultmann's analysis of Paul's antithesis in man between "flesh" and "spirit" concludes that these terms only describe what Heidegger has better distinguished as unauthentic and authentic existence, the former describing that existence wherein one's under-

187

standing of himself leads to concern for the world and wherein one finds security in externalities and history, the latter describing that existence wherein life is lived in terms of the real potentialities of the personality, free from the past and open to the future, such an analysis gravely fails to penetrate into the Biblical meaning of sin and grace. Sin defined as human self-assertion in the world of relativity and perishability seems hardly to scratch the surface of the Bible's portrayal of sin as any want of conformity unto, or transgression of, the law of God (I John 3:4). Human misery viewed as mere involvement in this world of relativity hardly does justice to the much fuller description of human misery found in the Bible and depicted as *loss* of communion with God and *subjection* to God's wrath and curse, to all the miseries of this life, to death itself, and to the pains of hell forever. (Gen. 3:8,24; Eph. 2:3; Rom. 5: 12,14; 6:23; Matt. 25:41). Grace defined as that which is necessary to bring man into a state of freedom and the enablement of man to attain authentic existence fails to do justice to the Biblical depiction of grace as the unmerited love of God in action in the very presence of sin (Rom. 5:20), and manifested in a saving way in his acts of justification and adoption, in his work of sanctification, and in the benefits to the believer which accompany these, namely, assurance of God's love, peace of conscience, joy in the Holy Spirit, increase of grace, and continuing perseverance in the faith to the end (Eph. 1:7; I John 3:1; II Thess. 2:13; Rom. 5:1-5; Col. 1:10-11; Prov. 4:18; II Pet. 3:18).[50]

Certainly the salvation that is consonant with Bultmann's view of God and man fails to meet adequately the spiritual needs of man and is radically unbiblical. The Bible declares man's basic need to be the deliverance out of his state of sin and misery and a new birth into a state of salvation, this need being met only in the life, death, and resurrection of a personal Redeemer, the Lord Jesus Christ, as the benefits of his redemption are applied to the believer by the Holy Spirit.

These facts alone sufficiently indicate that Bultmann is not able to propagate the Biblical faith or to instruct the saint. And from the point of view of Orthodoxy this criticism could stop here. However, since Bultmann's demythologized kerygmatic theology raises several pertinent issues and contains certain definite inconsistencies and discrepancies, no criticism would be complete without some word concerning them.

Irrationalism. First, a basic irrationalism pervades Bultmann's theology. Bultmann is guided throughout his theological work by the very practical concern of removing all unnecessary obstacles to the faith of modern man. We should not, so he says, insist that modern man accept the pre-scientific view of the world, the New Testament teaching on miracles, spirits, etc., and the mythical idea of a Savior God-man dying on a cross for sinners. Yet it seems extremely arbitrary on Bultmann's part to stop with the kerygma as he formulates it, namely, that God acts for man's salvation in the death and resurrection of Jesus Christ, and not to demythologize it too. Thielicke is justified in remarking: "We are left wondering why the event of Christ is not myth like everything else. Surely '*logos sarx egento*' implies an intervention in the closed system of reality." [51] Is not such an insistence, particularly when Bultmann is unwilling to provide any objective basis for accepting the same, an unnecessary obstacle to modern man, if, as it would appear to be, the removal of unnecessary obstacles is Bultmann's desire. If obstacle there must be, why not simply retain the New Testament picture of things? Now it will not do to reply that this criticism misunderstands the nature of myth and the purpose of demythologization, and that while it is true that the New Testament is to be demythologized completely, yet only that which is myth can be demythologized, and since the kerygma is not myth, it must be retained. For there is absolutely no *defensible* criterion which Bultmann can produce which can demonstrate why his kerygma is not as equally mythical as the mythology which he regards as unnecessary. His kerygma definitely proclaims divine intrusion into man's affairs in order to provide the *only* remedy for man's lack of authenticity.

Bultmann, of course, attempts to skirt this difficulty by reminding his critic that God does not *actually* intervene. Only *by faith* is God made relevant to the human situation. Though the human existent knows that he lives in a world into which God *never* intrudes, *nevertheless* by faith God becomes real in the human situation. But herein as well is Bultmann's irrationalism evident. Either an event is or is not an act of God. It cannot both be and not be an act of

God at the same time, all of Bultmann's protestations to the contrary notwithstanding. If it is not, no amount of "faith" on my part makes it an act of God, unless, of course, God in this connection is my own little "fairy idol" subject to my every beck and call. If it is, it is so, regardless of whether I believe it to be so or not. Now, of course, in the Reformed view, everything that happens is decreed by God and either mediately or immediately governed by God (Eph. 1:11; Acts 4:27-28; Psa. 145:17; 104:24; Heb. 1:3). Bultmann's assertion that God does not intervene in human affairs is really a deistic view at best, which allows no room for divine providence, either general or special. Actually, there is considerable reason to wonder whether Bultmann even has a God at all, for is not Bultmann's call to believe that an act is the act of God even though the person concerned knows that it is not, perilously similar to Peale's call to positive thinking? "Just think positively and you will be amazed at what you can accomplish!" And is not the "crucifixion of our passions" which is purported by Bultmann as being accomplished when we believe in the cross of Christ (even though we know that Jesus did not really die for us), as Schniewind suggests, nothing more than a "striking euphemism for self-mastery, which is the quest of all the higher religions and philosophies"? [52] It definitely seems to be so!

The irrationalism which pervades Bultmann's theological pronouncements, as Pinnock notes, is representative of a much more extensive mood—never seriously considered as viable prior to Kierkegaard and Biblical criticism—to be found throughout modern theology, and expressed by a divided field of knowledge. The "upper story" contains concepts to be accepted without any kind of empirical verification but only on the grounds of a leap of faith since the "lower story"—the world of rationality and testable science—offers no key to the meaning and significance of man. In such a dichotomy man must leap to a faith commitment—which one being of little consequence—in which he can feel at home. Of course, in this leap the fact of faith seems to be the important thing, the object of faith inconsequential. This shift toward a divided field of knowledge, Pinnock analyzes as an attempt to escape the tangle of logic and history by creating one's own meaning of human existence by an act of the will.[53] Through this expression of will as "ultimate concern," man experiences "salvation." It is little wonder that such a mood is considered by the uninitiated layman as theological double-talk, "full of sound and fury, signifying nothing rational."

A misunderstanding of Biblical faith. Second, Bultmann's concept of faith is unbiblical in its assertion that faith, to be faith, must be devoid of all genuine objective knowledge content. He sees this to be simply a consistent application in the area of cognition of the Reformers' principle of justification by faith alone in the area of good conduct. As the Reformers demolished all human security in meritorious works, so he desires to remove a false confidence in human knowledge. But, as Pinnock rejoins, "The analogy is tragically fallacious. There is a world of difference between leaving one's moral bankruptcy and finding refuge in the objective and finished work of Christ, and turning from intellectual doubt about the veracity of Scripture only to leap into the abyss of blind faith." [54] How true!

Though a theologian's view of the nature of faith will always depend on the views he holds of Scripture, of God and man, and of their relationship, one with the other, yet if he is willing to heed the teaching of Scripture, the theologian will learn that the Bible does not repudiate an objective knowledge basis for faith. Rather, he will discover that the Bible regards faith as including rational assent grounded in certain specific objective facts and events. To illustrate this point, one could cite Hebrews 11:6: ". . . he that cometh to God must believe that he is [*estin*], and that he is a rewarder of them that diligently seek him." From this text alone one learns that Biblical faith involves intellectual assent to at least two affirmations of such a nature that they could become articles of creeds, namely, that God *exists* and that he is the *rewarder* of them who diligently seek him. But the assumption of the writer of this epistle in making this assertion (which he makes abundantly clear throughout his discourse) is precisely these things, namely, that God is and that he rewards the one seeking him, not that God does *not* exist or that he does *not* reward the one seeking him. He would never be so foolish as to demand that the one coming to God must believe that God exists if he knew that God did not exist. He would never be so irrational as to require the one coming to God to believe that God will reward his searching if he knew that God would not reward him. Yet Bultmann seems to be just this foolish and irrational when he asks the modern man to *believe* that a given act is the act of God when he

191

knows (whether the modern man knows or not) that that act is not and cannot be an act of God.

Another verse (among many) is Rom. 10:14: "How then shall they call on him in whom they have not believed? and how shall they believe in him of whom they have not heard?" This verse makes it as clear as it can be made that at least some knowledge of Christ is absolutely essential as a *precondition* to trust. Our Lord taught the value of objective evidence as the proper basis for faith when he instructed Thomas to thrust his finger into his wounds and to believe (John 20:27). Paul in the Damascus road incident, asked, "Who art thou, Lord?" (Acts 9:5; 26:15). The knowledge gained in each case cited led on to faith.

Of course, knowledge of objective fact as here described does not and from the nature of the case cannot refer to knowledge based on facts that can always be scientifically and empirically verified. Whether Jesus rose from the grave on the third day cannot be scientifically proven in the sense that the word "scientifically" conveys for modern scientism. But knowledge can be knowledge nonetheless if it is based on *trustworthy testimony*. As Packer correctly declares, "Whether particular beliefs should be treated as known certainties or doubtful opinions will depend on the worth of the testimony on which they are based." [55] And the objective events and facts in which the Bible urges that we place our faith rest on the testimony of a God who cannot lie (Titus 1:2) and which is, therefore, *absolutely* trustworthy. Now, of course, this last affirmation rests on a particular view of the Bible, but it is a view claimed by the Bible for itself and recognized by the Church (a *motivum credibilitatis*) as the only true view for nineteen and a half centuries. In the Bible God requires him who would be saved to recognize his need of salvation and to believe in certain objective historical events (the meanings of which are divinely interpreted), namely, that Jesus died (actually and literally on a particular calendar day on a particular hill in the land of Palestine) for our sins (which is the divine interpretation) according to the Scriptures (which is the testimony to be believed), that he was buried, and that he rose again (actually and literally) the third day (after the particular day on which he died) according to the Scriptures (which is the testimony to be believed, but which is abundantly supported by the eye-witness testimony of Peter [cf. I Cor. 15:5 and II Pet. 1:16-18], the twelve, five hundred disciples at one gathering, and finally James, the apostles, and Paul [I Cor. 15:5-8]). Now none of this testimony, of course, can be scientifically verified—none of these witnesses are present in person for interrogation; however, *no* reason has yet been advanced which must *necessarily* demand the denial of the veracity of any one of them. To the contrary, much evidence may be cited to show that they all gave trustworthy testimony. Certainly God did and must. Therefore, since the testimony of God is manifestly true, it is to be believed, and only rejected at the peril of one's own soul.

To rebut the testimony of Scripture to the resurrection of Jesus, the claim is often made that only the disciples saw Jesus after his resurrection, that, therefore, the event of the resurrection is of interest only to believers. Bultmann, in particular, insists that the early disciples' Easter faith gave rise to the story of the resurrection rather then the resurrection serving as the ground of that faith in the disciples. But such a claim is simply not true to the very witness on which the claim is based. First, many disciples found it extremely difficult to believe in Christ's resurrection even after the Lord "showed himself alive after his passion by many infallible proofs" (Acts 1:3; Matt. 28:17; John 20:25-28). Second, and perhaps even more important for the point presently being made, at least one *unbeliever* saw the resurrected and glorified Lord and as a result of that revelation believed, namely, Saul of Tarsus on the Damascus road. Ridderbos demonstrates the weakness in Bultmann's view when he writes: "If Christ did not rise from the dead and this story is a myth, the question confronting us is how this myth originated. It is undeniable that this 'myth' originated several days after the death of Jesus. A very abrupt change had to take place in the thoughts and deliberations of the disciples with respect to their dead Master. To think of this as the mythical formation of the significance . . ., which the disciples abruptly ascribed to Jesus' crucifixion without any new fact as it basis, a fact which originated outside of themselves, is a postulate that is dictated by Bultmann's concept of reality, but which is at the same time absolutely unintelligible from an historical point of view. It is especially incomprehensible if one remembers that this resurrection witness, in the primary sense of an eye witness . . ., was the starting point and center of the Christian proclamation and formed the foundation of Christian certainty." [56]

There can be no doubt whatsoever, then, in the light of this discussion that the Bible does set forth definite objective facts and events based upon trustworthy testimony as the knowledge basis of faith. The Bible knows nothing of a leap into the dark for no rational purpose. One cannot ignore the Bible on this point with impunity. To follow Bultmann in his concept of faith is to be misled completely; it is to be led away from the Biblical faith which is rationally defensible and pistically satisfying to a faith whose object is extremely difficult to define, whose authority is solely Bultmann himself, and whose verification is wholly subjective and non-verifiable.[57]

A false evaluation of modern science. Finally, Bultmann's claim that faith in God's acts must be based solely in the non-verifiable, non-rational, paradoxical revelation event itself and on nothing else because, besides the "fact" that this alone makes true faith possible, modern science has amply demonstrated that this is a closed world system operating on a cause-and-effect basis and into which the supernatural cannot and does not intrude—this claim, I say, is erroneous in that it ascribes powers to modern science which in fact it cannot and will never have. No scientific fact, in and of itself, can prove that this world is a closed system of cause and effect. It is invariably the interpretation which the scientist places on the fact which determines the meaning of the fact. Consequently, it is not with the specific facts of science that we take issue; rather, it is with the philosophy of science that controls modern science that we must be concerned. Obviously, Bultmann assumes the validity of the principles (the philosophy) which control the modern scientific enterprise and which guide it in all of its affirmations. But he fails to distinguish between an unbelieving philosophy of science and a truly Christian philosophy of science. The former, we readily admit, is unable (and unwilling) to allow a place for supernaturalism within its boundaries; the latter, however, is unable (and unwilling) *not* to allow a place for supernaturalism within its boundaries. As I have attempted to demonstrate elsewhere,[58] non-Christian scientism, in all of its efforts, *assumes* as pre-scientific givens the non-createdness and autonomy of man, the ultimacy of man's rational processes, and the non-createdness of every fact with which it has to do. Of course, all of its efforts will "prove" the non-existence of God or, at least, his non-intervention into this world's affairs. And this is so, even though the unbelieving scientist loudly claims that he makes, as a scientist, no religious value-judgments or moral decisions.

A truly Christian philosophy of science, to the contrary, delights in affirming the existence of the Creator, the createdness of all facts, human rationality as a divine gift, and a divinely-imposed cultural mandate to receptively "reconstruct" the universe as it thinks God's thoughts after him. Nor is there any incompatibility between this approach to science and science *per se*, as is evidenced by the fact that here in America several hundred highly trained, indisputably qualified scientists are members of the Creation Research Society, an organization dedicated to the highest expression of true science within the framework of Biblical revelation. Here are many scientific minds who insist that this world is not a closed system controlled solely by cause and effect. In fact, they insist that such a position as Bultmann maintains, as a universal negation, cannot be proven, while much evidence to the contrary may be cited which points by implication at least to the view that God has interfered, indeed, is constantly doing so, in man's affairs. Bultmann, as so many others in this day, has erroneously granted to modern science an infallibility and a finality which the modern scientist himself will admit it just does not have. Consequently, modern science need not be a hindrance to nor a reason for faith.

Bultmann speaks much of and shows great concern for "modern man." He means by the "modern man" that man who has "come of age," who can no longer tolerate the mythical elements of a pre-scientific age, who no longer believes in miracles, such as the resurrection, or a "three-storied universe"—heaven above, earth between, hell beneath. He seems to forget that unbelief in some forms of Biblical supernaturalism was as prevalent in the days of the events of the New Testament as it is today. Unbelief in miracle is not "modern"; unbelief in the resurrection is not the result of a sophistication newly learned in our day and unknown to the days of the Apostles. Ancient Gnosticism, for example, was unable to relate Christianity's insistence on the Incarnation to its philosophy of matter as evil so Gnosticism refused to believe in the Incarnation. It is the same today. Unbelief is in so many instances, particularly on the academic level, simply the result of the inability to cope with the truth of revelation in the light of a previously assumed position. If the previously assumed position were given up, and upon examination it can so often be shown that there is no valid reason for not giving it up, the truth of revelation is easily assimilated. All of this simply means that the idea of the so-called "modern man" has been greatly exaggerated. Man's nature has not changed basically since the fall of his first parents; his needs are the same. Always some, as in Paul's day, at the preaching of the Gospel will mock, others will say, "We will hear thee again concerning this matter," but some will believe (Acts 17:32-34). And those who believe, after instruction concerning the nature of the resurrection body as to its material nature, when confronted with the "three-storied universe" of Scripture, will quickly see the need for and the reality of a "place" (John 14:2) called heaven for the elect and a "place" called hell (Matt. 25:41; Rev. 20:12-14) for the reprobated wicked, though the need to observe carefully the possible use of phenomenal language in the descriptions also must be stressed. Certainly there will always be the need to interpret the statements of Scripture as a body of divinely-revealed truths, but one only casts himself out upon a subjective sea of conjecture with no guiding light when he denies that the Bible is the Word of God and declares, therefore, that man must fend for himself. The confusion with which modern theology is rife is abundant proof that every theological edifice so constructed is doomed at the outset to the ravages of time because its foundational planks are rotten. Feeling unable to accept the Scripture's claim concerning itself, Bultmann began with existentialist philosophy and constructed a New Testament theology in which the entire divine element exists only in the believer's mind. It is undoubtedly true that Bultmann is only listening to a "recording" of his own inner voice.

NOTES

1. Günther Bornkamm, "The Theology of Rudolf Bultmann," an essay in the book by that title (Edited by Charles W. Kegley; New York: Harper & Row, Publishers, 1966), p. 16.

2. John B. Cobb, Jr., *Living Options in Protestant Theology* (Philadelphia: The Westminster Press, 1962), pp. 227-228.

3. Rudolf Bultmann, *Jesus Christ and Mythology* (New York: Charles Scribner's Sons, 1958), pp. 37-38.

4. *Ibid.*, p. 16.

5. *Ibid.*, p. 15.

6. *Ibid.*, p. 15.

6. *Ibid.*, p. 35.

7. *Ibid.*, p. 36.

8. Rudolf Bultmann, "New Testament and Mythology," *Kerygma and Myth* (Edited by Hans Bartsch; New York: Harper and Brothers, 1961), p. 10.

9. *Ibid.*, pp. 1-8.

10. Bultmann, *Jesus Christ and Mythology*, pp. 64-65.

11. *Ibid.*, p. 85.

12. Herman Ridderbos, *Bultmann* (Philadelphia: The Presbyterian and Reformed Publishing Company, 1960), p. 73.

13. Bultmann, *Jesus Christ and Mythology*, p. 73.

14. Bultmann, *Theology of the New Testament* (Translated by Kendrick Grovel; New York: Charles Scribner's Sons, 1955), II, 239.

15. Bultmann, *Jesus Christ and Mythology,* p. 18.

16. Cobb, *op. cit.*, p. 232.

17. Bultmann, *Jesus Christ and Mythology*, p. 53.

18. F. F. Bruce, "Form Criticism," *Baker's Dictionary of Theology* (Edited by Harrison, Bromiley, and Henry; Grand Rapids: Baker Book House, 1960), p. 227.

19. *The New Scofield Reference Bible* (New York: Oxford University Press, 1967), p. 989.

20. Ridderbos, *op. cit.*, p. 11.

21. *Ibid.*

22. Bultmann, *Kerygma and Myth*, p. 191.

23. *Ibid.*, p. 193.

24. *Ibid.*, pp. 191-192.

25. Bultmann, *Jesus Christ and Mythology*, pp. 54-55.

26. Bultmann, *Kerygma and Myth*, pp. 24-25.

27. Cobb, *op. cit.*, p. 234.

28. Bultmann, *Jesus Christ and Mythology*, pp. 22, 25-26.

29. Bultmann, *Jesus and the Word* (New York: Charles Scribner & Sons, 1934), p. 8.

30. Bultmann, *Kerygma and Myth*, p. 35.

31. *Ibid.*, p. 117.

32. Cf. George E. Ladd, "What Does Bultmann Understand by the Acts of God?" *Bulletin* of the Evangelical Theological Society, 5, 3, pp. 91-97.

33. Actually, Bultmann has moved away from this emphasis in recent years.

34. Cobb, *op. cit.*, p. 241.

35. Bultmann, *Jesus Christ and Mythology*, pp. 72-73.

36. Bultmann, *Kerygma and Myth*, p. 34.

37. *Ibid.*, p. 35.

38. *Ibid.*, pp. 35-43.

197

39. *Ibid.*, p. 35.

40. *Ibid.*, p. 38.

41. *Ibid.*, p. 36.

42. *Ibid.*, p. 37,

43. *Ibid.*

44. *Ibid.*, pp. 38-39.

45. *Ibid.*, p. 41.

46. *Ibid.*, p. 42.

47. Cited by Ridderbos, *Bultmann*, p. 28.

48. Cf. Cobb, *op. cit.*, pp. 234-235.

49. Ladd, *op. cit.*, p. 91.

50. For Bultmann's definitions of sin and grace, consult Ridderbos, *Bultmann*, p. 44.

51. Helmut Thielicke, "The Restatement of New Testament Mythology," *Kerygma and Myth*, p. 154.

52. Julius Schniewind, "A Reply to Bultmann," *Kerygma and Myth*, p. 65.

53. Clark H. Pinnock, "The 'Upper' and the 'Lower' Story in Modern Theology," Classroom notes, New Orleans Baptist Theological Seminary.

54. Pinnock, *A Defense of Biblical Infallibility* (Philadelphia: The Presbyterian and Reformed Publishing Company, 1967), p. 6.

55. James I. Packer, "Faith," *Baker's Dictionary of Theology*, p. 209.

56. Ridderbos, *Bultmann*, p. 34.

57. It is for this very reason, namely, the absence of objectivity in Bultmann's theology, that the Bultmannian "school" has come upon "hard times" and has fragmented so until now his followers are known, for lack of a more precise name, as simply "post-Bultmannians." Many of Bultmann's pupils today are insisting upon more objectivity in theology.

58. Robert L. Reymond, *A Christian View of Modern Science* (Philadelphia: The Presbyterian and Reformed Publishing Company, 1964), pp. 12-22.

CHAPTER IX

TILLICH'S "CORRELATION" THEOLOGY

ABOUT PAUL TILLICH

Paul Tillich (1886-1965) was born the son of a Lutheran clergyman in Starzeddel, a small town in the province of Brandenburg, Germany. Upon completion of Gymnasium work in Berlin in 1904 with a strong background in Latin, Greek, the classics, and the history of philosophy, he continued his studies at the Universities of Berlin, Tübingen, and Halle, finally receiving in 1911 the Ph. D. degree from Breslau. His dissertation concerned itself with Schelling's philosophy of religion. In 1912 he received the degree of Licentiate of Theology in Halle and ordination into the Evangelical Lutheran Church. During World War I he served as a chaplain in the German army, spending his intellectual hours studying art and world cultures and becoming increasingly sympathetic to the religious socialist revolution, becoming himself one of the founders of German religious socialism.

From 1919 to 1924 Tillich served as *Privatdozent* of theology at the University of Berlin, lecturing on the relation of religion to politics, art, philosophy, depth psychology, and sociology, developing at that time what he termed a "theology of culture." He moved to Marburg in 1925 as a professor of theology and there began to write his *Systematic Theology,* although the first volume was not to appear until 1951. After brief teaching assignments at Dresden and Leipzig, in 1929 he accepted a professorship in philosophy at the University of Frankfurt and remained there until dismissed by Hitler in 1933 because his religious socialism brought him into conflict with growing Nazism.

That same year Reinhold Niebuhr invited Tillich to come to Union Theological Seminary, New York, as Professor of Philosophical Theology. So at the age of forty-seven, Tillich brought his family to America and assumed a teaching career at Union Seminary which continued until his formal retirement in 1954. Throughout his long career at Union, in addition to his teaching duties, he lectured, preached, wrote, and served in many organizations, both political and philosophical.

After his retirement he went to Harvard University as University Professor, continuing as before his lecturing, writing, and traveling. In 1962, he transferred to the Divinity School of the University of Chicago as Professor of Theology. Before his death, he completed his *magnum opus,* a three-volume *Systematic Theology.*

Also important among his published works, which include many books and hundreds of scholarly articles, are *The Religious Situation, The Interpretation of History, The Protestant Era, The Courage To Be, The New Being, Biblical Religion and the Search for Ultimate Reality, The Dynamics of Faith,* and *The Shaking of the Foundations.*

Books about Tillich of interest to the American reader are *The Theology of Paul Tillich,* edited by Charles W. Kegley and Robert W. Bretall, *The Existentialist Theology of Paul Tillich* by Bernard Martin, *Paul Tillich: An Appraisal* by J. Heywood Thomas, *Paul Tillich and the Christian Message* by George H. Tavard, and *Tillich* by David Freeman.

*　　*　　*　　*　　*

According to William Hordern, Paul Tillich was a "boundary line" theologian in several ways. After his arrival in America, Tillich continued to work with European refugees and served on the Council for a Democratic Germany. Thus he stood on the boundary between European and American cultures. Many qualified thinkers view his stand theologically as somewhere between Liberalism and Neo-orthodoxy. And he definitely stood midway between philosophy and theology.[1] Perhaps here should be noted too his concept of the "boundary line of human existence" as the region where man, pushed there by despair, is confronted through revelation (ecstatic reason) with the New Being in Jesus as the Christ. This attitude indicates in itself something of Tillich's cultural concern and breadth of dialogue.

Furthermore, as a "Christian apologist," Tillich thought of himself as an "answering" theologian, that is, a thinker addressing himself to the pressing existential questions of an age of radical doubt. No one familiar with Tillich and his writings can deny that he definitely interacted with the problems of twentieth-century man. So widespread has Tillich's influence become among academicians that no discussion of contemporary theology is complete without an exposition of his system of thought.

Tillich's Theological Method

Tillich regards theology as "concerned existential statement" in that it deals with the *meaning* of reality (being-itself) *for us*. At this point Tillich is severely critical of Barth, who, so says Tillich, has utterly failed to relate the Christian message to the cultural situation. Because of his refusal to find the Word of God in any sense in the cultural situation, contending rather that the Revelation comes "straight down from above," Barth, in Tillich's opinion, has fled the field of apologetics and has thereby failed to speak to his existential situation. Viewing this as a grave deficiency, Tillich makes this task central to his purpose.

In the construction of his theology—one which attempts to respond to "the totality of man's creative self-interpretation in a special period," a concept which he terms the "situation" [2]—Tillich employs the "method of correlation." By this he means the placing in fruitful juxtaposition an analysis of the human situation, which poses the existential questions, and the Christian message, which yields the answers.[3] "Systematic theology uses the method of correlation," explains Tillich. "It has always done so, sometimes more, sometimes less, consciously, and must do so consciously and outspokenly, especially if the apologetic point of view is to prevail. The method of correlation explains the contents of the Christian faith through existential questions and theological answers in mutual interdependence." [4] Still more to the point, Tillich affirms: "In using the method of correlation, systematic theology proceeds in the following way: it makes an analysis of the human situation out of which the existential questions arise, and it demonstrates that the symbols [5] used in the Christian message are the answers to these questions. The analysis of the human situation is done in terms which today are called 'existential.' " [6]

The method of correlation replaces for Tillich what he regards as "three inadequate methods of relating the contents of the Christian faith to man's spiritual existence." [7] Against Orthodoxy and Barthian Neo-orthodoxy, it replaces *supernaturalism* because this "aberration" looks upon the Christian message as "a sum of revealed truths which have fallen into the human situation like strange bodies from a strange world," [8] answering questions which man has not asked. Against classic Liberalism, it replaces the method of *naturalism* (humanism), because this deviation "derives the Christian message from man's natural state. It develops its answers out of human existence, unaware that human existence itself *is* the question." [9] By this method, he continues, "questions and answers were put on the same level of human creativity. Everything was said by man, nothing to man. But revelation is 'spoken' to man, not by man to himself." [10] Finally, against Thomism specifically and all natural theology generally, it replaces the *dualism* of this theological error's efforts to build a supernatural structure on a natural substructure.[11] "The method of correlation," Tillich declares, "solves this historical and systematic riddle [of welding the two structures together] by resolving natural theology into the analysis of existence and by resolving supranatural theology into the answers given to the questions implied in existence." [12]

Tillich's *Systematic Theology* is divided into five parts, with each part being developed through the application of this method. "The method of correlation requires that every part of the system should include one section in which the question is developed by an analysis of human existence and existence generally, and one section in which the theological answer is given on the basis of the sources, the medium, and the norm of systematic theology." [13] In this last connection, these *sources* of systematic theology Tillich holds to be the Bible, Church history, and the history of religion and culture in general; [14] the *medium* of systematic theology to be experience, that is, participation in the sources; [15] and the material *norm* of systematic theology to be the "New Being in Jesus as the Christ." [16] Thus Tillich's systematic theological structure may be schematized as follows:

(1) The first section is entitled "Reason and Revelation" [17] and contains an analysis of man's rationality (in unity with the rational

structure of reality as a whole) and of the questions implied in the finitude, the self-estrangement, and the ambiguities of reason. This analysis presents a "situation" answered by "revelation."

(2) The second section is "Being and God" [18] and consists of an analysis of man's essential nature (in unity with the essential nature of everything that has being) and of the question implied in man's finitude and finitude generally, thus raising the question of being which Tillich answers by his affirmation of "God as the ground of being."

(3) The third section is "Existence and the Christ," [19] which consists of an analysis of man's existence (what he is but should not be) as self-estrangement from his essence (what he ought to be) (in unity with the self-destructive aspects of existence generally), thus raising the question of existential self-estrangement which Tillich answers by the "New Being in Jesus as the Christ."

(4) The fourth section is "Life and the Spirit," [20] which contains an analysis of man's life (in unity with life generally) as the complex and dynamic unity of essence and existence and an analysis of the question implied in the ambiguities of life. This analysis Tillich answers in terms of the "Spirit."

(5) The final section is entitled "History and the Kingdom of God" [21] and is an analysis of man's historical existence (in unity with the nature of the historical generally) and of the questions implied in the ambiguities of history, which Tillich answers in terms of the "Kingdom of God."

By such a structure Tillich differentiates his theology from the traditional (Orthodox) and kerygmatic (Neo-orthodox) theologies as an "answering" theology employing the method of correlation. [22]

Although Tillich expressly declares that the answers which he gives to the questions raised by his analysis of the human situation are affirmed only from within the theological framework determined by the Christian faith,[23] Cobb correctly perceives that the material in the question sections and the material in the answer sections differ only in that "in the former the depth dimension of existence or the ground of being does not come explicitly to attention," the neglect of which dimension intended to show the dire difficulties which obtain, while in the latter Tillich seeks to show that a consideration of this dimension resolves these difficulties.[24] Furthermore, "the actual norms guiding the presentation do not differ radically between the sections dealing with the situation and those presenting the answers." [25] Cobb is convinced that there are actually three distinct sources of norms that are determinative, not only for the answers to the situation raised by Tillich's analysis, but also for all of Tillich's thought—namely, the phenomenological, the ontological, and the Christian (the "New Being in Jesus as the Christ"). He realizes that his distinction here between the phenomenological and the ontological as parallel sources is foreign both to Tillich and the philosophical existentialists, the former, for Sartre and Heidegger, for example, being the methodology by which the latter is formulated and affirmed, completely apart from *inference* from experience. Tillich too "develops his ontological doctrines in close conjunction with his phenomenological descriptions," but his ontology contains inferences unwarranted by phenomenology alone, inasmuch as it "deals with God as the ground of being of finite entities as well as with characteristics of the nonhuman world that are not directly open to phenomenological investigation." [26] A simple diagram will indicate the distinction which Cobb is making between Tillich and the two phenomenologists just mentioned.

Sartre and Heidegger	That which is accessible for direct description is *phenomenological*, including the ontological.
	That which is accessible by inference or speculative generalization is *metaphysical*, and is inadmissible in a scientific ontology.
Tillich	That which is accessible for direct description is *phenomenological*.
	The *ontological* includes both the above—the phenomenological—and that which is open to inference, though by the latter is not meant the "metaphysical," a term suggestive of another world alongside this one.

Cobb concludes, therefore, that "it seems less misleading to distinguish the phenomenological, as that which falls within the sphere of direct description, from the ontological, which can be warranted only by inference or speculative generalization. In this sense, man's awareness of his contingency is phenomenological, but the assertion that God as being-itself is the ground of being is ontological." [27] The question may be posed here, the full answer to be postponed until our criticism, whether Tillich's answer sections, determined, as Cobb has correctly seen, by ontology as well as by the theological norm of Jesus as the Christ, are actually affirmed only from within the theological circle determined by the Christian faith. A negative decision appears to be in order. But this much is clear from the discussion so far: Tillich starts with philosophy asking the questions and *wants* to allow Christian theology to give the answers to the philosophical "situation."

Tillich's Philosophical Beginning—Ontology

Tillich believes that the sum and substance of philosophy is ontology, that is, that philosophy is concerned with being-itself. In his *Systematic Theology* he calls philosophy "that cognitive approach to reality in which reality as such is the object." [28] And again, "Philosophy asks the question of being as being. It investigates the character of everything that is in so far as it is. This is its basic task, and the answer it provides determines the analysis of all special forms of being. It is 'first philosophy,' or, if the term still could be used, 'metaphysics.' Since the connotations of the term 'metaphysics' make its use precarious, the word 'ontology' is preferable." [29] Yet this ontology must emerge from the existential situation in which man finds himself: "The ontological question presupposes an asking subject and an object about which the question is asked; it presupposes the subject-object structure of being." [30] To make his ontology as scientifically accurate as possible, Tillich employs the phenomenological method of inquiry in his probe into being in its human expression. We recognize with Cobb that Tillich does not separate ontology from phenomenology in his system but rather "passes back and forth repeatedly between them, employing ontological categories in the phenomenological expositions." [31] But in order to show more lucidly the interrelatedness of his thought, this distinction suggested by Cobb serves a very useful purpose.

Tillich's phenomenology. At the phenomenological or human level, that is, in his analysis of human existence, Tillich is concerned with universal phenomena common and central to man's existence as such which do not presuppose specifically *Christian* existence. Three main areas of investigation for Tillich in this connection are reason, faith, and estrangement. We present here the conclusions of his analyses.

(1) Reason for Tillich is common and central to human existence as such, but he alleges that "under the conditions of existence the structural elements of reason [receiving and shaping] move against each other. Although never completely separated, they fall into self-destructive conflicts which cannot be solved on the basis of actual reason." [32] In short, the *essential* unity of reason (what it ought to be) is broken under the conditions of its *existence* (what it is but should not be). This moving of the structural elements of reason against each other Tillich speaks of as "polarities" and "polar tension," the former designating a pair of terms that face in opposite directions but that demand each other at the same time, the latter speaking of the inherent tension between the terms always present under conditions of existence. Actual reason in human existence is finite, self-contradictory, and relative, and hence can grasp only relativities. Thus Tillich sees in reason in its existential state the following polarities:

(a) *Between autonomous reason and heteronomous reason.* [33] *Autonomous* thought is reason subject only to its own structure without regard to its "depth" (the *logos* of being-itself). It tries to keep itself free from all outside impressions. *Heteronomous* thought is reason which imposes "another" law upon the structure of reason, justifying itself in the name of the ground of reason. It is a reaction against autonomous thought which has lost its depth and has become empty and powerless. There is endless tension between these two polarities, necessarily giving rise to the quest for *theonomous* reason, which is reason united to its own depth. Thus, concludes Tillich, the quest for revelation arises out of reason itself.

(b) *Between absolutism and relativism.*[34] "Criticism," both Socratic and Kantian, in philosophy was and is an effort to overcome the polarity between absolutism and relativism in reason, but in Tillich's opinion, "critical" philosophy has failed. Rather, this tension gives rise to the quest for the "concrete-absolute," which alone can relieve this tension.

(c) *Between the rational and irrational elements of reason.*[35] The tension between cognition and legal functions of the mind, on the one hand, and aesthetic and communal functions of the mind, on the other, gives rise to the quest for the *union* (or *re*union) of form (logic) and mystery (emotion).

Tillich concludes that in all three cases reason is driven to the quest for revelation. Precisely what the nature of this revelation is we shall see presently.

(2) Faith too for Tillich is a universal human phenomenon and thus a suitable topic for phenomenology.[36] "It is exhibited in all seriousness whether it takes the form of belief or doubt, of theism or atheism, of Christianity or paganism." [37]

Phenomenologically, faith to Tillich is "the state of being ultimately concerned." [38] But it may also be, as a philosophical expression of Mark 12:29, "the state of being ultimately concerned about the ultimate." [39] Thus faith may be considered in two ways: as ultimate concern with finite entities, such as a nation or "success," [40] or as ultimate concern about the infinite, the unconditioned, the ultimate. In several places,[41] Tillich attempts to show that the placing of faith in any finite entity is an attitude constituting idolatry. In fact, protestation against idolatry thus conceived is what Tillich calls "the Protestant principle of protest." [42]

Like reason, faith demands a transcendent dimension of depth which will overcome its finitude. As Cobb succinctly states: "The *concern* of ultimate concern may be directed toward objects or states of affairs in the spatiotemporal continuum of worldly events. But the *ultimacy* of ultimate concern points to a dimension of all existence that cannot be understood at that level." [43] Otherwise, there is no answer to the question implied in finitude. Tillich writes: " 'God' is the answer to the question implied in man's finitude; he is the name for that which concerns man ultimately. . . . The phrase 'being ultimately concerned' points to a tension in human experience. . . . Ultimate concern must transcend every preliminary finite and concrete concern. It must transcend the whole realm of finitude in order to be the answer to the question implied in finitude." [44]

This transcendent dimension must not only overcome finitude but also it must be holy. "Holiness," writes Tillich, "is an experienced phenomenon; it is open to phenomenological description. . . . The holy is the *quality* of that which concerns man ultimately. Only that which is holy can give man ultimate concern, and only that which gives man ultimate concern has the quality of holiness." [45] Thus "the experience of the holy reinforces further the view that the true object of faith is never a finite, conditioned entity. The mystery and fascination [46] of the holy points to the dimension that transcends the sphere of spatiotemporal subjects and objects." [47]

The two aspects of faith (as ultimate concern for the ultimate) which cause it to look for its depth or ground of being in a transcendent dimension are the experience of *finitude* and the experience of the *holy*. True faith points then beyond itself and conditional existence and demands a relatedness to an unconditional dimension of existence. It thus points us to a "theological" ontology.

(3) Estrangement is the third area of Tillich's phenomenological description. He bases his construction on the "creation/fall myth" of Genesis 1-3.[48] Tillich sees man as having "fallen away" from his true essence. Human existence is deeply divided in its totality: man is aware of an *ideal* or normative possibility for his being as his true being or *essence;* he is also aware of his *actual* being that falls short of his ideal being, which is his empirical actuality or *existence*.[49] This distinction between man's essence and existence Tillich terms alienation, estrangement, and "fall." (By the last term, it hardly needs saying, Tillich would not want to be understood as advocating the literal fall of Adam.[50])

How is man's "fall" to be understood with respect to its *possibility* and *motive*? Tillich states that man's freedom or power to contradict himself (that is, the ability to decide his destiny as an autonomous being) makes *possible* the transition from essence to existence. As for the *motives* that so drive men to exercise their freedom that the transition actually occurs, here Tillich turns for his answer to Freudian depth psychology. His discussion presupposes some image of the state of essential being. This essence from which men fall Tillich characterizes by the Freudian term "dreaming innocence," connoting lack of experience, lack of personal responsibility, and lack of moral guilt, or by the state of *undecided potentialities*. An "awakening" from this state is inevitable, for the state of dreaming innocence drives beyond itself, motivated by the awareness of finite freedom and by anxiety (*Angst*). When man becomes aware of his finite freedom, he is driven by anxiety (aroused freedom) towards efforts to actualize it. And this freedom produces a reaction with the destiny characterizing the state of dreaming innocence, which wishes to preserve itself. "Man is caught between the desire to actualize his freedom and the demand to preserve his dreaming innocence. In the power of his finite freedom, he decides for actualization." [51] In this "psychological fall," when man decides for actualization, he gains experience, personal responsibility, and moral guilt and *moves from essense to existence,* the latter characterized by unbelief, self-elevation (*hubris*), and concupiscence.[52] By *unbelief,* Tillich has in mind man, in his existential self-realization, turning toward himself and his world and losing his essential unity with the ground of his being and his world.[53] By *self-elevation,* Tillich simply has reference to the other side of unbelief: man becomes the center of himself and his world.[54] By *concupiscence,* Tillich refers to "the unlimited character of the strivings for knowledge, sex, and power." [55] This estrangement in man must be thoroughly understood since it is to this specific human condition that Tillich relates the "work of Christ."

Further phenomenological analysis shows essence and existence to be polarities. Out of the basic ontological structure of self and world [56] arise (1) the polarities of personality and community,[57] (2) the polarities of vitality and intentionality,[58] and (3) the polarities of freedom and destiny.[59] The ideal balance of these polarities Tillich conceives as being man's essential being, but man's actual and constant striving toward one pole away from the other is his existential being, which constitutes his "fallenness" and threatens the very humanity of his existence.[60]

Still further phenomenological analysis reveals in man an awareness of finitude (anxiety), radical contingency, and the certainty of death. "We experience our being as having no necessity, as not having in itself the ground of its being." [61] This lack of being in himself points man away from himself to a dimension of being-itself. Even when man, with "the courage to be," determines to live in the face of his finitude, this very courage points to a transcendent dimension of being.[62]

By way of summary, Tillich's descriptions of reason, faith, and estrangement seek to show that all three point away to another dimension, to unconditioned reality, indeed, to a theologically-oriented ontology.

Tillich's ontology. Tillich stands in the classic tradition of Western philosophy in its concern with the problem of being. However, by means of the phenomenological method, he seeks to develop a truly scientific theory of being. We have seen that Tillich in his phenomenological description of human existence detects polarities in reason, faith, and estrangement. Extending his analysis, Tillich declares that the polarities detected in human existence as such characterize finite being as such. Cobb elucidates Tillich's thought here: "What we grasped phenomenologically as our human situation is now seen as the universal characteristic of finite being as such, although only in man does it come to self-consciousness."[63]

With regard to *reason,* the phenomenological polarities of autonomous and heteronomous thought are reflected by the polarities of structure and depth at the ontological level. By structure Tillich means that which makes it possible for the mind to grasp and to transform reality; by depth is intended the expression of something that is not reason but which precedes reason and is manifest through it.[64] Tillich asserts that reality has a *logos* character. The mind is supposedly so constituted that it grasps and shapes reality on the basis of a corresponding structure in reality. Again, the phenomenological polarities of absolutism and relativism in reason are reflected by the polarities of static element and dynamic element at the ontological level.[65] The static element preserves the reason from losing its identity within the life-process; the dynamic element is the power of reason to actualize itself rationally in the life-process. Finally, the phenomenological polarities of rationalism and irrationalism are reflected by the polarities of formalism and emotionalism on the ontological level.[66]

With regard to *estrangement,* the phenomenological polarities of personality and community are reflected by the polarities of individualization and participation on the ontological level.[67] The phenomenological polarities of vitality and intentionality are reflected by the polarities of dynamics and form on the ontological level.[68] And the phenomenological polarities of freedom and destiny are "the human analogues of the universal polar elements of spontaneity and law."[69]

Tillich claims that the tension between essence and existence which he has shown to exist on both the phenomenological and ontological levels is one that has been recognized by and which has pervaded the whole tradition of Western ontological thought. For example, Plato conceived of essence and existence as the world of ideas and the material world which participates in that world. Aristotle conceived of them in the polarities of potentiality and actuality. (The Greeks generally spoke of the tension between Form and Matter.) In more recent times Kierkegaard contrasted essence and existence; Spinoza and Hegel derived existence from essence; and Dewey and Sartre derived essence from existence. In making this distinction, affirms Tillich, philosophy has taken cognizance of a real split or duality in being which everywhere manifests itself.

But philosophy has not been alone in recognizing this duality. According to Tillich, Christian theology reflects its own experience and vision of this duality, speaking of an *original* condition of the world and of man and the *present* "fallen" condition of the world and of man.[70]

Hence the duality, the tension, and the finitude of this spatio-temporal sphere all point away from this sphere to another dimension, to the unconditioned ground of being, to being itself, to that with which one should be ultimately concerned, where the togetherness of self and world is rooted in that which is neither subject nor object but the ground of both, where the togetherness of essence and existence is rooted in that which is beyond both essence and existence.[71] And it is in this major nuance of his thought that Tillich's ontology overtly becomes theology as well.

Tillich's Theological Response

Having ascribed, on the one hand, great powers to philosophy by formulating the human problem in philosophical (ontological) terms, Tillich denies, on the other hand, to philosophy as such the function of resolution and answer. He contends that philosophy deals only with the *structures* of being generally, while theology deals with the *meaning* of being for us.[72] So, for the "answers" to philosophically-framed questions, he turns to theology. But even here, as we shall see, he continues to frame the answers in philosophical categories, speaking, for example, of revelation as "ecstatic reason," of God as the ground of being, and of the reconciliation of existential self-estrangement as the New Being in Jesus as the Christ. Turning now to Tillich's understanding of revelation, God, Christ, and salvation, as the theological answers to the existential situation, we shall look at each of these in turn. Before we do this, however, we must say a word about Tillich's claim that theological language is symbolic.

Symbolic God-talk. Since God as the ground of being transcends the spatiotemporal sphere, Tillich contends that language about God cannot be understood literally but must be understood and intended as *symbols.* Except for the assertion that God is being-itself, Tillich affirms that "there can be no doubt that any concrete assertion about God must be symbolic." [73] For him, a term, when used as a religious symbol, represents something which is not itself but which has power to open up levels of reality otherwise incomprehensible. Thus, only a religious symbol can open up the depth dimension of reality itself, the ground of every other dimension. When religious symbols are not recognized as such but are taken literally, they become false and actually lead one away from an understanding of God. Thus, whereas Bultmann would insist that we demythologize the Bible, Tillich calls for a "deliteralization" of the Bible by which he means that one must reject "every interpretation of religious language that treats it as if it were speaking of events or entities at the finite level." [74] A proper understanding of Tillich's concept of religious language will explain why he draws the conclusions which he does pertaining to theological themes.

Revelation. We have already seen that Tillich maintains the existence of polarities or tensions in reason, both phenomenologically and ontologically, driving reason to quest for "revelation." This is so because it is Tillich's basic contention that the conflicts and tensions of reason are finally overcome only in the situation of revelation in which reason becomes "ecstatic" or "self-transcending." At this point Tillich clearly becomes the theologian as he seeks to correlate philosophy and theology into a philosophical theology. [75]

For Tillich revelation is the manifestation of the mystery of the ground of being, (1) mediated through the objective "miracle" and

212

(2) received through the subjective "ecstasy" of the mind. Genuine mystery appears when reason is driven beyond itself to its *ground* and *abyss,* to the fact that being is and non-being is not, to the original fact that there is something and not nothing. This is the manifestation of what concerns us ultimately.[76] But what drives reason beyond itself to its ground, to this ultimate mystery? Tillich responds with *miracle,* but refers thereby, not to the traditional understanding of miracle as God's active creative rearrangement of a divinely-controlled uniformity in nature, but to the expression of finitude (or threat of being overcome by non-being) to which everything is inescapably subject.[77] The *positive* side of the mystery of being is experienced as that which concerns us ultimately since it is the *ground* of our being; the threat of non-being, grasping the mind, produces the "ontological shock" in which the *negative* side of the mystery of being, namely, *abyss,* is experienced. Seeking the *meaning* of the mystery, Tillich interprets it theologically in its two essential elements—ground and abyss, thereby identifying this ground of being *symbolically* as God. What is revelation for Tillich, and what does it teach then? Basically, revelation is a situation in which reason becomes ecstatic, that is, transcends its ordinary structure through a simultaneous experience of the *shock* of non-being and of the *power* of being overcoming it. It produces the basic understanding that the actuality of God is being-itself, that is, the infinite ground of being in everything.

God as the ground of being. According to Tillich, philosophy, as ontology, raises the question, why does anything at all exist? Furthermore, why does it perpetuate itself? These questions necessarily drive one to the power of the being of everything, or to the ground of being. This ground of being (being-itself) Tillich symbolically designates as God.

How is this God's "existence" to be understood? Since being-itself is an abstraction from the concrete, finite entities that exist, dare we speak of the *existence* of being-itself? Tillich emphatically denies that we should so speak: "The being of God is being-itself. The being of God cannot be understood as the existence of a being alongside others or above others. If God is *a* being, he is subject to the categories of finitude, especially to space and substance." [78] "As being-itself God is beyond the contrast of essential and existential being. . . . Logically, being-itself is 'before,' 'prior to,' the split which characterizes finite being. For this reason it is as wrong to speak of God as the universal essence as it is to speak of him as existing." [79] Tillich continues: ". . . grave difficulties attend the attempt to speak of God as existing. . . . the question of the existence of God can be neither asked nor answered. If asked, it is a question about that which by its very nature is above existence, and therefore the answer—whether negative or affirmative—implicitly denies the nature of God. It is as atheistic to affirm the existence of God as it is to deny it." [80] He concludes: "God does not exist. He is being-itself beyond essence and existence. Therefore, to argue that God exists is to deny him." [81]

One might at first conclude that Tillich has simply redefined the meaning of the term "existence" so as not to include the being of Deity within it. But Tillich's denial of God's existence is more than simply an exercise in semantics, for Tillich's concept of God as being-itself excludes the Biblical doctrine of the ontological Trinity as three persons in the Godhead, "the same in substance, equal in power and glory," and postulates this being-itself as *neither supernatural nor natural.* Rather, he sees God's being in terms of "self-transcendence." "An idea of God which overcomes the conflict of naturalism and supranaturalism could be called 'self-transcendent' or 'ecstatic.'" [82] How is "self-transcendence" related to supernaturalism and naturalism? What do these terms mean in this connection? *Supernaturalism,* says Tillich, is that religious view that "separates God as a being, the highest being, from all other beings, alongside and above which he has his existence. In this position he has brought the universe into being at a certain moment (five thousand or five billion years ago), governs it according to a plan, directs it toward an end, interferes with its processes in order to overcome resistance and to fulfill his purpose, and will bring it to consummation in a final catastrophe." [83] Now though this is the Biblical picture of God, creation, and providence, Tillich rejects this "primitive form of supranaturalism" because "it transforms the infinity of God into a finiteness which is merely an extension of the categories of finitude. This is done in respect to space by establishing a supranatural divine world alongside the natural human world; in respect to time by determining a beginning and an end of God's creativity; in respect to causality by making God a cause alongside other causes; in respect to substance by attributing individual substance to him." [84] *Naturalism* is the religious view that "identifies God with the universe, with its essence or with special powers within it. God is the name for the power and meaning of reality." [85] Now though this is an accurate description of the materialist's, the pantheist's, and the "process" philosopher's views of God, Tillich rejects this too, because "it denies the infinite distance between the whole of finite things and their infinite ground, with the consequence that the term 'God' becomes interchangeable with the term 'universe' and therefore is semantically superfluous." [86] Tillich is now ready to define God as the self-transcendent ground of being: "God is neither alongside things nor even 'above' them; he is nearer to them than they are to themselves. He is their creative ground, here and now, always and everywhere." [87] Realizing that this could be understood as a form of naturalism, Tillich distinguishes his view from naturalism (or thinks he does) by stating: "The term 'self-transcendent' has two elements: 'transcending' and 'self.' God as the ground of being infinitely transcends that of which he is the ground. He stands *against* the world, in so far as the world stands against him, and he stands *for* the world, thereby causing it to stand for him. This mutual freedom from each other and for each other is [the sense in which we can] speak of 'transcendent' with respect to the relation of God and world. [This means] that, within itself, the finite world points beyond itself. In other words, it is self-transcendent. Now the need for the syllable 'self' in 'self-transcendent' has also become understandable: the one reality which we encounter is experienced in different dimensions which point to one another. The finitude of the finite points to the infinity of the infinite. It goes beyond itself in order to return to itself in a new dimension. This is what 'self-transcendence' means." [88] We shall not comment upon Tillich's understanding of God at this point. Rather, we shall follow Tillich in the development of his *Christian* understanding of God.

The New Being in Jesus as the Christ. To this point in our exposition of his thought, one might conclude that Tillich is simply a philosopher reflecting on the reason for all things, but Tillich thinks of himself as a *Christian* philosopher-theologian, takes his stand unabashedly within the Christian tradition, and earnestly desires to relate the Christian message to his age. Moreover, he does not think of himself as doing this in any liberal sense, inasmuch as he conceives of Christian theology as including the claim to its own finality,[89] this finality being found in Christ as the normative revelation of God.

What is Tillich's understanding of Jesus as this final revelation of God? "Christian theology in every age is the exposition of the significance of [the final revelation of God in Jesus as the Christ] in the context of the self-understanding of that age. If men perceive their problem as God's wrath upon them for their sins, Jesus as the Christ is preached as the forgiveness of sins. If men perceive their problem as the need of guidance and aid in the achievement of a nearer approximation to ideal life, Jesus as the Christ is preached as the ideal person. Today [in Tillich's view, on the basis of his phenomenological description of human existence] man perceives his problem in terms of alienation, despair, and meaninglessness. Jesus as the Christ [according to Tillich, then] must be proclaimed as the bearer of the New Being in which man is healed and enters a new level of life." [90] It is within this context that Tillich sets his Christology, constantly affirming the "New Being in Jesus as the Christ" to be the healing which modern man so desperately needs. As for Jesus as the bearer of the New Being being understood as the *final* revelation of God, Tillich means that Jesus, not as a person, but as a principle serves as the *norm* to judge the "wholeness" which the man who finds healing experiences.

The fundamental and paradoxical affirmation of the Christian faith, according to Tillich, is that "in *one* personal life essential manhood has appeared under the conditions of existence without being conquered by them." [91] In maintaining a permanent unity with God (the ground of his being) despite his participation in all the conditions and consequences of existential estrangement, Jesus becomes the actualization of essential manhood or essential God-manhood.

According to Tillich, critical historical study can neither verify nor destroy the foundation of the Christian faith, for the foundation of this faith is not some particular word or deed which a certain Jewish rabbi named Jesus spoke or performed in the early part of the first century. Rather the foundation of the Christian faith is the *picture* of Jesus as the Christ which lies on the pages of the

New Testament: "The power which has created and preserved the community of the New Being is not an abstract statement about its appearance; it is the picture of him in whom it has appeared. No special trait of this picture can be verified with certainty. But it can be definitely asserted that through this picture the New Being has power to transform those who are transformed by it." [92] But do we know this picture to be true? Tillich admits that we cannot, in the strict sense, know any such facts of history to be true. We do know, however, that the picture of Jesus recorded in the New Testament (whether or not it is correct as to detail, even the detail of the name of the person who inspired it [93]) points to the historical existence of a personal life capable of inspiring it. The skepticism of historical research may cast doubt upon every detail of the life portrayed in the Biblical picture, but it cannot, according to Tillich, "overthrow what is guaranteed by the experience of faith, namely, that this picture has a transforming effect upon those who are grasped by it and that the power of the New Being is expressed in and through it." [94]

Martin maintains that for Tillich Jesus as the Christ "is both a historical fact and a subject of believing reception, and that Christianity must assert both sides of this event on which it is based." [95] On the one hand, it must emphasize the historicity of the personal life designated by the name Jesus. On the other hand, it must also emphasize the believing reception of Jesus as the Christ by the disciples and subsequent generations.[96] Otherwise, he would not have been the Christ but only perhaps an historically and religiously important person and as such a preliminary revelation, but only that, a prophetic anticipation of the New Being, but only that.

In what sense is Jesus as the Christ the bearer of the New Being? "Jesus as the Christ is the bearer of the New Being in the totality of his being, not in any special expression of it. It is his being that makes him the Christ because his being has the quality of the New Being beyond the split of essential and existential being. From this is follows that neither his words, deeds, or sufferings nor what is called his 'inner life' makes him the Christ." [97]

Tillich emphasizes that the New Testament pictures Jesus as (1) being involved in existence, and yet (2) remaining unconquered by existence. Each of these points is important for a correct understanding of Tillich's construction of Jesus as the Christ. For Tillich

Jesus *is* not the Christ; he *becomes* the Christ. And this becoming the Christ Jesus accomplishes in his victory over existence. The New Testament pictures Jesus as participating completely in existence. This is depicted, first by his finitude: "In [the New Testament] he is portrayed as having to die and as sharply experiencing the anxiety connected with the awareness of this fact. In it he is also portrayed as subject to homelessness or lack of a definite place in the world; to want; to bodily, social and mental insecurity; to loneliness and separation from others; to uncertainty and outright error in his intellectual conceptions and beliefs; to doubt about himself and his work; and to the feeling that he has been abandoned by God." [98] It is depicted, secondly, by his involvement in the ambiguity of guilt: by making the Pharisees and the leaders of his people guilty in his tragic conflict with them, he himself becomes guilty.[99] But in the New Testament picture of his victory over existence, that is, over unbelief, self-elevation (*hubris*), and concupiscence (cf. the discussion of estrangement), the Christ-character of Jesus, that is, his character as the New Being (or as the One who—despite his being only finite in freedom and despite his involvement in all the negativities of the human predicament—does not lose his essential unity with God) is borne out.[100] This is not to say that Tillich believes in the sinlessness of Jesus: "There is, in fact, no enumeration of special sins which he did not commit, nor is there a day-to-day description of the ambiguities of life in which he proved to be unambiguously good. He rejects the term 'good' as applicable to himself in isolation from God and puts the problem in the right place, namely, the uniqueness of his relation to God." [101] The New Testament picture of Jesus as the Christ emphasizes, then, two basic elements: his subjection to the conditions of existential estrangement and his victory over them. By these Jesus as the Christ becomes the bearer of the New Being to men.

The cross- and resurrection-symbols. The dual relationship which Jesus sustains to existence is confirmed, according to Tillich, by the two central symbols in which the New Testament expresses its understanding of the universal significance of the event of Jesus as the Christ, namely, by the cross and resurrection.

The cross symbolizes Jesus' subjection to existence. Tillich accepts the historicity of the event of the cross,[102] but sees certain other "myths" or symbols of the New Testament corroborating this more central symbol. Among these are (1) the idea of subjection of self expressed in the Pauline "myth" of Philippians 2 (which he rejects as unhistorical [103]); (2) the "unhistorical legends" of the lowly birth of Christ in Bethlehem, his lying in a cradle, his flight to Egypt, and the early threat to his life by the political powers [104]; and (3) the scene of Gethsemane and his burial.[105]

The resurrection symbolizes Christ's victory over the existential self-estrangement to which he subjected himself. Tillich rejects the historicity of the resurrection event itself but does affirm an historical event underlying the "myth" of the resurrection, namely, the disciples' experience of the certainty of their own victory over existential estrangement which they received through participating in the spiritual personality of Jesus. After reviewing several theories developed to explain the resurrection accounts (such as the physical, spiritual, and psychological) and finding them all inadequate,[106] Tillich sets forth his own theory (which he calls the "restitution" theory) in terms of the negativity which is symbolized as having been overcome in the resurrection stories: "The negativity which is overcome in the Resurrection is that of the disappearance of him whose being was the New Being. It is the overcoming of his disappearance from present experience and his consequent transition into the past except for the limits of memory." [107] Martin has captured Tillich's thought quite precisely: "According to Tillich's theory, the power of Jesus' being impressed itself so sharply on his disciples as the power of the New Being that, after his death, they underwent an ecstatic experience in which 'the concrete picture of Jesus of Nazareth became indissolubly united with the reality of the New Being.' They then experienced him as one whom death was not able to push into the past but who is spiritually present whenever the New Being is present." [108] "This presence does not have the character of a revived (and transmuted) body, nor does it have the character of the reappearance of an individual soul," writes Tillich.[109] It is only a spiritual presence, but this presence is the event which was interpreted in the New Testament through the symbol of the resurrection; and the experience of the disciples of being grasped by his presence, thus "healing" them, is duplicated in all those who in every age experience his living presence here and now.

As in the case of the symbol of the cross, certain lesser symbols corroborate the more central symbol of Christ's resurrection. They are as follows: (1) Jesus' pre-existence, (2) the "myth" of the virgin birth, (3) the transfiguration, (4) the miracle stories, (5) the ascension, (6) his present intercession at the Father's right hand, (7) the second coming, and (8) the ultimate and final judgment of the world by Christ. None of these symbols, according to Tillich, should be understood literally (if taken so, they are "reduced to absurdities"); but if taken symbolically, they strengthen the New Testament picture of Jesus as the Christ gaining victory over existential estrangement.[110]

Salvation. Salvation for Tillich is to be interpreted in the modern period as "healing" in the sense of "reuniting that which is estranged, giving a center to what is split, overcoming the split between God and man, man and his world, man and himself."[111] Modern man, according to Tillich, is estranged from himself, that is, he has fallen away from his true essence and exists in unbelief, self-elevation, and concupiscence. The modern minister's task is to direct his hearer's attention to the New Being in Jesus as the Christ since Jesus as the Christ is one who *like* him was immersed in existence but who *unlike* him overcame his *existence* by remaining ever *essentially* united to the ground of his being. He then is hope; he then is example. But more than that, he is *real help* because those who are grasped by his living presence, as were the disciples, and participate in it, that is, for those who experience existentially the realization that his presence as "New Being" is theirs, experience salvation or healing, which assumes a threefold character: regeneration, justification, and sanctification—not three different events, but three aspects of the one "saving event." First, participation in the New Being is regeneration, or "new birth." Regeneration is "the state of having been drawn into the new reality manifest in Jesus as the Christ";[112] and in this state, ". . . the characteristics of the New Being are the opposite of those of estrangement, namely, faith instead of unbelief, surrender instead of *hubris,* love instead of concupiscence."[113] Second, acceptance of the New Being is justification, but specifically the *subjective* side of justification. "There is nothing in man which enables God to accept him. But man must accept just this. He must accept that he is accepted;

he must accept acceptance." [114] On the *objective* side, justification is the "eternal act of God by which he accepts as not estranged those who are indeed estranged from him by guilt and the act by which he takes them into the unity with him which is manifest in the New Being in Christ." [115] Third, transformation by the New Being is sanctification, distinguished from the former two as a process is distinguished from an event, in which the power of the New Being transforms personality and community, inside and outside the church.[116]

Both the individual Christian and the church, and both the religious and the secular realms as objects of the sanctifying work of the divine Spirit of the New Being, are the central concerns of the third volume of Tillich's *Systematic Theology* and receive detailed treatment there. Since the content of this volume is not germane to the present purpose, we will now turn to a criticism of Tillich.

Criticism

Until his death, Paul Tillich personally spearheaded the mid-twentieth-century urge to relate the Christian message to this age of radical doubt. The task he chose for himself was to decipher man's problems existentially and to find a new and meaningful way of speaking to him about God. To accomplish these ends, Tillich, among other endeavors, wrote his monumental *Systematic Theology*. He who spends much time in its pages will be forced to admit that its author was a brilliant philosopher-theologian, equally at home in both sciences. Nevertheless, the truly Christian man must also admit that Tillich's conclusions are, from the point of view of the Christian theism of Scripture, definitely sub-Christian. Of course, Tillich would freely admit his deviation from traditional Protestant Orthodoxy; nevertheless, he feels that he has retained the essentials of genuine Christianity. But has he? To this specific point we address the following remarks of this criticism.

The Bible. If Christianity is anything at all, it is a "book religion," that is, a religion which claims to base all of its teachings upon a particular body of writing, in this case, the Bible. This priority is given to the Bible, not only because of its own claims of necessity and authority, sufficiency and finality, but also because the

Lord of the Church, God manifest in human flesh, throughout his teaching placed his imprimatur upon it in whole and in part. The Christian Church has always felt that it held the advantage at this point over the other "book religions" of the world, since its Lord, "declared to be the Son of God with power, according to the spirit of holiness, *by the resurrection from the dead,"* vouchsafed its inspiration, veracity, and trustworthiness during his earthly ministry. And even the most liberal interpreters of Scripture have felt compelled to admit that the Gospels do depict a Christ who had the highest regard for Scripture, though they have aborted the significance of their concession by offering varying theories to explain why Christ's attitude need not be theirs. But all of them—the kenosis theory, the accommodation theory, the form-critical theory, and the "inadequacy of language" theory—fail to destroy Jesus' testimony to the Scriptures.[117]

Of course, Tillich would insist that this attitude toward Jesus' opinion concerning Scripture completely overlooks the "corruptions and contradictions" with which the Scripture is replete and which have been uncovered by the science of textual criticism. He would contend that the conservative Christian refuses to face all "the facts." To the contrary, the conservative does not evade these textual difficulties. He is simply *unconvinced* that the evidence for the many "corruptions and contradictions" is as incontrovertible as the text critic claims. Candidly admitting that textual difficulties have been introduced into the Scriptures through scribal negligence, he is even more concerned than the negative critic that these errors be ferreted out and the original text recovered. There is one thing of which the conservative *is* convinced however; he is persuaded that it is the liberal critic such as Tillich who has refused to face all the facts. Packer states the case ably: "[The liberals] accuse us of not facing all the facts. We reply that they think this is so only because they themselves do not face all the facts. The boot is on the other foot. They say we fail to meet the claims of reason. We say that they fail to meet the claims of *Christian* reason; and that it is they, rather than we, who weaken the Church's intellectual life, in that they discourage Christians from using their minds in a manner consistent with their faith."[118] The Christian man has faced one fact that the liberal establishment refuses to face: he has faced squarely the all-important claims of the Biblical Christ and his authentication of Scripture.

The upshot of the liberal attitude is clear; sheer unbelief is the only obstacle to accepting Christ's statements concerning Scripture; the liberal theories are transparently weak. Now either Jesus Christ is or is not God. If he is not God in the fullest sense of the word, there is no compelling reason to believe anything he said nor is he worthy of any man's trust or of such titles as "Lord" and "Master." If, on the other hand, he was and is God manifest in the flesh, his divine character guarantees the truth of his teachings, and he who would follow him as a disciple should not question his Master's word.

This is precisely the issue that Tillich has refused to face squarely. Though claiming as his context of theological utterance the Christian circle, he rejects the Bible as the revealed Word of God concerning man's sinful condition and the remedy provided in Christ's substitutionary atonement and self-consciously substitutes alien guiding principles, namely, existentialism, history of religions, and culture in general. Not only, as we have noted, does he reject the supernaturalism of Scripture as being "primitive," but also he finds it "impossible" in the writing of his *Systematic Theology* (because of "personal, practical limitations") "to make extensive references to the Bible." [119] Now no author should be overly faulted for omissions since personal limitations and space are definite writing factors, but for a professing Protestant Christian theologian to write a systematic theology and therein to treat the Bible as merely one source of several is unforgivable. It is apparent from a reading of Tillich that he simply has no real appreciation of Biblical study. Convinced as he is that theology must respond to the "situation," and equally convinced that the Bible, if understood in the traditional sense, has no applicability to this age, Tillich turns to philosophy in the effort to analyze contemporary man's deepest problems of existence. Admittedly, his description of man's plight as self-estrangement and despair is penetrating, but how far short it comes in comparison to the Bible's teaching on the nature of sin! Actually, if the orthodox proclamation of the Christian message has ceased to "speak" to modern man, it is due in part to such theologians as Tillich who have substituted "another gospel" for the Biblical message with the result that modern man has grown unaccustomed to the true message. The orthodox Christian contemns Tillich's (and every other modern theologian's) capitalizing on the "power" which has adhered to certain words such as "cross" and "resurrection" in order to propagate a false gospel. He is convinced, furthermore, that the sooner modern congregations hear once again the Biblical message preached in power and taught with clarity, both in Biblical terminology, the sooner this age's ills will be "healed." Tillich's theology fails utterly here.

Tillich's methodology. As we have seen, Tillich's methodology is that of correlating philosophy (ontology) and theology, the former asking the questions and the latter answering them. Also we have noted that Tillich expressly affirms that these answers are derived from the Christian faith and affirmed only from within what he calls "the theological circle" of that faith. But, as George F. Thomas, of the Princeton University Department of Religion, has rightly seen, "the main difficulty with Tillich's 'method of correlation' and with the 'structure' based upon it is that he seems to allow to philosophy in its analysis of the human situation an 'autonomy' which is not rooted in 'theonomy.' Only the 'theonomous,' the 'saved' reason, according to his own view, can be expected to see the truth of the situation clearly and profoundly. Only such a reason can properly formulate the 'questions' to which the Christian message gives the 'answers.' [But] can a philosophical reason which has not been fully 'converted' by the Christian faith correctly formulate the 'structure' and "categories' of Being and raise the deepest 'questions' implied in existence? If not, will not the Christian 'answers,' whose form is determined by the nature of the 'questions,' be distorted or obscured?" Thomas illustrates what he means: " 'God,' says Tillich, 'is the answer to the question implied in being,' a question which arises in 'the shock of possible non-being.' This is the 'question' raised by philosophy. What is the 'answer' given by theology? The being of God is 'being-itself.' " [120] And from this answer, as Thomas shows, Tillich draws the inference that God, contrary to the Christian message, is neither *a* being nor personal. Tillich's answer to man's self-estrangement in terms of the "New Being in Jesus as the Christ" is also informed by impersonalistic elements. Cobb's conclusion is correct: ". . . it is clear to the reader of *Systematic Theology* that the actual norms guiding the presentation do not differ radically between the sections dealing with the situation and those presenting the answers. Phenomenological analysis and ontological analysis are employed extensively in both sections, and the results of analyses in the sections on the situation are employed normatively in the sections in which the answers are presented." [121] Thus Tillich has not escaped the error of natural theology, namely, permitting the philosophical presuppositions of the system so to pervert the Scriptural revelation that the latter ceases to call men to turn from themselves to full faith in Jesus Christ as Savior from sin and as Lord of life. There is, in Tillich's case, grave doubt as to whether he has actually listened to the Bible or to the Christian faith at all. Where he does allude to Biblical events and norms, they are either completely reinterpreted as "symbolic" or so thoroughly reinformed with alien impersonalistic philosophy that they are not recognizable as Christian.

Tillich's doctrine of God. According to Orthodoxy, God is a "Spirit, infinite, eternal, and unchangeable, in his being, wisdom, power, holiness, justice, goodness, and truth" (*Westminster Shorter Catechism,* Q. 4), this God subsisting in three persons, equal in essence, power, and glory. Tillich finds this definition faulty in that it (1) assumes that God is *a* being alongside of and above everything else that is, and (2) ascribes to him personality. Tillich describes this as a kind of atheism. For him the word "God" is only a symbolic vocable for the power of the being of everything, that is, the infinite and unconditioned ground of all being; and though this ground of being is not less than personal in that it is the ground of everything personal, still it is not itself personal. Furthermore, a proper Trinitarian construction involves, not the mysterious relation of three persons in the one Godhead, but the mysterious *life union* of the *ground of being* (which transcends finitude) with *everything finite.*[122] Finally, the ground of being is neither supernatural nor natural.

All "theologians of the leap" are natural theologians in the sense that they begin with presuppositions alien to Scripture and, in order to make their case, require the granting of the pre-scientific "given" necessary to their respective systems, Tillich too can make his case only if his phenomenological analysis is accepted as correct when it concludes with the finitude of all things. If this be granted, as is the case with Mascall's system, it might be true (if one does not insist upon impeccable logic) that finitude ontologically drives on beyond itself to its infinite ground of being. But when a Bertrand Russell simply rejects Tillich's premise and denies (incidentally, on good grounds) that one can argue back from the existence of empirical data to an infinite ground, natural or supernatural or otherwise, Tillich is unable to show the superiority of his system. Human authority has simply been challenged by another of equal weight. Neither authority is able to show why his system is to be preferred, and the result is a standoff.

Only the Christian man with an authoritative message coming to him *ab extra* from God can present a system which is internally coherent and which accurately describes the true nature of things. Of course, he will be accused of simply arguing from his circle like Tillich does from his, but the Christian man is confident that his circle, based as it is on Scriptural verities, is in line with the universe and its internal causes, man's deepest needs and the meeting of those needs, and history itself since in the Scripture he sees the beginning and end of history. Of course, he gladly owns that it is grace and grace alone which has put him in possession of this circle of reasoning.

Tillich rejects the Biblical Creator-creature distinction. For him, "the doctrine of creation is not the story of an event which took place 'once upon a time.'" [123] (If he had accepted the Scripture's teaching on this point, he would have circumvented much of his very evident misunderstanding of God and supernaturalism.) But according to Scripture, the eternal, infinitely incomprehensible, sovereign God created the universe. Man, his crowning creation, though rational, was created with only finite, creaturely comprehension, however. How was this infinitely incomprehensible God to communicate with his creature? It is at this point that many philosophical systems go astray. Because they reject the Creator-creature distinction of Scripture, they see no possible way for communication to occur between the infinite and the finite. They ultimately conclude by denying either God's ability to communicate with his creature or man's ability to comprehend his Creator. But according to Scripture, God created man with an innate knowledge of his Maker and with the capacity to comprehend God's revelation of himself. Of course, any revelation about himself to man constitutes a condescension on God's part. That is to say, when God came to man, of necessity he came in human form (at times) and by human speech. Later, when he superintended the inscripturation of revelation, that revelation was again anthropomorphic, that is, in human language at the level of finite comprehension. Admittedly, Biblical revelation produces a knowledge of God in man, the image-bearer, which is only analogical to God as he is in himself; but it is nonetheless true knowledge for the creature, since it is knowledge resulting from the Creator's revelation of himself to the creature, even though it comes to man at the level of finite comprehension. It must be kept in mind that the Creator has never expected from his rational creature anything higher than creaturely comprehension of him; in truth, he is satisfied with such knowledge on his creature's part *if such knowledge is based on his self-revelation.* Knowledge of him based on any other source God regards as idolatry.

Of course, this construction of the relationship between God and man has at its heart the Creator-creature distinction of Genesis 1. But it is only in this way that meaningful dialogue can be carried on between the Creator and his creature. Yet the creature in covenant with God, that is, the creature who freely and gladly owns his creaturehood, does not find his creaturely knowledge of God a burden to him. Rather he glories in his incomprehensible Maker. But this is Tillich's problem. Apparently, he finds his creaturely knowledge a burden to him, so he looks elsewhere to another revelation which will allow him to construct his own God. He rejects the only true God of Scripture and substitutes his ground of being. He concludes that revelation is nothing more than an activity of the mind transcending itself and that God is nothing more than a quality which man may discern in all beings in his encounter with them.

It is difficult to see how Tillich thinks that his understanding of God is going to be able to overcome Orthodoxy's "inability" to speak to this age. Frankly, it has nothing to commend it, for it is less than intelligible. It is nonsense! What kind of a God is the God beyond theism? What kind of a God is the God who is neither supernatural nor natural? David H. Freeman shows the absurdity of all such talk in his Tillich monograph, concluding: "Tillich apparently does not want to choose between the possibilities open to him. A geometrician may have a concept of a square and he may have a concept of a circle. But he cannot have a square circle." [124] Also since Tillich's revelation about God is not from God at all, one wonders where and how Tillich learned so much about the ground of being.

Tillich's doctrine of Christ. Tillich's Christology is a matter of real heartbreak to all orthodox Christians. He reduces Jesus of Nazareth to the level of mere man, making him hardly worthy of anyone's concern, much less worship. He rejects the literalness of the Son's pre-existence and deity, the virgin birth, Jesus' miracles and his atoning death, his resurrection, ascension, and present high-priestly ministry at the Father's right hand, and finally, his second coming and the final judgment. His claim to be a Christian he can justify only on the basis of a "leap."

His understanding of Jesus "becoming" the Christ rather than *being* the Christ is completely unscriptural. Jesus looked upon himself as having been sent as the appointed representative of the Almighty. He was no amateur Christ. He was the Anointed One sent from God. While it is true that Tillich does speak of Jesus as the *final* revelation of the New Being, he does not want to be understood as affirming any supernatural quality about the man Jesus. He simply means that the principle of wholeness was manifested in the human Jesus (how he can affirm this in the light of his attitude toward Scripture is without explanation; the "picture" concept is absurd) as he overcame his existential situation; and wherever this principle, accessible to all men, is experienced to any degree, the New Being in Jesus as the Christ is present and is serving as the norm by which the resultant "healing" is judged. For Tillich, then, God has not acted in any unique way in Jesus; we may all participate in the same principle of wholeness. Jesus is simply Tillich's norm for judging the degree to which someone overcomes the split between his essence and existence.

Tillich's doctrine of salvation. Tillich's soteriology is another example of the use of Scriptural terminology, such as justification and sanctification, to describe an existential experience which has no relation to the living God. What it basically amounts to is an awakening in man to a new self through "meditating" upon the death and resurrection "symbols" of Jesus. Those uncommitted to the Christian faith can and have claimed to find equal saving power, by applying Tillich's methodology and answers to their thought, in contemplating the life and death of Mahatma Gandhi and Buddha.

In fact, Tillich's theology reminds many authorities of the "contemplation" religions of the Far East. Surely Christianity is more than these! Actually, such a Christ and such a salvation will carry conviction only for those modern minds who can participate with Tillich in his sophisticated, yet very mystical, faith. But even then, the human heart will not have had its need met. What man needs above everything else is the forgiveness of sin and a righteousness in and about him which will give him acceptability in the presence of a holy God. Neither Tillich's Christology nor his soteriology helps man one iota in these regards.

Pictured on the cover of the October 13, 1967, issue of *Christianity Today* is a stack of books, among which are Gabriel Vahanian's *No Other God,* William Hamilton's *The New Essence of Christianity,* Thomas J. J. Altizer's *Toward a New Christianity, The Gospel of Christian Atheism,* and *Radical Theology and the Death of God* (the last co-authored by Hamilton), and Paul M. van Buren's *The Secular Meaning of the Gospel.* These authors constitute the leadership in the contemporary theological movement known popularly as the "death of God" theology and more technically as the "radical (or secular) theology." At the bottom of the pile, supporting the entire stack, is Tillich's three-volume *Systematic Theology!* Whether intentional or not, this picture graphically illustrates as words can never do the direction which Tillich's influence has taken in modern theology. It is undoubtedly true that Tillich would disavow any leadership in the "radical theology" as he did the night before his death in a heated debate with Altizer. But it is equally true that Altizer himself professes to have simply followed Tillich's directional thrust, though more consistently and more doggedly, in arriving at his conclusions. This similar directionality may be easily sketched, although of necessity in broad strokes, by a consideration once again of Tillich's doctrine of God as the ground of being.

It will be recalled that kerygmatic theology has long talked about a God who is so transcendently "wholly other" that he is *Deus absconditus.* Of course, it spoke too of *Deus revelatus,* but even in his "revealedness" God is still wholly hidden. Since the early 1930's, however, some kerygmatic theologians, notably Barth, have been steadily adding "objectifying" elements to the kerygma to combat an existential take-over of their thought. Tillich thinks that Barth is in danger, however, of becoming orthodox in his willingness to speak more and more of the "historicity" of such saving events as Christ's resurrection. Barth, Tillich feels, is too literalistic. Tillich, to the contrary, insists that all language about God, including his existence and personality, is symbolic, that the only thing one can postulate about God that is not symbolic is being-itself. Thus Tillich advances beyond Barth. Whereas Barth is willing to speak about God as being so wholly other that he is absolutely hidden, Tillich denies even his existence and personality. He is simply the power of being in everything. From this it is only a short step to the affirmation that "God is dead," with the need arising, of course, to explain his death and how man may get along without him.

Thus Hamilton, rejecting the idea of God as a "problem-solver" or "need-fulfiller," equates Christian existence with such things as the civil rights movement and the Great Society's "war on poverty." *God, as a very present help in time of need, is dead.* While preserving those human experiences that have a kind of sacredness about them, such as death and sexual experiences, we should move out of the Church and into the world. Such "worldly" responsibility, for Hamilton, is equated with standing with Jesus, who is "the place to be," in our neighbor's struggles and sufferings. In Hamilton we have a "theologian of secularism" taking his place by a leap of faith in the "Christian" circle with Tillich.

Altizer, employing Blakean mysticism, Hegelian dialecticism, and Nietzschean "eternal reoccurrence," teaches that God, in order that man would not be too other-worldly conscious, graciously turned himself into his opposite—man—in Jesus and in Jesus died, thereby self-negating or self-annihilating himself. Viewing the incarnation as a process, Altizer claims that God gave up his immutability and impassibility for the flux and processes of time and history. God's death, then, opens up entirely new possibilities of existence for man. No longer need he be concerned with the other world; he can now devote himself completely to the betterment of this one. And every force for such betterment, including Marxian communism, is "incarnational" or a Christ event. Thus, concludes Altizer, the only truly Christian man is the atheist, for only he can be absorbed by the needs of this world. In his understanding of the Christ event,

Altizer too leaps into the "Christian" circle as a "theologian of secularism."

Van Buren, under the influence of Ludwig Wittgenstein and analytic philosophy, simply insists that God-talk is non-sense, and the sooner the theologian stops talking about God altogether and begins to talk about man's experiences and expectations, the more honest he will be; the sooner he devotes himself to secularism, the better off he will be. Van Buren too, however, joins the "theologians of the leap" by making a Christian confession of the lordship of Jesus, though all he means by this is a commitment to live the freedom which he perceives in Jesus.

Thus the "radical theologians," for no compelling reason, all leap into the Christian circle by variously employing Jesus in their respective systems, all the while preaching a gospel of secularism. Tillich is not one whit different in this respect.

Tillich, no doubt, would view with horror the suggestion that his system even remotely resembles the radical theology; but when it is considered in the light of Flew's now-famous parable, in which he shows that a non-corporeal, non-sensational, non-verifiable gardner in no way differs from a non-existent gardner, we must conclude that there is little difference between a God who is non-existent and non-personal and no God at all. Nor is there any necessary reason why any one of these theologians has to speak from the Christian circle. It is simply dishonest for these men, as we have said before, to capitalize upon the power with which certain words have become freighted by usage and tradition in order to make a case for their non-Christian thought.

In Tillich's theology one sees a prime example of the effort to relate the Christian message to an alien culture. Every man, of course, must judge for himself as to Tillich's success in preserving the essence of Christianity while relating its message to his culture. But from the Biblical viewpoint there is no doubt but that he has indeed lost its essence, if indeed he ever had it.

NOTES

1. William Hordern, *A Layman's Guide to Protestant Theology* (New York: The Macmillan Company, 1955), p. 165.

2. Paul Tillich, *Systematic Theology* (Chicago: The University of Chicago Press, 1951), I, 4.

3. *Ibid.*, pp. 59-66.

4. *Ibid.*, p. 60.

5. The term "symbol" in Tillich's thought is a technical one which will be explained later. It should only be observed at this point.

6. *Ibid.*, p. 62.

7. *Ibid.*, p. 64.

8. *Ibid.*

9. *Ibid.*, p. 65.

10. *Ibid.*

11. *Ibid.*

12. *Ibid.*, pp. 65-66.

13. *Ibid.*, p. 66.

14. *Ibid.*, pp. 34-40.

15. *Ibid.*, pp. 40-46.

16. *Ibid.*, pp. 47-52.

17. *Ibid.*, pp. 69-159.

18. *Ibid.*, pp. 161-289.

19. *Ibid.*, II, 17-180.

20. *Ibid.*, III, 11-294.

21. *Ibid.*, III, 297-423.

22. John B. Cobb, Jr., *Living Options in Protestant Theology* (Philadelphia: The Westminster Press, 1962), p. 261.

23. *Op. cit.*, I, 8-11, 106-107, 132, 135; II, 14-16.

24. *Op. cit.*

25. *Ibid.*, p. 262.

26. *Ibid.*

27. *Ibid.*, p. 263.

28. *Op. cit.*, I, 18.

29. *Ibid.*, p. 163.

30. *Ibid.*, p. 164.

31. *Op. cit.*, p. 268, fn.

32. *Op. cit.*, p. 83.

33. *Ibid.*, pp. 83-86.

34. *Ibid.*, pp. 86-89.

35. *Ibid.*, pp. 89-94.

36. Cobb, *op. cit.*, p. 264; cf. Tillich's *Dynamics of Faith*, p. 126.

37. Cobb, *loc. cit.*

38. *Ibid.*; cf. *Dynamics of Faith*, pp. 1-4.

39. *Systematic Theology*, I, 11-12.

40. *Dynamics of Faith*, pp. 2-3.

41. *Systematic Theology*, I, 13; *Dynamics of Faith*, p. 12; *The Protestant Era*, pp. 226, 233, 239-240.

42. Cf. Cobb, *op. cit.*, p. 265.

43. *Ibid.*, p. 264.

44. *Systematic Theology*, I, 211.

45. *Ibid.*, 215.

46. These are technical terms from Rudolf Otto's *The Idea of the Holy*.

47. Cobb, *op. cit.*, p. 265.

48. *Systematic Theology*, I, 202-203; II, 29-44.

49. Cobb, *op. cit.*, p. 266.

50. *Systematic Theology*, II, 29.

51. *Ibid.*, p. 35.

52. *Ibid.*, pp. 47-55.

53. *Ibid.*, p. 47.

54. *Ibid.*, p. 49.

55. *Ibid.*, p. 53.

56. *Ibid.*, I, 168.

57. *Ibid.*, p. 176.

58. *Ibid.*, p. 180.

59. *Ibid.*, p. 182.

60. Cf. Cobb, *op. cit.*, p. 267, for concrete examples of the imbalance constantly present in the polarities.

61. *Ibid.*, p. 268.

62. Cf. Tillich's *The Courage To Be*.

63. Cobb, *op. cit.*, pp. 269-270.

64. *Systematic Theology*, I, 75, 79.

65. *Ibid.*, p. 86.

66. *Ibid.*, p. 89.

67. *Ibid.*, p. 174.

68. *Ibid.*, p. 178.

69. *Ibid.*, p. 185.

70. *Ibid.*, pp. 165, 203.

71. Cf. Cobb, *op. cit.*, p. 270.

72. *Systematic Theology*, I, 22.

73. *Ibid.*, p. 238-239.

74. Cobb, *op. cit.*, p. 272.

75. *Op. cit.*, pp. 106-118.

76. *Ibid.*, I, 110.

77. *Ibid.*, p. 116.

78. *Ibid.*, p. 235.

79. *Ibid.*, p. 236.

80. *Ibid.*, pp. 236-237.

81. *Ibid.*, p. 205.

82. *Ibid.*, II, 5.

83. *Ibid.*, p. 6.

84. *Ibid.*

85. *Ibid.*

86. *Ibid.*, p. 7.

87. *Ibid.*

88. *Ibid.,* pp. 7-8.

89. *Ibid.,* I, 15-16, 132.

90. Cobb, *op. cit.,* p. 275.

91. *Systematic Theology,* II, 90-94.

92. *Ibid.,* pp. 114-115; cf. Bernard Martin, *The Existentialist Theology of Paul Tillich,* pp. 160-161.

93. *Ibid.,* p. 114.

94. Martin, *op. cit.,* p. 161.

95. *Ibid.*

96. *Ibid.,* pp. 161-162.

97. *Systematic Theology,* II, 121.

98. Martin, *op. cit.,* pp. 162-163.

99. *Systematic Theology,* II, 132-133.

100. *Ibid.,* p. 126.

101. *Ibid.,* pp. 126-127.

102. *Ibid.,* p. 153.

103. *Ibid.,* p. 158.

104. *Ibid.*

105. *Ibid.,* pp. 158-159.

106. *Ibid.,* pp. 155-156.

107. *Ibid.,* pp. 156-157.

108. Martin, *op. cit.,* p. 167.

109. *Systematic Theology,* II, 157; cf. Wieman's similar understanding of the resurrection of Jesus.

110. *Ibid.,* pp. 159-165.

111. *Ibid.,* p. 166.

112. *Ibid.,* p. 177.

113. *Ibid.*

114. *Ibid.,* p. 179.

115. *Ibid.,* p. 178.

116. *Ibid.,* pp. 179-180.

117. Cf. my article, "Our Lord's View of the Old Testament According to Matthew," *Biblical Viewpoint,* I, 116-121.

118. James I. Packer, *'Fundamentalism' and the Word of God* (Grand Rapids: Wm. B. Eerdmans Publishing Company, 1959), p. 127.

119. *Systematic Theology,* I, vii.

120. George F. Thomas, "The Method and Structure of Tillich's Theology," *The Theology of Paul Tillich* (Edited by Kegley and Bretall; New York: The Macmillan Company, 1964), pp. 103-104.

121. Cobb, *op. cit.,* p. 262.

122. *Systematic Theology,* I, 228-229; 250-251.

123. *Ibid.,* p. 252.

124. David H. Freeman, *Tillich* (Philadelphia: The Presbyterian and Reformed Publishing Company, 1962), p. 19.

EPILOGUE

THE ONLY TWO OPTIONS

Many voices are crying to be heard today on the theological scene. The world, both academically and spiritually, is in a state of confusion and turmoil. No one man has the answers to all of the world's ills. There does appear to be, however, in the breasts of modern men a hope and longing for a voice and a message to lead them out of the morass of modern despair and meaninglessness. In the foregoing pages we have discussed six attempts to proclaim just such a message.

Mascall, as we have seen, attempts to construct a theological system in which he begins with a reinterpretation of Thomas's theistic proofs. Reducing them to a basic affirmation that finite entities exist, Mascall affirms that reflection on this fact forces one to conclude that an infinite and intelligent (but impassible) being exists. Then to this basic conclusion he relates Biblical revelation. Here is clearly a natural theology in which rational conclusions are given priority over Biblical verities. In Wieman's thought, God is viewed as the process of creativity of good operating in the world toward the production of value or worth. His allusions to Jesus are, of course, completely sub-Christian—another clear example of philosophical presuppositions—in this case, radical empiricism—distorting revelation. Both Brunner and Barth, although claiming to be listening to the voice of God, actually allow the voices of Kant and Kierkegaard to drown out God's. Brunner consciously substitutes for Biblical authority the Kierkegaardian dialectic between God and man with the result that a non-verifiable, indescribable religious experience dominates his thought at the center. Barth as well assumes a religious autonomy over the Scriptures and by means of an unscriptural Christomonistic hermeneutic resolves all of history into the covenant of grace within which God is granted an unscriptural freedom and man possesses reality only as he is already caught up in a universalistic reconciliation in Jesus Christ. Bultmann, heeding an unscriptural scientistic claim of inviolable authority over what God can and can not do in his universe, a form-critical understanding of the New Testament, and Heidegger's existentialistic analysis of man, demythologizes the New Testament kerygma to the point that it becomes meaningless and irrational. And Tillich, demanding that his existential and cultural analysis of man be allowed to frame the questions which theology is to answer, reduces Jesus Christ to merely a man whom the New Testament pictures as one who overcame existential self-estrangement, and salvation to the awakening of a new self in man through meditating upon the overcoming principle exemplified in Jesus.

One might conclude at first blush that these are diverse and unrelated systems. Actually, their differences are those of degree and not of kind. While no one will deny that Mascall is "more Biblical" than Wieman, Barth than Brunner, Bultmann and Tillich, yet it is still a fact that everyone of them has assumed to himself the role of autonomous man, and in the development of his respective theological system has made himself the first and final reference point from which all predication is made. His own cultural background, academic training, religious affiliation, and existential point of view become his "Archimedian point of beginning" and determine for him what the Word of God should and should not say. In each of these systems man begins with man, reasons to God, and determines for himself the content of the "revelation" from that God.

It is only in the theology of the Reformers that God's voice is heard above all the noise and din of men's weak counterfeits. For it is only in the theology of the Reformers that the Bible is allowed to speak forth its message to man in certain terms. If there is one thing that the Reformers consciously sought to do above all else, it was to remain silent in the presence of the Lord of the Temple and to let him speak to them. As children of the Reformation we honor them most when we stand upon their shoulders better to hear God's Word.

While it is only in the theology of the Reformation that the special principle of grace is re-enthroned and a Scriptural understanding of revelation is honored, it is sadly true that some who claim to be children of the Reformation have not listened as intently as their fathers to God's voice in Scripture and have not sought self-consciously to think God's thought after him. Some of them grant to man autonomy in the decisions relative to salvation and spiritual development. They even make God's *eternal* purpose dependent upon man's *temporal* decisions, since they view God's elective decree as determined by rather than determinative of man's faith. This is not an unimportant point for in so doing they unintentionally strike at the very heart of the Christian gospel— Christ's substitutionary atonement. For when God's elective purpose is made dependent upon man's actual decision to gain salvation through faith in Jesus Christ, then in the order of decrees God's decree to distinguish among men logically follows his decree to redeem man through Christ's atonement. This means that God's decree to redeem men through Christ's death either applies to all men (which no Christian believes actually occurs historically, and which God himself must consequently limit in either his distinguishing decree or in his application of the Son's redemption) or to no one specifically. As Benjamin B. Warfield has correctly seen in *The Plan of Salvation,* the highest view of the atonement which such a view of man and God will logically allow is the governmental view, but it can never affirm a real substitutionary atonement. It has thus wounded Christianity in its very heart. It appears that even the Amyraldian, the Pajonist, and the Arminian have united, albeit unintentionally, with the autonomous man in these matters.

There are, in fact, then only two real options: one may claim for himself religious autonomy and determine for himself what God has said and done, or he can renounce such autonomy as sinful and live self-consciously under the Lordship of Christ as that Lordship is revealed in the written Word. But this means, of course, that he must renounce his own self-righteousness, admit his creaturehood, and genuinely worship the Creator rather than the creature. And this, apart from a sovereign work of God in his heart, man in his rebellion is unwilling to do.

INDEX

INDEX